"Circumstances are destiny"

CIVIL WAR IN THE NORTH

Series Editor, Lesley J. Gordon, University of Akron

"Circumstances are destiny"

An Antebellum Woman's Struggle to Define Sphere

Tina Stewart Brakebill

The Kent State University Press

Kent, Ohio

© 2006 by The Kent State University Press, Kent, Ohio 44242
Library of Congress Catalog Card Number 20065031674
ISBN-10: 0-87338-864-X
ISBN-13: 978-0-87338-864-1
Manufactured in the United States of America

10 09 08 07 06   5 4 3 2 1

LIBRARY OF CONGRESS CATALOGING-IN-PUBLICATION DATA

Brakebill, Tina Stewart, 1962–
    Circumstances are destiny : an Antebellum woman's struggle to define sphere / Tina
Stewart Brakebill.
        p.   cm. — (Civil war in the North)
    Originally presented as the author's thesis (master's)—Illinois State University, Normal,
Ill., 2002.
    Includes bibliographical references and index.
    ISBN-13: 978-0-87338-864-1 (pbk. : alk. paper) ∞
    ISBN-10: 0-87338-864-x (pbk. : alk. paper) ∞
    1. Colby, Celestia Rice, 1827–1900. 2. Cherry Valley (Ashtabula County, Ohio)—Bi-
ography. 3. Cherry Valley (Ashtabula County, Ohio)—Social conditions—19th century.
4. Ohio—History—Civil War, 1861–1865—Social aspects. 5. Ohio—History—Civil War,
1861–1865—Women. 6. United States—History—Civil War, 1861–1865—Social aspects. 7.
United States—History—Civil War, 1861–1865—Women. 8. Women—Ohio—Cherry Valley
(Ashtabula County)—History—19th century. I. Colby, Celestia Rice, 1827–1900. Diaries. Selections. II. Title. III. Series.
    F499.C384B73 2006
    977.1'3403092—dc22   2005031674

British Library Cataloging-in-Publication data are available.

To the memory of Celestia Rice Colby
and strong-minded women everywhere who endeavor
to "elevate and redeem woman."

Contents

Acknowledgments

CELESTIA RICE COLBY lived a life surrounded by people, yet she often felt isolated and unsupported. Luckily, my experience has been quite the opposite. Since the autumn of 2000, I have spent countless hours in archives, at libraries, and at my computer preparing this book, and much of that work was solitary; nevertheless, I never felt unsupported. The idea that a project of this nature could be accomplished alone is—of course—far from being truthful. From the moment an archivist said, "I think I have something you might be interested in" through this very moment I have been supported, encouraged, and informed by teachers, colleagues, friends, and family. Without them, this project never could have seen completion.

I owe a debt of deep gratitude to the staffs of many underfunded, understaffed, and often underappreciated archives, historical libraries, historical societies, and museums. Time and time again, these organizations have provided me with the "stuff" that ignites my historical curiosity, and this project was no exception. First and foremost, I am obliged to Illinois State University Archivist Jo Anne Rayfield, who graciously introduced this material to me and offered her time and expertise throughout the long process. Thank you also to the several semesters of Illinois Regional Archives Depository interns, who happily put up with my constant presence, offered help whenever they could, and perhaps most appreciated when long hours of manuscript reading were involved—they let me have the "good" chair as well. Special acknowledgments also are due to the staffs at the Andover Public Library in Andover, Ohio; the Ohio State Historical Society; and the McLean County Historical Museum and Library in Bloomington, Illinois. Illinois State University's Milner Librarian Vanette Schwartz also deserves a special acknowledgment for her help and encouragement. I truly appreciate Troy Olson, Jan Johnson, and Skyler's Pictures in Bloomington, Illinois, for their help with the technical aspects of gathering illustrative material. In addition, in these days of e-mail and Internet research, I often received help from people whom I never met nor got to thank in person. Consequently, individuals, as well as the staffs, at numerous facilities deserve credit for their help, including Ashtabula County (Ohio) historian David Lepard; the Bentley Historical Library at the University of Michigan; the Schlesinger Library at Radcliffe University; Darrol Pierson at the Indiana State Library; The Historical Library of Western Pennsylvania; Flint Public Library; Miami County Museum in Indiana; and the county clerk's offices in Livingston, Genesee, and Washtenaw counties in Michigan.

Of course, gathering the necessary material is only part of the process—writing requires enormous support as well. Working with Kent State University Press has been an enjoyable experience, and a first-time author could not have asked for better editors than Joanna Hildebrand Craig and Tara C. Lenington. I owe an immense debt of gratitude to the many people who have read drafts and offered advice since the birth of this project. Any mistakes or missteps the book still may have are not from lack of guidance. Mark Wyman and Sandra Harmon have been on board since the very beginning. They read almost as many rough drafts as myself, and each time they graciously offered their invaluable wisdom, editorial suggestions, and critiques; perhaps more importantly they also supplied consistent encouragement and support. My gratitude to them cannot be adequately expressed. Kent State University Press's anonymous readers provided very useful direction, which resulted in a change in organization that improved the narrative immeasurably. Stephane Booth and Stacey Robertson's careful critiques helped me to improve both the narrative flow and various areas of interpretation. Along the way, many other readers stepped in and offered help when I needed it, including Paul Holsinger, Kyle Ciani, April Schultz, and David Chesebrough, who sadly lost his battle with cancer before he could see this project completed. My appreciation to them all is enormous.

Celestia Rice Colby struggled to find friends and family who consistently supported her efforts to change her destiny. Fortunately, I have been luckier in that regard, and I owe thanks to many people. I am particularly indebted to my friends who are also fellow historians, especially Gina Kieffer, Mary Alice Wills, and John Poling. They listened, read drafts, offered comments, drank coffee, joined in my political ranting, supplied encouragement, and their eyes didn't glaze over when I start talking "history." I also send my love and gratitude to my family and friends who stuck around through the ups and downs of the last few years, even when they may have thought I was crazy for quitting my job. My parents—Janey and Silas Stewart—are a source of constant love and support. Scott Stewart offers equal amounts of pride and antagonism in the way that only a "little brother" can, and I appreciate almost every minute of it. I am grateful to Gordon and Sandi Brakebill for their consistent encouragement. To Ore and Heather, thanks for the incentive: see, I told you I had a job-e-job! Thank you to Christy Michalec and Hollis Stewart for being—in Colby's words—"sisters in all but the name." You all helped make this experience one that I cherish. Finally, thank you to Brian for everything always.

Introduction

"CIRCUMSTANCES ARE DESTINY."[1] This terse statement was the entire entry made for October 24, 1857, in the private journal of northeastern Ohio native Celestia Rice Colby. Her entries were normally much more loquacious, but this brief observation represents both her fears and hopes for her future in one succinct statement. Colby's life in many aspects was entirely ordinary. She was a native-born, aspiring middle-class, literate, white, rural mother and housewife. She never achieved fame or fortune. She was one of the supposedly inconsequential people of history who receive attention as part of a statistic or type, but commonly garner no individual consideration. Colby's life gains notice over a century after her death by virtue of her somewhat extraordinary effort to find time to write extensively, not only as a means of self-reflection, but also for publication. These words demonstrate that in the autumn of 1857, on the cusp of her thirtieth birthday, Colby began in earnest a struggle to establish a sense of personal identity that went beyond her immediate situation of housewife and mother.

The most intense span of Colby's effort to change her circumstances, and thus her destiny, occurred in the decade leading up to and into the Civil War, and the largest part of this book is devoted to this time period. However, a broad view of her entire life is necessary to truly understand her struggle. To that end, her life story is presented in three stages. The first part lays out her formative years from childhood through the first decade of her marriage. These chapters serve as foundation to illustrate what she likely expected from her future and why. My goal is to set the stage, so that the reader understands the influences at play in constructing Colby's expectations as well as those influences that had a hand in her growing desire to deconstruct those expectations. The centerpiece of the study, Part II, begins in the autumn of 1857 at the time in which Colby's attempt to change those expectations accelerated. Her most obvious efforts to alter the course of her future continued until about midway through the Civil War. During this time, Colby wrote extensively in her private journals as well as producing many essays, stories, and letters for publication—all of which help to illustrate her ongoing efforts to alter the expected path of her life. Each chapter uses these works to move her journey forward in time and highlight the ebb and flow effects of her evolving private and public attitudes on a myriad of issues. Midway through the Civil War, Colby's struggle to change the course of her life seems to have stalled. This point marks the beginning of Part III, in which her increasingly infrequent journal entries and published writings supplement the examination of the remainder of her life in an effort to determine whether she resolved her struggle or merely accepted defeat.

Colby hoped to alter her conditions in order to elevate her future. However, over the years, the intensity of her struggle varied as her belief in her ability to change her circumstances, and thus her destiny, often wavered. "My destiny is to act, to do life's humblest duties, in a narrow, unknown sphere, to crush back the upspringing aspirations that rise in my soul, and to strive for the mastery over my own spirit. Shall I ever attain this victory? Ah no!"[2] Colby was well aware that her "uprising aspirations" put her at odds with accepted societal thoughts about women's roles. The "narrow, unknown sphere" of which she spoke is the notion of separate spheres—men in the public realm and women in the private one—an ideal that gained wide popular acceptance in the nineteenth century. Simplistically stated, as the nineteenth century progressed, trends such as industrialization, urbanization, and the rising market economy increasingly meant that men's labor was performed at a location separate from their homes. This physical division between workspace and home contributed to an increased emphasis on the importance of the differences between public and private, which in turn fed into a wider societal acceptance of the separate-spheres ideology. This notion of separate public and private spheres was in reality primarily a prescription for a cultural ideal rather than an actual description of real life; nonetheless, it was a powerful ideal, which has endured, in only a somewhat modified form, into the present. Its mid-nineteenth-century meaning implied not mere separation, but more importantly, the so-called naturalness of this division based on innate male and female character traits, which meant that behavior that fell beyond those limits was unnatural, and thus wrong.

An important component of this gender separation was the differentiation between the perceived nature of men's and women's responsibilities: men "worked" in the public realm while women "tended" the private home. This distinction between working and tending was more than merely semantics. Among other real consequences, it began the validation of the idea, which lingers into the present, that tasks done by men outside the home, particularly for a wage, were properly thought of as work, and tasks done by women inside their homes were the result of the natural nurturing instinct and therefore not work and not of any monetary—or real—value.[3] Thus Colby charged that her destiny as a woman involved "life's humblest tasks" and her fear that any greater aspiration would then necessarily be "crushed." Mainstream societal norms maintained that this "destiny" was a natural one—for all True Women.

As the 1850s unfolded, however, Colby's views about her own life as well as her gender's natural role increasingly were affected by a small but growing antebellum movement that countered some of the core tenets of separate-sphere ideology. These "strong-minded" women—and men—spoke out against gender inequality. They maintained that nature had little to do with the creation of the woman's sphere; society had created the boundaries on women's roles. They declared that all humanity, including women, had the innate—natural—right to equality. This idea was not without some precedence, but by the 1850s it was so antithetical to the emerging popular consensus regarding women's roles that mainstream society considered it quite radical. During the mid-century years these two rival views—true woman versus strong-minded woman—could be heard most definitively in New England, New York, and northeastern Ohio, because the underlying cultural and economic changes that helped to spawn these views emerged initially and quite forcefully in the urbanizing northeastern United States. Despite the undeniable presence of both views, those voices that prescribed the so-called proper behavior for true womanhood had a powerful advantage. Economic, legal, and social parameters strongly supported the notion of separated gender spheres; consequently, this idealized picture of womanhood gained status as the model for all women. In this model, ordinary—that is, normal—women gladly tended the private sphere, and thus the "housewife" was born.

Colby battled both internal and external forces in her effort to reconcile her personal hopes and ambitions with society's expectations and obligations. This evidence of her struggle challenges as well as corroborates some conventional thoughts about how ordinary, white, mid-nineteenth-century women reacted to conflicting role messages. In the nearly two centuries since the term "separate spheres" gained popular acceptance, its meaning, its use, and its varied implications for the past as well as historical interpretation have devolved, evolved, and sedimented in many ways. As knowledge about the actual lives of women has increased, ideas about the historical reality of the ideal of separate spheres, as well as its validity as a labeling term, have changed. Earlier women's history scholarship emphasizes the notion of gender-separated spheres as both a historical situation and a tool for interpretation. Since that time, other factors such as class, race, region, and family have been layered into interpretations. Scholarship that focused on women's endeavors as factory workers, farmers, pioneers, reformers, writers, students, teachers, friends, citizens, and mothers—to name just a few—demonstrated that separate spheres and the concomitant labels of public and private must be considered within a wider framework. The labels' function as scholarly descriptors has gone through many stages, particularly in the last several decades. Many years of scholarship have produced an evolution and maturity in women's and gender history that has flourished and branched out in unforeseen ways with the addition of depth and detail. Because this study looks at one woman's life from both a broad contextual perspective and a narrower individual focus, this abundance of scholarship informs this study in a myriad of ways.[4]

Although scholarship centered on subjects ranging from dairy techniques to female higher education enhances our understanding of Colby's life, the concept of separate spheres is a vital consideration in any interpretation of her experience. Some current scholarship questions whether separate spheres ever represented more than a metaphorical concept, but regardless of whether history defines the concept as figurative or literal, Colby felt real effects. In reality, Colby's life was not separated physically into strict divisions of male/female or public/private; however, this fact did not mean that the idea of a proper woman's sphere was an academic or a metaphorical concept. In Colby's world, it was a set of real ideological constructs that affected how she viewed herself and what she believed was possible as well as how society viewed her actions. Colby's publications and private journals provide a window enabling us to see how she perceived her role as a woman. This view reveals juxtaposition between her self-described ideal "inner life" and her actual day-to-day actions, or self-described "outward world." We will see that Colby saw her life as irreparably divided, not necessarily between public and private, but between her ideals and her reality, or her inner life and the outward world, both of which in reality involved intertwined public/private and male/female spheres. External and internal forces—pushes and pulls—operated in and on Colby's life and helped to form a conceptual framework that affected how and why she made the decisions that she did. With the benefit of time, we can see more clearly how this framework was constructed. The shifting cultural context that defined much of the antebellum United States as it attempted to grow from infancy and to establish a uniquely American identity provides the broad beams that this framework rested on. These broad societal forces and their differing views of what represented the natural state of humanity fueled much of the despair, tensions, and conflict evident in Colby's rhetoric.

Publicly, Colby wrote eloquently and forcefully about the natural equality of all humankind and directly confronted subjects such as slavery, temperance, education, and women's rights. Privately, however, her actions were not always as bold. Her public views regarding women's place in society, when compared to her private unpublished thoughts about the reality of her own life, offer poignant examples of her conflict. Publicly, she lamented women's continued subjugation: "To elevate and redeem woman—those who have been crushed and bruised, trampled underfoot by the world, by society, too often less pure than those whom it makes outcasts, and of whose very name it makes a by-word of scorn, loathing and contempt, is an effort worthy of the loftiest powers of woman's genius, and ennobles it, and makes it sacred and holy—and yet it is an effort that requires a noble and fearless daring, for it is not always a safe thing to say 'yes,' when the world says 'no.'" Beyond platitudes, however, she had very pragmatic demands based on her thoughts regarding innate human rights: "But the most zealous advocates of woman's rights ask for nothing more than simple justice, and will never be willing to submit to anything short of it." Ironically, her impassioned pleas for equality, which were written during the late 1850s and early 1860s, coincided with journal entries that reflect a sense of deep doubt about her own worth and the value of her existence: "Another day has passed in the same monotonous way in which all my days are passing. I've done nothing worth recording." Her private words of hopelessness, contrary to her words in the public sphere, revealed that her passionate belief in the possibilities of change frequently did not play a major part in her everyday life. As she put it bluntly: "Circumstances are destiny."[5]

As her story unfolds, we witness her evolving sense of social justice and the budding rise of personal goals while simultaneously exploring the apparent inconsistencies within her life. Her powerful published words would seem to show that she had been an early crusader of sorts, brandishing the sword of equality, consequences be damned. Her diaries, however, provide evidence of her frustrations and hopes, a picture of perhaps a victim—a potential shining star dimmed by overlaying clouds. The truthful answer is a somewhat more complicated and multifaceted picture, complete with contradictions, accomplishments, frustrations, joys, and sorrows. Each facet of her written legacy offers different perspectives that often beg more questions than they answer about what it meant to be a woman in nineteenth-century America. The final portrait is of a woman not easily definable, but infinitely real and—like many women today—conflicted about her place in the world. This examination of Colby's efforts to establish an identity for herself serves as more than just an interesting look at one woman's past amid the changing goals and expectations of nineteenth-century America. Celestia Rice Colby's documentation of her own struggle provides us with the opportunity to view details of how an ideal can operate to shape the beliefs and behaviors of one woman. In many ways the nature, and even some of the particulars, of her struggle are familiar to women of the present who still receive conflicting societal messages regarding their roles. The nineteenth-century ideal of gender-separated spheres is embedded in those modern messages. An examination of the complex ways that those roles assigned to women in the past actually were incorporated into their lives provides a foundation on which to better understand the continuing struggle of modern women and adds valuable depth to our broad perspectives regarding women and their perceived roles. In order to accomplish this in-depth investigation, we must continue to add detail harvested from the lives of individual women—women whose experiences spun the threads of life that make up the intricate fabric of the past.

Before continuing with our examination, a few clarifying notes may be helpful. first, for the sake of simplicity, I refer to Celestia Rice Colby as "Colby" through-out the book, even when writing about her childhood and pre-marriage years. I introduce other family members and friends with their full names and then refer to them by their first names. For example, Colby's husband, Lewis Colby, is called "Lewis" throughout. Second, because Colby's writings are the founda-tion for this book, some explanatory context may be helpful to the reader. The Colby Collection actually encompasses material from several members of her family. Her youngest daughter, J. Rose Colby, was a professor at Illinois State Normal University, and it was upon her death in 1941 that the collection of personal and family papers came to the Illinois State University Archives, Illi-nois State University, Normal, Illinois. The largest part of the collection focuses on Rose's professional career, but it also contains various remnants of other members of her immediate family's past, especially her mother's writings. The material directly traced to Colby includes personal journals, scrapbooks of published writings, and many other pieces of miscellaneous writings.

Colby's personal writings, which I refer to interchangeably as journals and diaries, consist of more than 680 pages of handwritten, bound material from the mid-1840s to 1865. Unlike many farmwomen's diaries, these journals are not merely a litany of tasks and weather reports, but rather are an intimate explo-ration of her inner feelings about her life. This self-reflection makes them of special importance, but this value does not eliminate the challenges common to the use of personal writings. Any interpretation that relies on handwritten documents intended as personal reflection must contend with a myriad of con-cerns, including worries concerning the "completeness" of the available docu-ments due to the lack of a clear beginning or ending; illegible, faded writing; unfamiliar language and writing style; the veracity of entries; the ambiguity as to motives; and uncertainty about the context in which they were written.[6]

The issue of completeness is of special importance because a change in writ-ing habits can be as vital a piece of evidence as the writing itself. In Colby's case, informed interpretation lends itself to the conclusion that the collection contains the whole of the diaries. The extant journals span the mid-1840s through 1865. Entries often appear daily in the years from 1849 to 1850 and from 1857 to 1860 and frequently range from half a page to several pages or more. The rest of the time, entry frequency varies from weekly to monthly or less, and the entry length is inconsistent as well. Despite the inconsistency in frequency and length, the journals are for the most part coherent and chronological with the possible exception of entries made in the early and mid-1840s. Colby's first diary begins with material—most of which is poetry, often undated—that apparently was written during this early time span. In addition, some of this writing may have been recopied from loose sheets, so exact composition dates are not always verifiable. It is also impossible to know definitively whether a journal ever existed for the years between 1854 and 1857. She ended one journal in 1854, and then in October of 1857, she commenced writing in another one with no notable fanfare, although the book itself seems to represent a new purchase. It is a smaller lined book designed for writing, instead of an oversized ledger, as is the previous journal. Contextual information, primarily the fact that during those three years she had three children under the age of five, supports the idea that she simply lacked the time or energy to write. When the entries do eventually stop in 1865, well over half of the book remains empty, so it is possible to conclude that her journal writing ended as well.

As for the actual reading challenges, I was lucky. Although much of the ink is very faded, I became accustomed—after numerous readings—relatively easily to her prose style. Colby's writing style and techniques indicate a certain level of sophistication. She used proper grammar and syntax, and the actual script itself usually is clear and well formed. In addition, the sprinkling of foreign phrases, quotes, and references to literature, history, geography, and philosophy allude to education. Because Colby's apparent motive was to explore her innermost feelings, she wrote relatively infrequently about more mundane topics. Consequently for my purposes, her choice to share these feelings represents both a challenge and an advantage. For example, as I read the journals, I was immediately aware of her personal feelings, but it took considerable research with other sources to reconstruct the basic framework of her everyday life. So although Colby's journals do not provide a clear contextual outline of her life, they do provide abundant anecdotal evidence and tantalizing clues that inspire further research as well as a gripping emotional framework.

In addition, unlike many ordinary women who write journals, Colby's private voice is not the only one available, as she also wrote frequently for publication. These works also represent a distinct set of challenges. The sheer number and variety of antebellum newspapers, as well as the difficulty in obtaining extant copies today, make the task of tracking one individual's contributions extremely time consuming and difficult. Luckily, Colby's habit of clipping her own publications and saving them provides invaluable access to her public writings today. However, perhaps to an even greater extent than with her private writings, it is impossible to know whether those published pieces that survive today represent the whole or only a part. Between 1853 and approximately 1870, Colby kept scrapbooks that contain over 275 pieces that were published in a number of publications. She wrote both fiction and nonfiction and covered a diverse scope of topics that included not only reform movements such as abolition, temperance, and women's rights, but also themes like child-rearing, education, cheese production, reading, and nature.

I located a number of these pieces in their original publications, and the scrapbook clippings apparently represent the greatest part of the whole in these cases. In addition, if Colby noted in her journal that she had sent something to a newspaper, then a corresponding clipping usually can be located in a scrapbook. Until the mid-1860s the clippings also appear, for the most part, in chronological order. Occasionally, a clipping will appear out of order, perhaps indicating that it took her longer to obtain a copy. finally, like her personal journals, her habit of clipping and pasting her writing ended in 1865, which left a good portion of the scrapbook empty. She inserted several articles that originated in the late 1860s and early 1870s into the book, but unlike the others, these items are not pasted in. This fact indicates that she had access to the book. All of this evidence lends credence to a conclusion that her scrapbooks represent the greater part, if not all, of the whole for the years between 1853 and 1870.

Even with this conclusion, the use of this material presents other challenges, chiefly the inability to always ascertain the exact date or publication in which the material originally appeared because her clippings often eliminated newspaper names and dates. This fact, along with the inability to locate extant copies of some of the newspapers, resulted in a failure to read all the pieces in their original published form and context. Fortunately, prior research that focused on antebellum newspapers helps to provide contextual information regarding the different publications' standard subject, content, and tenor. As for the undated material, frequently the subject matter provides a good indicator of the timing. Regardless of these occasional obstacles, the existence of these original essays, articles, and editorial letters provides a vital window from which to view her public sentiments on many issues, especially when her diary entries are few or nonexistent.

The collection also contains a great number of unbound pieces of writing produced mainly in the 1880s and 1890s that fall generally into the categories of miscellaneous manuscripts and miscellaneous correspondence. Frequently, archives receive material that an individual or family has stored away for years—forgotten and unorganized—and as such it is impossible to know the extent to which they represent the whole. Much of these miscellaneous papers fall into that grouping and consequently present even greater challenges regarding dating, placing into context, and at times even definitively identifying authorship. Fortunately, some of this material is dated and its purpose clear; for example, manuscript drafts of essays written for hopeful publication and letters received from family and friends that include dates and names. Other items, such as drafts of letters and bits of prose and poetry that Colby wrote, cannot always be completely verified as to date or ultimate purpose, but often can be categorized partially through contextual references. This uncertainty does not render these materials always unusable, however. Ambiguity as to whether letters or manuscripts were mailed or published does not alter their authenticity as a powerful guide to help understand Colby's state of mind when they were written. Although often challenging because of the lack of clarity, this portion of the collection serves as vital anecdotal evidence for interpretations of Colby's postwar life.

Colby produced over 680 pages of diary entries and 275 newspaper and periodical publications as well as a myriad of miscellaneous manuscripts and correspondence. Although space precludes including even a fraction of that total, I frequently provide long quotations. Several reasons are behind this need for extended quotes. first, her private words are not published, thus by and large are unavailable to the general reader; second, her public words, although published, appeared in newspapers and periodicals that currently, at best, are available in a limited fashion; third, Colby's own words are vital in order to attempt an interpretation of her perceptions about her own situation. So, in order for the reader to gain a fair representation of Colby's views, which are this book's primary focus, it is frequently necessary to include the full extent of those words. Consequently, I have done minimal editing of Colby's writing. Any emphases within the entries, such as underlining in the diaries and italics in published works, are Colby's or appear in the original published sources in that style. Punctuation, grammar, spelling, and style are unchanged, so occasionally a word or phrase may seem quaint in its usage or misspelled because of changes in writing style and standardized word spelling. Common differences include: "staid" for "stayed," "vail" for "veil," "to day" for "today," and "woman's rights" instead of "women's rights." However, because Colby's writing is highly readable in its original style, these occasional aberrations are *not* indicated with the usual notation of [*sic*]. Brackets are employed *only* if I felt that the addition of a word or phrase is necessary for readability or clarification. finally, perhaps the most important justification for not only the extensive use of quotes, but also the book itself, is the hope that the reader will gain sufficient understanding of Colby's perceptions about her life to realize the importance those thoughts can have in our ongoing efforts to interpret women's history. Although she was not famous or important in a traditional historical sense, her life provides a vivid illustration of an essential link in the ongoing historical process that shapes women's present lives and future possibilities, and as such serves as a valuable connection between the past and the present.

PART I

An Expected Life

CHAPTER ONE

1827–1848

"The impress of the Connecticut character"

In February 1865, after several sleepless nights following the decision to sell their home and move the family from Ohio to Illinois, Celestia Rice Colby noted in her journal that her angst was "not because I regret the sale or wish to stay in Cherry Valley. But every tie of my life has been formed in this humble town."[1] As we examine her life with the perspective of time, Colby's observation proves astute. Her location in this small, rural, northeastern Ohio community played a large part in her formation of self-identity. Her sense of self was so strongly imbedded within the context of family, community, and country that even when some of those ingrained patterns were at odds with her personal hopes, she often seemed resistant to break completely from the established norms in her life. Ironically, this past not only acted as a limiting force, but it also helped lay the groundwork for the strong views that eventually broadened her desires for the future.

Understanding the foundations beneath Colby's outlook on her life's expectations is important if her later struggles are to be placed in any greater context. Unfortunately, attempts to reconstruct the early years of any ordinary person's life from the first half of the nineteenth century, particularly a woman's life, present difficulties, and Colby is no exception. The nineteenth century produced very little in the way of official documentary evidence of women's lives. Fortunately, however, Colby's recorded memories provide a starting place for interpretation. Sometime after having children of her own, Colby wrote an essay—of which only an incomplete version survives—describing her early childhood. She nostalgically recalled "my father who lived in the 'new settlement' in northern Ohio. Indeed I believe he was one of *"the first,* who came into the unbroken wilderness in the town of A. [Andover] and the humble location in which I was born." Her mother she described as "the gentle wife, who with her woman's love had left home and kindred in the old Bay State, to create by her presence a new home in this wilderness. Here were born unto them four little girls who did not even imagine that their humble home was not a palace."[2]

Her depiction of her home as "one of love and peace," represents a truthful, albeit idealized, account of her early family life. She was the last of four daughters born in rural Andover, Ohio, to Joel Rice and Flavia Rice, née Bradley. Three girls preceded her birth: Celestia Resign, Cordelia, and Cirlissa, born in April 1822, September 1823, and July 1825, respectively. Only two of the girls survived until Colby's birth. Celestia Resign—the first Celestia—died in July of 1825, just two weeks before Cirlissa's birth. Two years later, on December 19, 1827, Colby—she was christened Celestia M.—arrived and inherited her deceased sister's name. Eighteen months later, in July of 1829, Flavia gave birth to a boy named John Bradley Rice. Colby failed to mention this fifth and final child born to Joel and Flavia; perhaps he was left out of the story because only two months after his birth, Flavia Rice passed away. Her mother died when Colby was only eighteen months old; consequently, she could have no real memory of her. Despite this fact, her writings consistently demonstrate how profoundly her mother's early death affected her. Colby's draft of her nostalgic rendition of her childhood reveals that she tried several alternate beginnings that incorporated her mother's death. Ultimately, she chose to discard those versions and continued the essay with an uplifting story of a happy home with an intact mother. Failure to completely come to terms with this loss may have contributed to her inability to incorporate her death into a story for her own children, preferring instead to garner an idealized account of her childhood based on her wishful assumptions.[3]

Colby continued her childhood reflections with descriptions of their "of course few and scattering" neighbors who, like her family, were working to build a life in this sparsely settled landscape in northeastern Ohio. The majority of settlers in this section of the new nation had started life in New England and eventually moved west to look for new opportunities, and Colby's parents were no exception. Her father was born in 1796 in Granby, Connecticut, and her mother spent her childhood less than ten miles away in Southwick, Massachusetts. In December of 1819, Joel Rice and Flavia Bradley married at Feeding Hills, just outside of Springfield, Massachusetts, at "the home of Elder Shepherd." According to family history, Flavia Bradley was descended from an "Irish gentlewoman of property" who had refused to take her husband's name. The veracity of this defiant step is unknown, and although the tradition did not live on in the New World, several generations later the genealogical notes made by her great-granddaughter proudly related this bit of family history. Sometime after their marriage, Joel and Flavia Rice, like many people looking for land in the early nineteenth century, moved west to Ohio. By 1830, the couple was settled in Andover, a pioneer community in southeastern Ashtabula County, Ohio, which borders Pennsylvania on the east and Lake Erie to the north. The young couple was one of very few families. In 1830, only about twenty-five other families lived in this newly settled portion of the county.[4]

Ashtabula County was part of the Western Reserve and, as such, had strong cultural and social ties with New England. The Western Reserve, a small section of the larger Northwest Territory, consisted of land that Connecticut had claimed as its own. The preexisting inhabitants of the area—the American Indians—had contested this claim. Several years of fierce competition for dominance meant many deaths on both sides before the native tribes of the area acquiesced to the greater firepower and white influx. The 1795 Treaty of Greenville, among other concessions, led to the removal of the tribes from the area. Connecticut ceded the territory that is now northeast Ohio to Congress in 1800. Congress then officially opened the land to settlement. A few pioneers had set out even before this time, but between 1795 and 1800, the total number of white adult men resident in the whole of the Northwest Territory was likely only five thousand. The first permanent settlers arrived at what would be Ashtabula County from Connecticut in 1798. The total number of residents of the Western Reserve in those two years before 1800 was probably not over 125, so these twenty-five Connecticut transplants to Ashtabula made up about a fifth of the Reserve total—a significant addition.[5]

The Connecticut foundation's effect cannot be underestimated. An 1878 history of Ashtabula County claims proudly that "Ashtabula County may well be considered the legitimate offspring of Connecticut. At least two-thirds of the pioneer settlers of the different townships were born within the boundaries of that State. Full one-half of her population to day [sic] can trace their lineage to the enlightened people . . . of the Connecticut. . . . It was but natural that the new colony should bear the impress of the Connecticut character."[6] What this "Connecticut character" meant was that unlike some sections of Ohio whose strong economic and family links to the Southern states lent them a more rustic feel, New England transplants considered themselves more urbane. They had brought their culture with them, which included orderly communities with schools, libraries, and churches connected by a strong sense of Puritan pride and work ethic.

The settlers would need that work ethic. Colby's essay describes the "unbroken wilderness" and the "humble log cabin" in which her family lived. The "surroundings demanded sturdy toil to fell the giant trees, and make the farm—that *was* to be when its crop of oak, chestnut, maple, beech and elm trees were removed—productive." Her words capture the essence of the struggle that these early settlers faced as they attempted to claim farmland from the "gently undulating," abundantly forested, and predominantly clay soil. Although farmers eventually grew wheat, corn, and oats, these products never would be sufficient to sustain a family. The area's future lay in its cows. Once the land was cleared, Ashtabula County primarily, and very successfully, produced and sold butter and cheese.[7]

Despite the challenges of the environment, occasional deadly skirmishes with the last remnants of American Indians, the fear linked to Tecumseh's attempts at forming an American Indian federation, and the few battles fought in nearby Lake Erie during the War of 1812, New England settlers continued their trek into northeast Ohio. By 1804, the Western Reserve population grew to between 400 and 500 people, and by 1812 this number surged to 1,500. Ashtabula organized as a county in 1811, and in the years after the war its population grew steadily. In 1820, approximately 7,400 people called it home, and by 1830, it boasted approximately 15,000 residents. In 1860, this number had doubled to 31,805 people. These new arrivals were a very homogeneous group—white, native-born, Protestant, farm families. The census information for the county at large from 1820 through 1870 lists no slaves and only a handful of immigrants and "free blacks." As Ashtabula County grew, new communities were born. In 1827, the village of Cherry Valley, initially an offshoot of Andover, officially broke away and elected its own local governing body. By 1829, the year Colby's brother John Bradley Rice was born and Flavia Rice died, it even boasted its own postmaster. The Rice family still lived in Andover when Flavia Rice died, but just over a year later in November of 1830, Joel Rice remarried, and sometime between 1830 and 1832, Joel Rice and his new wife Evelina Rice, née Johnson, moved the entire family several miles west to this new community—Cherry Valley, Ohio.[8]

Cherry Valley was fairly representative of what was considered the northwest at this time, in which transplanted New Englanders strove to recreate ordered communities within their still predominantly rural environments. True to this end, the first settlers to the Cherry Valley Township established an organized society in which they constructed their homes and businesses along several intersecting roads. The area's first road, Hayes Road—named after the man instrumental in its construction, Col. Richard Hayes—was built in 1812. The first frame barn was built in 1818, the first frame house in 1825, followed by a sawmill in 1829. By the time the Rices arrived from Andover in the early 1830s, Cherry

Valley was not merely a town legitimized by the act of a petition to separate, but an already viable community.[9]

Today, Cherry Valley consists of a few houses surrounded by woods and grape arbors identified by a sign at the intersection of Routes 90 and 11, but in the early and middle nineteenth century it was a thriving rural community. Initially, Cherry Valley was typical of many frontier settlements, as many people came and went during its first decade of existence. It eventually coalesced, as those residents who could afford to purchase and improve land stayed and those who could not moved on. In 1840, the year that Colby turned thirteen, Cherry Valley's population was 690 people—approximately a third each of men, women, and children. Throughout Colby's residency, this population remained fairly steady before starting to drop in the decade after the Civil War. By 1920 it had plummeted to only 256 people, and today it lacks a separate census figure or a post office of its own.[10]

Families like the Rices, who arrived in the 1830s and 1840s and settled, kept the population relatively stable. When the children and grandchildren of these families became adults, however, many of them either migrated to more urban areas or moved west. Although mobility typified the late nineteenth century, an additional factor contributed to Cherry Valley's lack of growth and eventual decline as compared to Ashtabula County as a whole: no railroad lines entered the community. Other parts of the county were connected by rail to each other and eventually to the rest of the country, but a rail line did not enter into the southeastern section of the county until 1873. In an age of transportation revolution centered on train travel, Cherry Valley's fate was sealed when the rail line passed to the east through Andover.[11]

Joel Rice, somewhat of an entrepreneur, worked at times as a peddler, a merchant, a farmer, and a speculator. He owned dairy-farm real estate and participated in the rising market economy by opening in 1832 the "second store" at the corner of Hayes and Center roads in Cherry Valley. Census reports show the family's assets to be among the highest in the community. The Rice family also continued to grow after their arrival in Cherry Valley. Three more children, Napoleon, Flavia E., and Jay Joel, were born in December 1831, November 1840, and March 1842, respectively. They also housed an occasional hired hand or young male relative who helped with the farm. During Colby's preteen years the household fairly consistently included two adult men who worked primarily on the farm, one adult woman who worked in the house and the farm, five children in school, and several under five years old. Young families dominated the community, so although the Rice household was typical, all indications also point to a certain level of prosperity.[12]

In basic character, Colby's family was much like those of her neighbors—typical northeastern pioneers who valued religion, education, and family. As will be discussed at length, her adult writings show quite a high level of discontentment with this typical life. These writings also indicate that, at least in Colby's view, other members of her family and community apparently did not experience this same sort of unhappiness. Why? Although discerning the inner workings of their minds is, unfortunately, not possible, we are privy to some of Colby's thoughts. Colby's self-reflective words provide evidence that those very factors so important in her community underpinned much of her later discontent. Ironically, those values assessed to be core to the "Connecticut character" of which Ohio was so proud contributed to her eventual struggles. An entire chapter of the previously noted 1878 Ashtabula County history describes the many laudable character qualities inherent in its "parent state." "Education was cherished. . . . Religious knowledge was carried to the highest degree of refinement and applied to moral duties. . . . There was mutual trust. . . . The widest latitude was given to forms of belief. . . . Connecticut from the first possessed unmixed popular liberty . . . kept active by the constant exercise of elective franchise. There was nothing morose in the Connecticut character. Life was not somber. . . . Religion itself sometimes wore the garb of gaiety."[13] The manner in which those themes of education, religious freedom, and personal liberty as a citizen manifested themselves throughout Colby's life affected many of her life goals as well as her level of happiness. Their initial embodiment occurred in her childhood.

Despite the cheery tenor of Colby's essay on her childhood, other evidence disputes this interpretation. Happiness was not a constant. In Colby's own estimation, her mother's early death serves as a turning point. Her father's second wife—he eventually would marry again and outlive his three wives—inadequately filled the void left by her mother's absence. Colby's extensive writings never mention Evelina Rice, who entered Colby's life in the role of stepmother in 1830 when Colby was only three years old, and remained in it until her death in December of 1863. Colby's descriptions and references to her father neglected to mention a spouse. This omission is especially ironic; prior to the marriage Evelina was already a part of the family. She was Flavia Rice's half-sister, thus Colby's aunt. Colby's daughter, J. Rose Colby, who as an adult wrote about her mother's early life, did describe Evelina Rice: "A strange form had taken the lost mother's place. Unloving eyes looked upon the child, harsh words filled her ear."[14] Apparently, Colby did not refer to Evelina Rice in a loving "motherly" way. Rose's own memories of the woman, which would have ended in 1863 when Rose was only aged six, must not have been positive enough to counteract those negative impressions.

Colby's early religious experiences did not foster happiness either. Colby's memories of her childhood church experiences could not even remotely be described as wearing a "garb of gaiety." Colby's father, Joel Rice, his successive wives, and various members of the extended Rice family are buried in the Congregational cemetery in Andover, which was where the Rices apparently attended worship services. Joel Rice was originally from Connecticut where the Congregational Church was the official state religion until 1818 and still dominated until well into the 1840s, so the family's membership in what could be a rather conservative denomination was not surprising. Congregationalism, when supported by a strong Puritan strain of Calvinism, with its emphasis then on the total depravity of humanity and the unconditional salvation of the elect, could have been a depressing force on a young girl unsure of her place. Colby's daughter validated this interpretation with her assertion that Colby's childhood religious experiences were indeed unhappy ones: "A stern religion beset her. John Calvin's gloomy soul inspired all about her, his dark fancies lowered over their lives. Terror and wonder and ignorant faith dwelt together in her mind." In her later life, Colby disavowed many aspects of this style of orthodox religion by repudiating the notion that God's presence was captured in the "gloomy" aspect of John Calvin. Her adult view that God's love was better seen and felt in a flower, however, came after a hard-fought battle against her Calvinistic religious influences. Looking back over his life, radical abolitionist Parker Pillsbury blamed the "drapery of gloom," which was his Calvinistic Congregationalist upbringing, for his poor self-confidence as an adult.[15] Colby also struggled with lifelong self-esteem issues, so perhaps like Pillsbury she never really threw off its effects.

Calvinism strongly influenced Colby's childhood home life, and Congregationalism was the area's first religious denomination; nevertheless, Methodists and Baptists soon predominated in Andover and Cherry Valley. Methodists met in people's homes in Cherry Valley as early as 1825, and a Baptist church was established in 1830. So although the Rices apparently remained practicing Congregationalists, Colby was exposed to other religious forces. Additionally, since Baptists and Methodists dominated the area, their influence played a significant role in the local culture as well as in the formation of societal norms of acceptable behavior. Colby and the Rice family must have felt this presence, even if they attended the Congregational church, as many of their closest neighbors—the Colbys, Cornells, Giddings, Greens, Higbees, McDaniels, and Sweets—were members of the Regular Baptist Church of Cherry Valley. David Colby, Colby's future father-in-law, was a leading member of the church and frequently took a major role in the decision-making debates of the Baptist church.[16]

The Regular Baptist Church's minutes validate the church's involvement in many aspects of people's daily lives beyond their spirituality. In June of 1837, a church committee deliberated on what to do about two members involved in a civil lawsuit. After one party to the suit claimed that "all that what I have done I view to be wrong" and asked for forgiveness, the church accepted his apology and allowed him to retain membership. Members were also regularly removed for infractions such as dancing, hunting on the Sabbath, and neglecting the church as well as more specific wrongs such as an "attempt to injure the character of Henry Andrew's wife," and "repeatedly getting intoxicated." Several members of the Regular Baptist Church were removed from church membership because they "violated their covenant obligations" by attending service at another church that appeared in Cherry Valley in the later 1830s: the Freewill Baptist Church.[17]

The existence of the Freewill Baptist denomination illustrates that even the dominating presence of established churches could not stop other religious influences from entering the community. The formation in 1839 of the Freewill Baptist Church, as the result of a theological difference with the Regular Baptist Church, represented the influence of a societal force that swept through the northeast United States in the first decades of the nineteenth century: the Second Great Awakening. The initial Great Awakening, one hundred years prior, gave birth to the Baptists, Methodists, and Presbyterians. The second incarnation, with its emphasis on a more individualistic and evangelistic form of worship, was given fire by the "father of modern revivalism," Charles Finney. Evangelical churches added the spirit of reform and perfectionism to church worship. Finney's arrival and presence as president at nearby Oberlin College in 1835 brought this spirit even closer to northeastern Ohio.[18]

The Second Great Awakening attracted far more women than men, and women dominated the benevolent efforts of the churches. Ideas about how to solve complicated social problems sometimes collided with patriarchal religious tradition and complicated spiritual choices. Antislavery reform efforts provide a prime example. Slavery became an important issue in the Western Reserve area of Ohio in the 1830s, and women formed numerous antislavery societies including the first female Ashtabula County Anti-Slavery Society in 1832. During this decade, many reformers experienced growing dissatisfaction regarding the methods proposed for ending slavery as well as the attitudes of the more conservative element that insisted on increasingly secondary roles for women. In particular, the Congregationalists experienced a certain degree of lost moral authority with their precept that women should not take an active or public role in the fight against slavery. For women involved in benevolent antislavery societies, this attitude made evangelical churches that more attractive. As the nineteenth century continued to unfold, social issues increasingly intertwined with religions practice and altered people's expectations regarding their church's role and their role within the church.[19]

Evolving personal and community ideas about religion and social issues played an important role in Colby's future struggles, but education proved one of the most important keys to both her satisfaction and dissatisfaction. Like religion, education was an early priority in Cherry Valley. Unlike her early church experiences, school brought happiness and a sense of well being to Colby's childhood. The first postmaster's wife taught the first school out of her home in the winter of 1829–30. Between that time and 1877, six separate "district" or common schools came into being. According to census records, most of the county's children between the ages of five and about sixteen years attended school. Like the majority, Colby likely received her initial schooling at one of these common schools, but unlike many of her cohorts, she also received further education during the early 1840s at a private seminary school, the Grand River Institute (GRI), located about twenty miles northwest in Austinburg, Ohio. This highly regarded institute opened its doors to female students in 1840.[20]

GRI apparently admitted women "on equal conditions with young men." The available course catalogs show no distinction between male and female curricula. Students had to be at least fourteen years old and furnish "satisfactory testimonials that they possess a good moral character; and that they are sufficiently acquainted with the elements of Orthography, Reading, Writing, English, Grammar, and Arithmetic" to complete a four-year curriculum in either the English or the Classical Department. Both departments required algebra and geometry. The English Department added courses such as rhetoric, chemistry, botany, universal history, political economy, logic, moral philosophy, and natural philosophy. The Classical Department concentrated on subjects such as Latin and Greek grammar, exercises, and translation before moving on to reading and analyzing selections from Cicero, Virgil, Homer, and others in the later years. Today's high school students likely would have found the curriculum quite challenging.[21]

The addition of females to the school was quite successful, especially in the 1840s when few other educational options for girls would have been available. As the decade unwound, the number of female students grew. The official 1850 roster of students lists fifty-four "Gentlemen" and forty-eight "Ladies" in attendance. Students hailed from various locales besides Ashtabula County, or even greater Ohio. Pennsylvania, New York, and Michigan were well represented as well as the occasional student from Canada. These students could not have been attracted by the luxury or the ease of life at the school. The catalogs describe the men's rooms as furnished with only stoves and bedsteads. The ladies received the addition of tables, chairs, and washstands, and at times the "Ladies' Hall was so full that trundle beds were made to run under the old fashioned high post beds . . . so the capacity of the rooms might be increased." The students were also expected to work off part of their room and board. The catalogs note that "From one-half to three-fourths of this expense is ordinarily paid from the avails of two to three hours daily labor." Since over twenty miles separated Austinburg and Cherry Valley, the best land route to the school was described as an ox-cart trail; travel was still horse drawn at its best, and Colby likely boarded there at least during the week.[22]

Colby's time in Austinburg at Grand River must have affected her in ways beyond mere formal education. GRI may have helped establish the foundation for her future progressive leanings. Austinburg was a community in which the "abolition sentiment" was always quite strong, and it served as a well-known station for the Underground Railroad. Today, Betsy Mix Cowles—an early GRI teacher, administrator, and pioneer in women's higher education—is remembered as much for her antislavery work and devotion to the cause of women's rights as her role in education. In addition, American Anti-Slavery Society speakers, including Abby Kelley, spent the summer of 1845 in the Western Reserve promoting their progressive brand of reform. Their radical stances included a call for "disunion" with the slave-holding states, abolition of Ohio's Black Laws, disseverment from all involvement with politics, and a complete break from religious organizations that did not openly condemn slavery by ending ties with Southern branches. In 1857 Colby noted the fact that she had seen Abby Kelley speak earlier in life, which most likely occurred during this visit.[23]

A broad movement encouraging children's education existed in nineteenth-century, northeastern, dairy-farm families. Families with below average-sized farms or with numerous daughters saw further education as a means to provide a plan for the gap between girlhood and marriage by training young women to teach school. In addition to its role as a stopgap, teaching could bring in extra money for the family. Nevertheless, whether any of Colby's siblings attended Grand River Institute is not known. Their names do not appear in any available student rosters, and contextual evidence lends itself to a conclusion that they did not attend GRI. Sons and daughters were crucial to dairy farming, which was very much a cooperative effort that needed both male and female help. Colby's brothers, John Bradley and Napoleon, turned fourteen in 1843 and 1845, respectively, and as the only boys, their labor would have been essential. In addition, Evelina Rice, who turned forty in 1842, bore a child in both 1840 and 1842. Cordelia and

Cirlissa would have been seventeen and fifteen years old, respectively, when the school opened its doors to women in 1840. However, with two new additions to the family, extra responsibilities beyond the usual tasks associated with their dairy work likely fell to the teenage girls, which may have made leaving home less likely. Cordelia remained in the Rice household until her marriage in May of 1848. Cirlissa remained for another fifteen years until her marriage in October of 1862. The continued presence of both Colby's older sisters may have allowed for Colby's absence. If that is the case, then her place as the third daughter and fourth woman in the family hierarchy was an important factor in her opportunity.[24]

The community's "Connecticut character" as well as the family's history may have been an impetus to provide continued education for the children when possible. According to family lore, great-grandfather Peter Rice—the original Rice immigrant—had been a lawyer. Evidence also indicates that Joel Rice had more than a common school education. An extant math notebook from his childhood demonstrates his knowledge of advanced algebra. Whatever the final reason, Colby's attendance was a high point in her young adulthood. Ironically, it also served as a foundation for later dissatisfaction with her life. Many dairy farmers wrestled with the decision of providing further education for their children precisely because of this fear that their children, especially their daughters, would develop a future dissatisfaction with farm life and view it as "drudgery." Education did complicate the perceptions of available roles, particularly for women, in the mid-nineteenth century. In this rural area, in particular, the pride in their New England character sometimes clashed with their need for the whole family to labor on the farm, as education conflicted with farm needs.[25]

Regardless of the potential clash, some farmers did send their sons and daughters away to school, and the Grand River Institute served this increasing need. Biographies of several former students clearly show they viewed their attendance with pride. One student, who went on to serve as an Ohio senator, referred to the school's curriculum as "college prep." Another former student noted that he took classes on alternate terms while teaching at a district school. The institute obviously allowed for those students whose plans did not include direct entrance into college. This group included female students, who had almost no avenues to pursue any higher education, but likely a significant number of males as well. Through the end of the 1840s, Ohio had only eleven colleges, and up until the 1870s, only about 1 percent of college-aged Americans—men or women—attended college.[26]

By 1840, female common school education was rapidly becoming the norm, particularly in the urban northeast, but Colby's further education at this institution must be placed in broader context. As 1840 opened, Ohio had only two female seminaries and five normal schools, or academies, including Grand River Institute. GRI was roughly equivalent to the high schools of today, but as the school's own history described, "It will be remembered that at this time [1840] the higher education of women in America had scarcely reached its experimental stage and there was not a co-educational school in existence of any importance. Mary Lyon had just founded Mt. Holyoke." This statement was not completely factual, but only a handful of avenues for women's higher education existed. Even the most famous example, Oberlin College, which by 1840 admitted women, expected those early female students to follow "ladies [*sic*] courses" and receive special degrees. Those two institutions, however, were vital to GRI's inclusion of female students; the first two preceptresses of the school's "Ladies [*sic*] Department" were Mount Holyoke graduate Katherine Snow and Oberlin graduate Betsy Mix Cowles. As Colby attended school sometime between 1841 and 1847, her time may have coincided with one or both of these women's tenures. Cowles held the post from 1843 to 1848, so Colby likely spent at least a year under her tutelage.[27]

Pinpointing Colby's duration at Grand River proved difficult, but likely was limited to the early 1840s. She turned fourteen years old—the minimum age for attendance—in December of 1841. She is not included in the available GRI rosters of students for the school years ending in July of 1846 or June of 1848. Although Colby made her first decisive reference to school in an August 1847 poem, "On the death of C.A. Weeks," in which she wrote sadly on the death of a school friend, her earliest extant writing, much of it poetry, appears in a journal dating back to 1844. As students were required to read and analyze poetry, perhaps this experience was the catalyst for her own writing. These poems are not intermingled with schoolwork, so possibly she began keeping her writing journal after finishing school or during breaks. Unfortunately, most of these early poems were sentimental works that provide no direct clues about school attendance. Typical examples of this early work include an undated poem most likely written around 1844 entitled, "My Sister's Grave," which romanticizes the positive aspects of a death in childhood:

> Where not grief can reach thee sister
> For thine's a happy lot.
> Sweet Sister would that *I* like thee
> In infancy had died,
> From sin and sorrow I should be free
> If sleeping by thy side.

Numerous other poems are somewhat sentimental or romantic portraits dedicated to friends and family, but other maudlin pieces similar in style to the
above included this acrostic devoted to her mother:

Mother ever dear, thy name dwells with me here
Oh! May thy fond spirit linger near;
To comfort and console and cheer my lonely way
Here oft at the calm sunset hour
Each evening come. I'll own thy power,
Return to thy native skies with sun's last ray.

This is one of the earliest of many poems that clearly demonstrates the lingering loss Colby felt for years after her mother's death.[28]

True to society's intended purpose for further female education, Colby also
taught school for an undetermined span during the 1840s. During her tenure,
she attended in October 1847 a ten-day Ashtabula County Teachers' Institute
course as a Cherry Valley common-school instructor. Although Colby attended only one session between 1846 and 1851, this fact does not necessarily lead
to a conclusion that she taught only for one year. In 1846, Ashtabula County
sponsored its first Teachers' Institute, and although sessions were held annually
from that point, attendance varied. Repeat attendance was not uncommon, but
often not in succeeding years. Two other Cherry Valley teachers, Henry Green
and Jesse Higbee, attended only in 1846 and 1848, and 1847 and 1850, respectively. Regardless of the exact timing of her teaching tenure, Colby rode the
leading edge of the rise in female teachers. In 1847, Ohio employed less than
2,000 female teachers, but over the next decade women swelled the ranks and
pulled almost even with male teachers. In 1854, over 6,400 women taught at the
common school level and sixty-three women at the high school level as compared to just under 7,500 men in the common schools and seventy-one at the
high school level. By 1866, Ohio's public schools certified over 11,000 women
and just over 7,600 men.[29]

If the Teachers' Institute's attendance rosters provide an accurate indication
of the evolving Ashtabula County male-female ratio, then the county was also
on the leading edge of the rise in female teachers. In 1846, 75 "gentlemen" and
60 "ladies" attended the Institute. In 1847, the balance shifted to 70 men and 84
women, and in 1850, this imbalance became even more pronounced with 125
women in attendance compared to only 69 men. This ratio may help explain why
the following resolution appeared in the 1850 Teachers' Institute's minutes, but

not in the 1840s: "Resolved, that we deem the qualifications of Female Teachers underrated by the small compensation allowed them for teaching; and in our opinion the same amount of labor performed with equal ability should be equally rewarded, whether performed by male or female." Ashtabula County female teachers' longevity may have been different than the rest of the states in the Northeast in general. Contrary to the norm, evidence shows several of Ashtabula County's female teachers may have taught for at least a six-year stretch from 1847 through 1851. Most young women's teaching careers fell far short of that mark, and Colby likely fell into that norm.[30] By the summer of 1847, her days as a teacher were over, as her life continued to head down the expected path.

In April of 1848, Colby wrote a poem-styled letter to a school friend, titled, "Ever dear Nette." This letter obliquely addressed this coming change, as well as the subject of GRI. She spoke fondly of their days there.

> With "kind regards" my love to you I send.
> My loved, my cherished school day friend.
> Memory oft winds her [illegible] to those days that are past
> Too bright and joyous were they to last.

She continued with an implicit reference to her reason for no longer attending classes:

> For school days are passed, and never again shall I
> Mingle with student, a student of "G.R.I"
> The "obvious reason" that you mention
> I think must be your own intention
> But such reasons do not work in every rule.[31]

This letter apparently alluded to the next major event in Colby's life. In August of 1847, she had become engaged to Lewis Colby. They were both nineteen, and their families were longtime neighbors. In honor of their engagement, Colby described her hopes for the future in an acrostic.

> Lewis for thee I wish much joy
> Ever happy be, without alloy.
> Wealth, I ask not; for I know full well,
> In contentment superior pleasure dwell.
> Sweet content be thine, and joys no longer can tell.

Celestia Rice penned this August 1847 acrostic in honor of her impending marriage to Lewis Colby. Used by permission Colby Collection, Illinois State University Archives, Illinois State University, Normal, Illinois.

Her engagement and pending marriage would seem to be the "obvious reason" for not attending further classes or teaching. Interestingly, if that is the case, Colby seems to caution Nette not to leap into marriage herself. The above letter also makes clear that by the spring of 1848, Colby had attended her last class. She also wrote numerous poems between her engagement in 1847 and her marriage in the summer of 1848, indicating that she may have spent the winter months in Cherry Valley, not teaching or matriculating.[32]

Colby's life to this point dovetails neatly with what has been characterized as the "domestic life cycle" of a proper, northeastern, native-born, white woman. This domestic life cycle had its beginnings in childhood, where games, toys, children's literature, and education were gender specific and designed to instill proper norms and cultural beliefs. After the completion of a girl's available educational opportunities, which at mid-century terminated at no higher than the secondary level, a proper young woman's next steps were quite limited. She frequently stayed home and apprenticed at her mother's side until her early twenties or in some cases, particularly in the New England area, she taught school for a short period of time. The ultimate goal for a true woman, however, was to marry and move to the next stage of the cycle. This phase of a woman's life—marriage with the roles of wife, mother, and household manager—was even more directly set by law and societal norms than was childhood. Married women's legal rights were strictly limited. Prescriptive literature that spelled out proper guidelines for behavior saturated nineteenth-century material culture, and societal pressure to conform was intense.[33]

This domestic life cycle was purported to be the expected course for all women. This supposed ideal for all women, the "True Woman," served as the linchpin that kept the quickly emerging and changing modern world from becoming unmanageable; all women were to aspire to this status. Only a small percentage of real women—primarily from the northeast, urban, white middle-class—would have realistically had the resources to maintain the type of lifestyle recommended by the prescriptive literature. For the most part, the reality of working women, rural farming women, and the poor was ignored. The message was a powerful one, however, and it affected even those women who were not its primary targets. The urban middle class did not enclose the only literate women in the nation, and this supposed ideal of womanhood reached women whose real lives did not have the capacity to embrace it, even if they desired. As a working member of a rural farm family, Colby would not have been a prime target of the message. Nevertheless, she was educated, intelligent, and well read, and over the years she felt its pull and reacted to it, regardless of its intended audience.

Research shows that rural women indeed reacted to the social construction of the feminine ideal, but they experienced the ideal in a different way because their day-to-day lives diverged in significant ways from their urban sisters. Despite the present-day acknowledgment that the idealized separate woman's sphere was not an actual physical reality for rural or urban women, it had real effects on all of society's—and the individual's—definition of womanhood, not just those in the urban northeast. In July of 1848, Celestia Rice started down the path to the next stage of womanhood, as envisioned by society, when she married Lewis Colby. As one historian notes, most nineteenth-century women possessed the expectation that marriage was the first step toward fulfilling their "destinies," and all indications were that Colby was happy to continue along this expected domestic path.[34] Her marriage marked the end of an old life. She had been a young working woman whose life had been dominated for the last several years by learning and teaching. She now began her new life as a wife, a live-in daughter-in-law, and a soon-to-be mother. During the next few years, her experiences in the outward world and her slowly evolving personal goals began to diverge and challenge her ability to achieve happiness in that socially defined role.

CHAPTER TWO

1848–1853

"It is my *first desire* to be a blessing to my husband and . . . train up my child in the way of virtue and religion"

IN AUGUST OF 1851, four years after her summer 1847 engagement, Colby noted in her journal, "Oh that I might live the past over again! How little would its record be like that which it now is. How very little would remain unchanged." It is unclear what aspects of her life she specifically regretted, but other entries made that autumn show a general dissatisfaction with her life. "Visited Mrs. N . . . this afternoon. It was quite like the generality of my visits. I do not know but that I am *unsocial* in my disposition. I seldom have a *good visit*. I go more for customs sake than with any expectation of pleasure. There are exceptions, but as a general thing, I find more real pleasure in solitude with pen, ink & paper and books than the majority of visits afford me." In 1848, as a twenty-year-old girl, Colby happily chose marriage and membership in a new family. By late 1851, she had matured into a young wife and mother, and that happiness seemed somewhat compromised. Somewhere along the early journey from girlhood to womanhood, her reality either failed to live up to her expectations or her expectations began to change because the theme of dissatisfaction became more common in her private writings. In the years after 1851, Colby clearly articulated that she felt a void in her life. She tried to fill it with reading and writing, and although she enjoyed these pastimes, she continued to hope for emotional and intellectual satisfaction beyond that provided by pen and paper. She wanted higher human contact and worried that she "might not find the gem I seek, a *kindred heart*."[1]

Initially, Colby expected that Lewis would fill this important role. From Colby's view—which is the only one we are privy to—their union began as one based on love; however, even that love did not ensure a smooth transition. In July of 1848, Lewis Colby and Celestia Rice officially married, but it would be three months before Colby "left [her] *youthful home* to share the joys and sorrows of another." The reasons behind this delay can only be speculated. Lewis, as a male under twenty-one, was a minor and needed the consent of a guardian to wed. Their marriage application contains this permission form; Converse G. Colby—Lewis's older brother—signed this form rather than their father, David Colby. Several reasons could be behind this aberration. Perhaps David Colby, who was sixty-six at the time, was unavailable or sick. He even may have been reticent about the decision. Lewis was the youngest male child and the only able-bodied son still at home; David may have desired that he wait to marry. Family expectations may have entered into the picture on the Rice side as well. Daughters were integral to the family dairy process, and Colby's sister, Cordelia Rice, had recently married and left the Rice household in May of 1848. Perhaps Colby's family needed her to remain at her childhood home through the end of the cheese-making season, which culminated in October. Regardless of the reason for the three-month wait, when the couple finally began living together in the autumn of 1848, it was at the home of David and Naomi Colby where they would remain until Lewis's parents died.[2]

Colby lamented this living arrangement almost from its inception. She never felt free to truly live an authentic family life. "I have just been rambling in search of berries. We passed an old deserted log house surrounded by woods and once the *home* of a large family . . . and I longed for some quiet retreat from the cares of the world, some *sweet solitude* that I could call *our home* where no sounds would reach us but those of *harmony* & *love*."[3] Colby "longed" for some place to call "our home." Although at the time of this particular lament she had been married only two years, her dissatisfaction with her living situation is already obvious. She feared the environment infringed on the couple's greater potential for "harmony & love." Lewis's obligations to his parents truly may have limited his ability to offer Colby a "kindred heart." She clearly felt this connection was compromised, and although the couple's romantic bond lasted past their courting period, she felt growing frustration regarding the totality of her living situation. She had willingly and happily entered into married life, so questions come to mind when reading the discontent evident in her journals. What had she likely anticipated from her life? Where did her notions about her future arise that her reality spawned such disenchantment? And was there more behind her unhappiness than merely living with her in-laws?

Colby's ideas about her future likely amalgamated from various sources. Her teenage writings, including her engagement acrostic, show her to be a romantic. She obviously had an emotionally based idea of what to expect from her marriage. Historical scholarship concludes that romantic love had a significant place within marriage choices for many Northern middle-class couples by the 1830s. It is impossible to know how many nineteenth-century couples actually married for love, but the idea of romantic love was certainly a popular cultural ideal by this time. Colby was an avid reader, so her images of marriage no doubt were fed by the popular domestic novels of the time, by authors such as Catherine Maria Sedgwick, E. D. E. N. Southworth, and Lydia Sigourney, whose romantic leading heroines were epitomized not only as idealized caretakers of home and community but also as women who were immersed in epic love stories. In addition, these popular depictions of romantic courtship emphasized what was considered an important facet of the idea of romantic love: the "self-revelation and disclosure" between couples. This "identification of inner states" encouraged romantic ideas about married life.[4] These ideas clearly provided the emotional foundation for Colby's belief that Lewis would be that longed-for "kindred heart."

Another avenue of information that likely affected Colby's expectations regarding her marriage was encompassed in societal ideals. By the middle of the nineteenth-century, prescriptive literature, legal limitations, and mainstream societal norms provided a rather unified picture of the role that women were expected to play in order for the ideal home to function as modern society envisioned. A modern woman's role incorporated the performance or overseeing of all of the tasks necessary to produce a safe and happy home in which her husband could retreat in calm and contentment from the public pressures of work and politics, and her children could receive the moral education and support necessary to become future ideal male citizens and female republican mothers. A true woman, although submissive, was portrayed as the heart in the center of the family; it was her duty to keep them all on the proper path. Whether a woman hailed from the northeastern urban United States, the Midwestern "prairie," or the Great Plains "frontier," her perceived duty was the same: she served as the "housekeeper": morally, socially, and in the physical sense of housework. In addition, as the perception crystallized that this housekeeping role was every woman's natural duty, women's own visions of their tasks were reshaped. If it was "natural" then it was not "work." The notion that a "magical transformation" took place within a woman's household grew into an overall view that women's responsibilities could be categorized as nonlabor. As historical research documents, chief among the repercussions of this "pastoral fantasy" regarding women's daily lives was the "growing devaluation of their contributions . . . in the family economy." Regardless of the actual labor invested

in housework, it was considered to have no intrinsic—or monetary—value in
the growing market economy. "Housekeeping" was considered fundamental to
a woman's role, so regardless of its unrealistic base and the demeaning message
regarding its so-called real worth, deviation from societal norms engendered
criticism, rejection, and increased efforts at social control. So, in many homes,
expectations regarding the ideal were not necessarily lowered, but rather, effort
was increased.[5]

Societal and romantic ideas aside, the reality of marriage was very different
from either the ideal of the wife creating—effortlessly—the peaceful sanctuary for her family or the epic love story of fictional marriages. This fact was
especially true in pioneer farm families like Colby's. Frances Trollope, an Eng-
lishwoman and writer who lived for several years in Cincinnati in the 1820s
and 1830s, described the life and the "enormity" of work done by an isolated
farmer's wife. She "spun and wove all the cotton and woolen garments of the
family, and knit all the stockings. . . . She manufactured all the soap and candles
they used, and prepared her sugar from the sugar trees on their farm. . . . The
life she leads is one of hardship, privation, and labour." In Trollope's opinion,
these rural women married too young, bore too many children too close together, and were generally old before their time. Later in her life, in much the
same spirit as Trollope, Colby described the "multitude of little chores" as the
base from which the "the history of my life—my outer life," was made.[6]

Colby grew up as part of an extended farm family, so responsibilities similar to Trollope's descriptions would have been part of her childhood. She witnessed the married life and working arrangement between her father and his
wife; she also likely knew Lewis Colby and his family for most of her life. The
Colbys had moved from New Hampshire to Cherry Valley in 1834 and, like the
Rices, were also dairy farmers. Lewis's brother, Orrin Colby, was also a common-
school teacher in Cherry Valley during Colby's teaching tenure.[7] So she would
have been familiar with the lifestyle as well as with the family life of her new
in-laws. Despite this supposed realistic familiarity, a strong cultural framework
prescribed her duties from an idealistic and unrealistic viewpoint, and she, no
doubt, had romantic ideals of marriage. In addition, to further complicate expectations, she had experienced at least a brief period of limited autonomy as a
student and teacher. Given these various influences, what could Colby reason-
ably expect from her married life as she entered a world in which she was to
function in the role of married woman—all under the auspices of her in-laws?

No extant personal writings that directly address her premarital expectations survive, so it is impossible to truly know her mindset as she began married life. Realistically, she should not have been too surprised by the direction

her life took. In most aspects, her life had followed society's ideal of the domestic life cycle: she was born into an aspiring pioneer family, educated through secondary school, taught for a short time, and then married. Her life path was remarkably similar to her mother's path as well as the path taken by most girls her own age: marriage was the expected outcome for a young woman. Rural women, like Colby, who came of age in the 1840s, were immersed wholly in a culture that structured women's identities through their husbands and as such they fully expected that adulthood would bring marriage. In addition, they expected that marriage offered their best chance for contentment. Beyond its place in forming women's identities, marriage functioned in another important way not only for the couple, but also for the community at large. As one historian notes regarding marriage in rural communities, it "served as both a manifestation and a symbol of social relations that bound the larger community." In short, marriage was a "given" for most antebellum women and men.[8]

This status was well reflected in Colby's community. At the time she began her married life, the vast majority of her neighbors between eighteen and thirty years old also were beginning their lives as newly married couples and parents. In 1850, of the twenty-five females living in neighboring Cherry Valley households who were in their late teens to their late twenties, only two were unmarried, and almost 70 percent of the young married couples had children. Many of these couples—like the Colbys—were unions of neighboring families. Commonly, these newly married couples set up a household near their parents, but in separate space. In this respect the Colbys were a bit out of the ordinary, but not overly so. They were not the only young couple to board with parents. In most respects, the Colbys' lives were entirely normal.[9]

Despite this normality or perhaps because of it, after two years into her marriage, Colby clearly articulated disillusionment. Her words demonstrate that her life clearly did not match the "pastoral fantasies" that she held before marriage. "A day of toil has passed. . . . A train of pleasing memories, and some sad ones, throng my heart filling it with visions of the past. With what glowing colors did imagination once paint the future, clothing every scene with unreal brightness, till life appeared a fairy land of bliss; but reality, *stern reality*, too often shows the falsity of our youthful *dreams*." Colby's initial expectations obviously laid a foundation that led to future tension and dissatisfaction with her so-called normal life. Her expectations at this point, whether they had been realistic or not, were not being met. However, even before this two-year mark, Colby's actions—specifically her choice to embrace evangelism—also can be interpreted as an indication that she was dissatisfied, or unprepared, for the reality of her new life. Although her early words do not indict Lewis for emotionally failing her, he traveled frequently, so his ability to sustain her was compromised not only by his parents' apparently unsupportive presence, but also by his physical absence as well. Considering Colby's clear attempts just a few years later to establish a greater sense of individuality, it is important to note that the stress she experienced during her early married years apparently stemmed not from a fear of the loss of personal independence or identity, but rather, it arose from her anxiety regarding her place within the context of her new family. Her sense of self was imbedded deeply within the concept of belonging to a whole, and her place within this new family was inadequately satisfying to her.[10]

Her new life, particularly the first several years, represented an in-between stage in her maturity. Her duties were unclear; she was no longer only a daughter, nor was she a student or a teacher, but she did not have a clear position within adulthood. She was a wife, but she did not live in her own home or have children, so it is unlikely that she was allowed or expected to assume the role of "woman of the house." This state of flux provided a perfect foundation for a crisis of identity, or rite of passage. Rites of passage accompany changes in social position, status, or role and are the process in which an individual leaves a known role and adapts to a new one. Anthropologists usually describe this process as having three stages: separation; liminal, or between; and aggregation. Separation involves a symbolic behavior, such as marriage, that moves a person from one set of responsibilities to another. The between stage can be characterized by temporary disorder. The person feels "outside of social restraints and norms" and may attempt to find a guidepost or anchor. Finally, aggregation occurs when society integrates the person into the new role.[11]

In Colby's case, the liminal stage may have manifested itself as an evangelistic religious conversion. The timing certainly supports the idea that she was looking for something to provide emotional confirmation. One year after moving to her new home, Colby recalled the initial stages of this conversion. "One year ago today, for the first time in my life, I attempted to tell the feelings of my heart on the subject of religion in public. Words could not express them but bitter tears bespoke the agony of my heart. Prayer was offered in my behalf. . . . For two days my peace was as a river . . . but told no one. . . . Soon unbelief fell its soul-chilling influence upon me. . . . For months did I groan beneath the bondage of sin." By January of 1849, her soul seeking reached the next level of resolution, as she "first dared to believe that God for Christ's sake had forgiven my sins, and first confessed to the world my faith in Jesus." She achieved the next phase in March of 1849 when she "experienced the pardoning love of god, and felt my sins forgiven." Finally, in June of 1849, she noted, "Baptized in the 'name of the Father son and Holy Ghost.' It was a solemn yet happy time."[12]

Spiritual self-examination, or as one historian characterizes it, "exposure of oneself to God," was a common impetus for journal writing in the nineteenth century, and, apropos to that fact, Colby's declaration, in March 1849, of God's pardon initiated her regular practice of writing. Over the next eighteen months or so, although she noted such things as attending worship services, or "class meetings," and her role as a Sunday school teacher, she used her journal almost exclusively as an avenue for personal, spiritual self-flagellation and glorification of God. "My greatest desire is that I may be wholly conformed to the will of God, that I may have no will of my own." Denial of self-worth was quite a contrast to her writings from the mid-1840s, which although sentimental and occasionally maudlin, were often notably happy in tone. An 1847 poem offers self-affirmation:

I am not what I seem,
That careless gay and thoughtless one
Which many deem;
The course of thought will sometimes run
Across my giddy brain
Swift as the clouds pass o'er the sun
And all is thoughtlessness again.

Her writing in the years before her marriage lends itself to an interpretation that she was relatively content with what she perceived to be her life's path. This attitude is especially evident in those works related to her school days. Only a year prior to her March 1849 conversion, her poem to "Nette" was lighthearted in its tone and made a positive statement on her life.[13]

However, from the first entry in March 1849 until late in 1850, her entries, which were made at least weekly, illustrate an attitude of personal and spiritual worthlessness. "Why is my heart so prone to unbelief—so prone to doubt the goodness of my heavenly Father. I feel that I am living *far below* the Christian's privilege—far below the *bible standard* of piety. I do not enjoy that 'peace which passeth understanding,' nor am I filled with 'joy, unspeakable and full of glory.' I feel that I fall *far short* of what I *ought* to be. My faith is too weak, my love too cold. Sin mixes with all I do. Shall I give up and go back to the world? *Never no never.*" She attended frequent "class meetings," but she worried that her "slavish fear" regarding public prayer was standing between her and God. She noted that when "I pray in the presence of others . . . my mind becomes confused so that I scarcely know for what I am asking." She berated herself for pride and selfishness, but she also concerned herself with the personal sins of other people's nonbelief.[14]

She attempted frequently to "introduce the subject" of religion to friends and family and worried about her potential responsibility if someone she cared for died without accepting conversion. "Had a conversation with E. [possibly Eunice Linsley, a neighbor] on the subject of religion. . . . I called her attention to the great Author of all things and our own obligation to him. She seemed to think there was *no reality* in religion and *no truth in the bible*, but acknowledged she seldom read it, and knew but little of what it contains. I can but pity her and pray that God may open her eyes." A month later she noted, "Yesterday I visited at Mr. K's. While conversing with F. I tried to introduce the subject of religion but I did not succeed in conversing freely on that most important subject." A few months later, she attempted to raise the subject with a visitor and berates herself for not maintaining the level of discourse. "Yesterday Mrs. E.H. came here and staid all night. I tried to introduce the subject of religion and partially succeeded, yet I fear I joined too much in light conversation for my own good." She asked herself if one of them should be "eternally lost, would I be guiltless? I feel not."[15]

Colby's love of reading is obvious throughout her life, and during this period she struggled with the church's dictate that she should stop reading fictional novels and newspaper stories because they were sinful. She declared fiction to be "Literary Poisons draped in a fascinating form to make them pass. . . . Their influence on the soul is slow and imperceptible but not the less deadly to all that is good." She determined that "by the assisting grace of God, I resolve, never to indulge in reading that class of writing so aptly styled 'light Literature.' It is mortifying that I should be so attached to them." And although a reading of the entire New Testament in the summer of 1849 must have provided sufficient material to fill her time, by autumn she had broken her promise. "This resolution has to day been broken, O how frail I am!"[16]

Colby fixated on her prior religious weaknesses, such as the failure to "earlier seek my Savior" and her regrets over "how long I resisted his holy spirit," as well as doubts over her depth of current belief. Despite this personal intensity, no evidence indicates she was concerned with the wider world's "social sins." Those topics, such as intemperance, morality issues, or Sabbath reform, were frequently a focus of the more urban sects of evangelical revivalism, but she does not mention involvement in benevolent reform efforts. Instead, Colby's reflections, which marked her second wedding anniversary, reveal the parameters she hoped would guide her life: the fulfillment of her personal duties within her sphere of influence as given by God. "It is two years this evening since I became a wife. I have tried to perform the duties of a wife with faithfulness and fidelity. It is my *first desire* to be a blessing to my husband and to be enabled to train up my child in the way of virtue and religion. What higher and important duties rest upon me. O that I may receive grace from on high to aid me. May the Lord be with me guide and direct—*all* my acts." [17] Her conversion experience has a very personal, almost self-indulgent, tone to it. Even her concerns over other people's sins intertwine with her feelings of guilt over her own failings to save them. This observation, along with the timing of her most intense involvement, which spanned from her move to the Colby household in 1848 until after the birth of her first child in 1850, corroborate the idea that her conversion was part of a crisis of identity, or "rite of passage," from childhood to womanhood.

In the spring of 1849, Colby had noted, "I believe the first desire of my heart is holiness." By the spring of 1852, after "looking over the record of the past," she inquired of herself, "Where is the blessedness I knew, when first I saw the Lord." Colby had noticed her faltering faith. The peace she had once hoped that her belief would provide seemed only a memory. "A quiet Sabbath . . . but my heart does not feel its sweet influence as it often has in other days. Restless desires, and longings that may not be satisfied on earth are ever flitting before me." She struggled with where to turn to fill the void she felt in her life.

> Thus far the day has been passed in working, reading, writing, and *think-ing*. Happy thoughts & sad ones have alternately thrown their sunlight and shadow upon my heart, though the shadows are sometimes *too deep* for a momentary gleam of sunlight to dispel. There are feelings in my soul that *will not slumber*, *aspirations* that I *cannot crush*, and longings that are never satisfied. O the struggle within, which I sometimes endure. O woman, earnestly do I pray that a brighter day may dawn on thee. Truly thou wert not made for an idle toy, for the sport of an idle hour, or yet for a *slave* to toil on, and on, through life hopelessly and unrewarded.[18]

Evangelistic religion no longer satisfied her higher aspirations, if it ever truly had. In addition, she questioned society's prescriptions for a married woman. These questions could have been prompted by her dissatisfaction with her own role within her family and the church and likely had foundations reaching back to her school days.

As Colby became more comfortable with her adult duties, the role of evangelism became less significant. However, this growing familiarity with her new role did not translate into gracious acceptance of the inherent responsibilities. In addition, contrary to what may have been accepted and expected behavior, she showed no signs that she was embracing a more orthodox form of worship. Her journals illustrate that she resisted submitting to her expected societal role. At this time, this hesitancy manifested itself primarily as private thought, but

her dissatisfaction was laying a foundation for future and more public resistance. Research analyzing rites of passage in terms of women's involvement in
evangelistic religions offers an interesting look at why some of these women
"aggregated" back into the fold when patriarchal hierarchy reasserted itself, and
why some women chose to embrace even more radical forms of religious or
reform expression.[19] These ideas add insight to our interpretation of Colby's
choices as her life unfolds.

During the first several decades of women's nineteenth-century participation in antiritualistic evangelistic religion, it served as an avenue for women to
assert power and autonomy. Women were, for the first time, not only allowed,
but also encouraged to speak or pray out loud in church and to create public
roles for reform purposes. However, throughout the 1840s and 1850s, church
leaders, almost exclusively men, increasingly reasserted their authority and expected women to take more "traditional" or submissive roles, in essence, to
aggregate into their expected roles. The women who were most likely to resist
that push back into submission were within the categories described by historical research as "socially inferior" and "socially marginal." Of course, it can be
argued that all women increasingly fell under the label of socially inferior as
white men gained greater egalitarianism. Obviously, not all women embraced
radicalism in any form; however, smaller subsets of women were, or felt, socially marginalized because they were different from the supposed norm of the
urban middle-class wife and mother. These women, for example, single women
or women from rural, economically pre-industrial families, were often among
the core of radical thinkers.[20]

As a rural-based dairy farmer, Colby fits into the latter class category. In
addition, she often expressed the feeling that she was different from not only
the supposed norm, but her own neighbors. The timing of Colby's evangelistic
experiences and her eventual public acceptance of progressive views offer cor-
roboration for this interpretation. Although Colby may have been drawn to religion as a means to ease her transition, evangelism also served as the means to
assert her autonomy and power as a woman during this transformation from
her previous role as a student, daughter, and friend into her new role as a wife,
daughter-in-law, and mother. It acted as an anchor during a period of disruption. The church gave her personal power in that she was individually responsible for her worthiness in God's eyes, but at the same time it reinforced ideas
of submissiveness. A fear of lost identity and independence had not necessarily predicated her evangelistic involvement, but her experience added fuel to a
simmering sense of growing individualism, and when the immediate tension
of the new situation resolved itself to a degree, Colby did not simply return to

the fold. She still felt unsettled, but evangelistic religion no longer provided the buffer for a reality that was increasingly unsatisfactory. From the spring of 1851, her entries demonstrate clearly her dissatisfaction, which she initially thought of as a crisis of faith; nonetheless, although she was aware of her disquiet, she was unclear as to how it would resolve itself.

She rebelled, at first privately, against quietly assuming the expected role of submissive "housewife," but eventually Colby's dissatisfaction took on a more public form as she turned to radical reforms and progressive religious expression. A closer look at different aspects of her early married life offer other possible factors that helped push her to her more radical and public positions. From the spring of 1849 to the winter of 1850, her journal provides, at minimum, weekly thoughts on her spiritual life. These entries, which read almost like prayers, report very little about her day-to-day life and make tracking the arc of her spiritual feelings much easier than framing her thoughts on the ordinary aspects of her daily life. By the summer of 1851, however, she focused more often on earthly aspects of her life and less on the spiritual, and with some additional extrapolation, a different light can be shed on her newlywed years.

As noted, from all signs, Colby's marriage began as one based on love. Unfortunately, after the first several years, it becomes more difficult to ascertain the nature of the relationship as Colby only seldom mentioned Lewis. Men frequently received little attention in nineteenth-century women's private writings, so this fact alone is not necessarily telling. One historian notes, in regard to Midwestern women's private writings, that when men do appear they are often "blurred, just out of focus to one side." Although evidence clearly alludes to unhappiness in the later years of Colby's marriage, nothing indicates that her dissatisfaction through the early 1850s was with her husband. Journal entries in those first years speak to a loving relationship; nevertheless, Lewis was frequently absent and these trips may have contributed to his inability to supply her the desired emotional support. Her entries made in the very early 1850s regarding his trips are revealing, not only because they display her loving feelings, but also because they provide foundational context for comparison to later years when his absences are less lamented. "Yesterday Lewis left home to be absent several weeks. Everything wears an aspect of loneliness when he is gone. May the Lord be with him to protect him from harm and return him in safety." A week later and still alone: "An air of loneliness rests in all around me. . . . Be thou also with my *beloved husband*. Guide him in his wandering—protect him from harm—save him from all sin and return him in safety."[21]

Although the extent to which Lewis joined in her evangelistic fervor is unknown, her conversion experience apparently did not alter her feelings for him.

Soon after publicly embracing God, she wrote about her changing perspectives on death, "not that the ties that bind me to the Earth are loosened, for I love my friends as well as ever, and he the *dearest* of them *all*, seems dearer now." Frequently, her written prayers contained loving references to Lewis: "I prayed for . . . my *dearest companion*" and "Still blessed of my Heavenly Father with life and health and the society of *one I love*." She also occasionally made reference to time they spent together talking or interacting as a couple: "Last night Lewis and I walked in the woods and called at his brothers. The walk back was truly delightful. . . . We talked of the *past*, the *present*, and *future*. We looked at the *past*, the *far off past* and spoke of those long months of absence and *uncertainty* which served to test our hearts. The present alone is ours, and it is our constant aim, together to seek that wisdom from on high to guide us right." All indications point to their interaction as a recently wed, happy couple. Those "long months of absence and uncertainty" may be a reference to the span between their marriage and the time they began living together. If so, it lends credence to the thought that forces beyond their own desires kept them apart for the first months of their marriage. Colby's assessment that "the present alone is ours" was accurate in more than a spiritual sense. Their little family was about to grow. In April of 1850 she was "blessed with a little boy," her first child, a son named Montie Plummer Colby, who was always called Plummer.[22]

Colby's pregnancy gave rise to a distressing sense of fear that religious devotion was inadequate to quell. She desired something more immediate and earthly: her mother. Although never specifically mentioned, Colby's evident fears reveal that she definitely felt the absence of a mother's support and presence. Her mother's death only two months after childbirth, no doubt, exacerbated Colby's primal fear of dying during the process. Weeks before her delivery, she noted, "How imperceptibly my life is gliding away. Soon, perhaps very soon, it will be gone forever." Several weeks later, she called to her faith in an attempt to subdue her fears of "death and the grave." She hoped that "surely that same *power* that can bring from cold dull earth such delicate and beautiful flowers, can preserve *my body* through *all its* changes." Even weeks after Plummer's birth, she worried about her survival. "I feel that my life is fast passing away, that death will soon close my time of probation."[23] This fear was in no way irrational or simply a byproduct of her mother's death; women and children died during and soon after childbirth with alarming regularity in the nineteenth century. Death was a harsh and common reality throughout early America.

Colby also felt emotionally unprepared for motherhood. This fear was more complex, but was due, at least in part, to the fact that she had no mother to guide her. In early March, she wrote, "The future too, rises before me with its cares and responsibilities for which I feel *unprepared*." And just one week before Plummer was born, she wrote, "Alone in my chamber, a feeling of sadness settles on my soul. . . . Thought turns to the future; the dark unknown future. . . . Oh how much need have I of wisdom on high, to guide me in the discharge of these new duties which are soon to be mine, and of which if neglected will turn that which was designed as a *blessing* into a *curse*." Unfortunately, her transference from motherless daughter to mother did little to fill the void left by her mother's death; it perhaps even widened it, as parenting highlighted what she lacked for herself.[24] Nevertheless, despite her fear, motherhood brought considerable joy into her life. Plummer replaced religion as the main focus of her days.

In June of 1851, the busy year after Plummer's birth was capped off with another pivotal event. The *Ladies Repository* published her original essay titled, "Flowers." The Methodist Church sponsored the *Ladies Repository,* which "sought to stimulate and develop feminine interests in religious and intellectual matters." This periodical and this first published essay represent a considerably different venue and goal than much of her later writings; nevertheless, it was a seminal event in her life. Her diary entry marking the publication provides an early illustration of the developing struggle to obtain a harmony between family and personal ambition. "Yesterday for the first time in my life I read my own thoughts and words in print. The composition which I sent to the Editor two months since was published in the Repository for June. I had scarcely anticipated that the result would be so favorable, as I was hardly satisfied with the production when I sent it. Yet it was the best I could do under the circumstances, it being written with a babe in my arms, while one hand held the pen, the other was employed in soothing my little one to slumber and as mother of course the mind was divided between both."[25]

No evidence indicates that in those early days of marriage and motherhood, Colby turned to her mother-in-law or her stepmother for support. She did, however, depend on her older sister Cordelia's support. She was the only one of her siblings about whom Colby regularly wrote in her journal, and they had a close bond. Her absence even for a short time caused Colby sadness. "Sister Cordelia left the place this morning for Pa. I shall miss her much. Months must pass ere we meet again." So Colby was very distressed when in September of 1851, Cordelia and her husband Zophar Davis moved their family west to the town of Geneva in Kane County, Illinois. Colby despaired that she had "parted with sister Cordelia to night perhaps *forever*." From the very earliest of Colby's writings, her deep and sentimental feelings in regard to a select group of female friends, as well as her sister, are obvious. Even before regular entries into her diary began, she featured them in highly sentimental and emotional poems and essays that romanticized their friendships. Cordelia, especially, served as a partial remedy to the empty space left by her mother's death. Colby, from young adulthood, attempted to create for herself what she lacked growing up: a supportive network. Historical scholarship finds that these networks, such as Colby desired, commonly developed from within a female sphere characterized by continuity, shared experiences, and mutual affection.[26] For Colby, however, cultivating friendships with women who shared daily experiences was less important than bonding with someone who shared her view on life, someone "like-minded." This attitude complicated her attempts to find the affection and support that she deemed adequate.

Her intensely religious entries during the early years of her marriage reflected this mindset. She worried that those whom she cared for most did not share in her spiritual feelings. Colby fretted that a friend's unhappiness stemmed from her lack of faith. "I have just been reading a letter written one year ago today from a youthful friend whom I have not often seen for several years. How it recalled the 'memory of the past' in all its freshness, and disclosed the *deep feelings* of the writer. Alas what a *change* has one short year wrought. . . . Young and talented, yet she is not happy. Oh that she might fall at the foot of the cross and find the only balm for a wounded heart in a *Savior's* love." Colby felt that only releasing the hold that earthly cares held could bring consolation. "Received a letter from Cordelia yesterday also one from 'Vine.' C. [Cordelia] seems to be enjoying the peace of mind that the world cannot give, the consolation of religion. Vine has strange feelings on the subject. She acknowledges her belief in experimental religion yet seems to think that there is enough '*native religion*,' as she terms it, to redeem us. Oh that she might know by experience the joys of believing." The concepts of experimental religion and native religion were part of a growing interest during this period in the idea that the scientific method could produce rational evidence of God. Natural theology brought the spiritual and the material world together with the idea that science could confirm religious truths and that God operates, and therefore could be seen, in Natural Law. The concomitant idea that this rational evidence could supersede biblical revelation would have been particularly troubling to Colby. Traditional Calvinists and evangelical revivalists viewed spiritual science, as the various incarnations of these ideas were known, as a dangerous practice that gave nature and rational thought precedence over God as the ultimate moral regulator.[27]

Over the years, Colby's religious feelings—including her thoughts about the spiritual sciences—changed, but her desire for her friends to be like-minded did not; in fact, it gained importance over time. During Colby's teen years and early twenties, along with her sister Cordelia, two other women stand out as vital connections: Cynthia and Vine. Their friendships represented a special bond that Colby desired in her life, especially after her evangelistic faith dulled. Unfortunately, these three women did not remain a constant in her life. Cordelia moved and Vine and Cynthia both died at a young age. Colby noted in early November 1850, "I have just heard the sad news of the death of my friend Cynthia. I loved her as a sister and can but mourn her early death." Both women were memorialized in poetry as well as with a living namesake. Colby's second child and her first daughter, Vine Cynthia, was born in September of 1852.

> Till we meet in spirit land
> Ah yes, I ever think of thee;
> Thy name is now our household word,
> My little Vine with artless glee
> Lisps the sounds so often heard
> ... And memory holds her sway
> Thoughts of thee and the sunny past
> Shall cheer me on my way.[28]

By the time of her daughter's birth, Colby's intense religious involvement had somewhat cooled. In the year preceding Vine's birth, she wrote much less in her diary. When she did write, she occasionally commented on her concern regarding her lack of spiritual fulfillment. She mused, "I have wandered from the only *true source* of happiness," and "where is the blessedness I knew, when first I saw the Lord." These occasional remarks reflect her awareness that her life no longer centered on total religious submission, but more often she merely reported receiving a letter, reading a book, or other miscellany. If she feared the birth of her second child, she did not record it in her journal. Nothing she wrote even clearly indicates her pregnancy or Vine's birth. Her last entry before Vine's birth complained about daily responsibilities. "The cares of Earth absorb too much of my time, and the necessary labor that depends on me leave but little time for the pleasanter occupation of reading and reflection. I grow dull and stupid."[29] Despite her joy regarding Plummer's addition to her life, obviously her responsibilities—as well as the literal burden of pregnancy no doubt—weighed heavily and resentment was surfacing.

Between that entry in August of 1852 and November of 1853, Colby made only five entries, of which two were poems, not reflections. In March 1853, she attended a lecture given by her brother-in-law Orrin Colby on "Education &c," which illustrates that her interest in secular education was reasserting itself. That same day, she also added a rather lackluster mention, "We moved last week into our future home. Perhaps in time, the sacred associations of home will cluster around it and endear it to the heart."[30] It is not clear whether this move included only the immediate family or if it also included her in-laws. Given her previous complaints about her living situation, undoubtedly a move into a home on their own would have received a more happy notice. Although during this year Colby wrote only very sparingly in her journal, she was writing. Her scrapbook contains approximately ten essays written and published in 1853 alone.

Life was moving forward and she was, no doubt, extremely busy with her growing family responsibilities. Personal diaries often are used to reflect on unhappiness with certain aspects of life; Colby's journal writing certainly at times follows this pattern. Colby's lack of private journal writing during this year may have been a sign that she had arrived at some sense of contentment and no longer felt the need to purge privately in her journal. It also simply could reflect limited time in which to write, so she chose public venues instead as an outlet for some of her creative tension. If indeed any sense of contentment had emerged, it should not necessarily be equated with a happy acceptance of societal ideals as to her role. The fact that she was writing for publication belies any notion of her complete aggregation into the role ordained for an ordinary woman. Ordinary antebellum women did not use their limited extra time to write for the purpose of publication. Many contemporaries considered it not only a wasteful endeavor, but also beyond the bounds of acceptable female behavior. Additionally, any sense of balance between the duties of a rural housewife and the inclinations of a budding author must have been extremely difficult to achieve, let alone maintain. And, in fact, during the next four years, that precarious balance between her everyday life as an ordinary woman and the inner life represented by the woman writing would be increasingly tested.

CHAPTER THREE

1853–1857

"Her influence at home . . . may sway the destinies of the world"

IN NOVEMBER OF 1853, a tragedy destroyed any sense of contentment Colby may have achieved. She simply noted, "Our sweet little Plummer is gone." Colby's three-and-a-half-year-old son, Plummer, had died. She was devastated. Over the next eight months, her journal contains only five entries, but her grief is palpable. Only weeks after his death she exclaimed, "How my heart yearns for the presence of my sweet child. I listen in vain for the music of thy voice, for it shall greet me no more on earth. Oh why wert thou taken? Earth is dark and dreary without thee!" Her next entry, in January of 1854, was in poetic form, but its message was the same. "I long for the presence of my angel boy." Three months later she simply recorded, "Weary months have passed since he exchanged the sport of infancy for the joys of heaven."[1]

Despite her overwhelming grief, those "weary months" were not empty ones. At the time of Plummer's death, Colby was already pregnant with her third child. Another son, Branch Harris Colby, was born in July of 1854. She clearly did not expect this child to fill the emptiness left by Plummer's death. She perhaps even resented the intrusion on her grief. Four days before Branch's birth, Colby lamented her wish to "lead thee [Plummer] back . . . to cheer my earthly home." A month after Branch's birth, Colby chastised herself in an entry that is clearly a comment on the new arrival. "The changes of this world sometimes prove to be blessings in disguise, yet our selfish hearts will murmur because we cannot see the 'silver lining' to every cloud." Branch's birth forced her to place her grief behind the needs of her growing family.[2]

Celestia Rice Colby's first
child, Plummer, died before
he reached his fourth birthday.
His gravesite—a simple stone
crowned by a lamb—was a
favorite destination for solitary
reflection. Author photo.

This growing family no doubt contributed to her lack of journal writing
as well. She had stopped almost completely in the previous two years, and at
this point she ceased writing in a journal altogether, not beginning again until
October of 1857. Regardless of her failure to record personal thoughts or document her life, many of her experiences during this period were important and
potentially life altering. She had given birth to three children—Plummer, Vine,
and Branch—between 1850 and 1854. In June of 1856, her second daughter, June
Rose, known always as Rose, was born. Colby also had a fifth child, a boy possibly named Thorn, who was stillborn or died immediately after birth. The exact
time and details of this event are unknown. Contrary to Colby's prolonged
grief following Plummer's death and her numerous references to him over the
years, no direct reference to this infant appears in her private or public writings.
His existence is deduced from two later sources: the 1900 census in which Colby
reports having five children, and an undated family tree constructed by Rose
that lists the name of a fifth child that can be read as "Thorn."[3]

The birth of a child approximately every two years meant that for at least six
years in the 1850s, Colby had at least one infant and/or one toddler while also
being pregnant. No wonder she lacked the time for recording private thoughts.

Her children were not Colby's only family responsibility either. Her extended family frequently added to her load. Her father-in-law, David Colby, fell ill and died from typhoid fever in February of 1855. Colby's mother-in-law, Naomi Colby, did not die until 1863, but her death notice commented that she had endured a lengthy illness. Possibly she was in poor health in the 1850s as well and likely looked to her youngest son, Lewis, and his wife for even greater support after David Colby's death. As early as the winter of 1849, Colby recorded staying home because of the "illness of Mother C." Lewis's brother Cyrus, who also lived with them, is listed in census reports as "crippled."[4] Colby's growing family and the changes in her household situation meant that by 1855 the mantle of primary responsibility shifted. Colby more often assumed the working role of "woman of the house." Regardless of her mother-in-law's continuing status as "matriarch," Colby took the lead role in accomplishing the majority of the actual tasks mandated as woman's work, including the house and dairy work.

The dairy responsibilities alone would have been extremely time-consuming because women—in particular their role as cheese makers—were integral to family dairy farms. Family dairy farms were a major force in the northeast, particularly in the first half of the nineteenth century. Sections of New England, New York, and the Western Reserve area of Ohio produced millions of pounds of cheese, not just for the United States, but for export as well. In 1866, the Western Reserve counties, known locally as "cheesedom," produced fifteen of the seventeen million total pounds of cheese in the United States. Clearly, a lot of money stood to be made, and throughout the nineteenth century, various forces operated to alter the nature of the business. After the Civil War, these changes quickly accelerated, and by 1885, cheese making for profit shifted away from home production and became almost completely centralized. However, from the completion of the Erie Canal in 1824 until the Civil War, cheese making provided steady business for many families like the Colbys.[5]

The daily life for a woman in Colby's position, as part of a dairy family, would have complicated any efforts to adhere strictly to contemporary societal ideals about women maintaining a separate home sphere. Home and work still intertwined in the quasi-preindustrial context of dairy farming, so the ideal of separate spheres would have been difficult to enact. Family was a key component of the dairy farm as the labor of both men and women was necessary to ensure its success. Although task sharing was significant and no strict division between home and work could realistically exist, much of the work still was organized around gender. Men did most of the planting, tending, haying, and harvesting of the grain and grass crops used for fodder. They also cut and hauled timber for winter use and took care of the livestock. Women, in addition to the usual and expected responsibilities to house and children, were almost exclusively responsible for the cheese-making process.[6]

The actual making of the cheese was a seasonal job when the intense work occurred in the summer and fall months, but the tasks involved in collecting the milk necessary to make the cheese—growing, harvesting, and storing food; feeding the cows; and getting them ready to calve—was a year-round effort. In addition to these outdoor tasks, other specific and prerequisite chores must be completed, which usually fell to the woman. Most importantly, the cheese house must be made ready. This process included cleaning, repairing equipment, and ridding it of possible vermin. Rennet, the key ingredient for cheese because it causes the milk to curdle, must also be prepared ahead of time. This job is a particularly unpleasant one as it involves killing a calf, removing its fourth stomach (the maw), and then curing it. Apparently, every dairywoman had a favorite recipe for this product. Colby wrote on the topic of rennet several times, and one article gave specific details for her recipe for success.

> The [three-to-five-day-old] calf should be allowed to suck in the morn-ing, and killed immediately after dinner. . . . When the rennet is extracted from the calf, it should be allowed to cool, after which pick off any loose particles of skin or fat which may adhere to it, turn the curd out upon a platter and pick out the hairs and grass, then salt it well. Turn the ren-net inside out and rub salt on both sides. Let them lay in this pickle over night, then turn the rennet again, add more salt to the curd, and replace it in the rennet, rub dry salt over the outside and hang it in a cool place to dry. Rennet when thus prepared will keep good for years and should not be used until they are, at least, one year old.

The process was not an easy one nor would it have fit neatly into the ideal of a woman's supposed refined and delicate sphere.[7]

The dairywoman's primary responsibility in the process was the actual cheese making. The cows calved around March of each year, and once their milk came in, cheese making continued into the early autumn. The process was very hard work as well as time consuming. As one historian describes, it was "an extreme-ly exacting, touchy, and laborious process, demanding unremitting attention." Colby depicts the process in several different essays and she, no doubt, would have agreed with this assessment. Each cheese required days of labor. The pro-cess began with the careful straining and storing of milk overnight and con-tinued for days through various stages that included adding rennet, skimming cream, cutting away curd, drawing off whey, and pressing the cheese, all of which were part of a carefully regulated time and temperature sequence. The process involved large vats, fire, boiling water, large presses, and various cutting tools. It was arduous, sometimes dangerous, work that according to Colby required years to learn and was best thought of as the "art of cheese making" if success was expected.[8]

Partly because of this view, changing dairy technology altered women's roles in the process less quickly than had other farm technology. New vats and fireboxes may have saved labor, but did not necessarily marginalize women's part in the process because cheese making was a learned skill perfected over time. Colby and her family dairy farmed during the time span in which the home industry peaked and then almost completely disappeared, so many of her cheese making tasks offered both continuity and change. Colby made cheese using the skills passed down to her by the previous generation of women, but she also consistently incorporated the new time- and money-saving tools and techniques. Eventually, the new ways became more mechanical and would override the art of the process and make her job obsolete, but for many years continuity and change worked together. In addition, cheese-making skills put dairywomen in a peculiar situation. Women's importance was enhanced in the dairy industry, but at the same time these skills, as one historian describes, "kept them under the patriarchal yoke—a situation that would eventually give rise to tensions within the family." At the heart of this tension was the fact that despite the skill women brought to the process, the value was still considered to be the land and the product, which were men's domains. Women's integral contribution was needed to produce cheese, but unlike smaller monetary enterprises like butter or eggs in which women may have had control over the earnings, the significant profits from cheese production were firmly in the grasp of the landowners, who were almost exclusively men. Akin to the devaluation of women's household work, the attitude that women's cheese work was an "art" had the possible resulting interpretation that it was not actual work.[9]

In reality, cheese making was very hard work performed in an environment that was not conducive to comfort or contentment. The "cheesehouse," where a dairywoman spent large blocks of time, was a "rather dim . . . close environment" frequently in a basement or cellar location with low ceilings and no doors. Perhaps the fear, or firsthand knowledge, of the results of such a mind-stultifying environment stirred Colby to urge farmers not to neglect the intellectual side of their lives. She wrote numerous essays admonishing farmers as to their responsibilities to read newspapers and books to raise their awareness of their world and their level of knowledge. In her opinion, farmers needed to study botany, natural philosophy, and chemistry. "Indeed there is no branch of knowledge that may not prove useful to him." Down time, such as rainy days or winter months, should be used to read because "to no class of persons is ignorance a blessing. Intelligence is the life of liberty and happiness." Her feelings about the inherently superior place of the countryside and the farmers of the nation over the urban market environment are obvious as she wrote of her "hope to see farmers as a class, occupy the place for which they were designed, and become in reality *Nature's noblemen,* the only aristocracy to be tolerated by a republican government."[10]

Despite her high praise for the farmer's way of life and her belief in evolving farming techniques, her dissatisfaction regarding the realities of her shared living situation may have been exacerbated by the very nature of the efficient, that is, progressive, farmhouse design at mid-nineteenth century. Home designs reflected the idea of "unity of home and work," which was very much part of the progressive dairy farm lifestyle. These designs separated public and private spaces, but in this context "private" did not refer to a separate, family-inclusive home sphere, but rather, it meant family, laborers, and anyone integral to the farm enterprise. In the same regard, "public" referred to others, such as guests who were not part of the farm "family."[11] This arrangement would have precluded Colby from having much in the way of private space in which to retreat. Her "chamber" gave her little real privacy as it encompassed the totality of private space allotted to her entire immediate family.

One of the primary reasons that Colby longed for a space away from "watching eyes" was so she could pursue her love of writing. Given her workload—which besides the dairy work and the children's daily care included the weekly washing and ironing of the family's clothes; daily baking and cleaning; planning, preparing, and cooking three meals daily; and the ever-present needlework—it is amazing that she found any time to write. The challenges that female diarists faced as they attempted to write were common to many women, including Colby. Women felt compelled to write only late at night or early in the morning while the rest of the household slept. The time required to accomplish their usual household duties allowed little time for writing, and their children's presence also created many distractions. Like Colby, these women's efforts to document their thoughts, experiences, and lives required supreme effort. Attempts to write for a wider audience required even more effort. Regarding female authors, as one historian notes, it is only with "both emotional, but more to the point, physical" support of other women that these women could accomplish their writing.[12] When Colby's apparent lack of both of those factors is considered, her output becomes even more remarkable, because although she was not writing in her journal during this period, she did write frequently for publication.

Many of these pieces were centered on the everyday interests of a dairy farmer, wife, and mother, but eventually, concerns beyond farming and childcare are revealed in these publications. Despite her rural context, Colby was well aware of changes underway in the wider world, and these sometimes revolutionary transformations increasingly influenced her views about her own life. The nation during the 1850s moved forward in an almost continuous state of flux: expansion; migration; immigration; economic and social upheavals; and increasing interconnection of people and markets via canals, roads, and railways. Frequently, this flux manifested itself in organized efforts to channel these societal changes in specific directions. Although reform efforts aimed at the abolition of slavery would turn out to be the most pressing in the short term, other marginalized groups, such as women, free blacks, immigrants, and laborers, also agitated for change, and all of these challenges were complicated by the implications they had for orthodox Protestantism, which had traditionally ruled on the larger moral questions.

A quasi-sense of nationalism had been building since the War of 1812, but by the 1850s this sense of unity was giving way to an increasing sense of sectionalism, partly in response to key legislative moves that were seen, especially in the northeast, as favoring the Southern slave states. According to disgruntled Northerners, the rise of "Slave Power," as this perceived bias in government was coined, was evidenced by, among other acts, the Fugitive Slave Act of 1850 and the Kansas-Nebraska Act of 1854. The Fugitive Slave Act, as part of the Compromise of 1850, gave added protection to slave owners. The Kansas-Nebraska Act repealed the 1820 Missouri Compromise's ban on slavery in the northwestern territories and put the decision in the hands of settlers. Both of these resulted in increased tension as free states saw slavery's hand reaching into the North. The nation in the 1850s was on the edge of a dangerous cliff. Although some public figures struggled to keep the nation from going over that precipice, their efforts often were drowned out by increasingly heated rhetoric and sectionalism.

As tensions rose, the northeastern antislavery movement in the 1850s agitated more fiercely as various factions vied for the hearts and minds of the region. The 1850s represented a time of change in the antislavery movement as antislavery proponents endeavored to choose their own level and type of involvement. The voices of antislavery men, who saw legislation as the only realistic means to affect change, grew louder during this period. This shift toward electoral politics meant that women, as nonvoters, increasingly were marginalized from the mainstream antislavery battle. As a result female membership in organized, male-led group reform significantly decreased in the 1850s. However, this decrease did not mean that women stopped contributing to the fight against slavery. Instead some women chose to spread the antislavery message through more fluid and self-directed efforts, such as sewing circles, fairs, and purchasing only food and clothing uncorrupted by slavery. For a number of women, however, fairs and sewing circles represented an inadequate level of involvement. For these women, the more progressive minded "ultras" offered a chance not only for direct involvement in the fight against slavery but also an increased level of acceptance as fellow warriors in that fight. Ultras demanded the immediate abolition of slavery and did not see legislation as the key to change; rather, they felt that the basic social structure of the country must be altered in order to realistically change the country's practices and attitudes. William Lloyd Garrison was perhaps the most famous, or infamous, member of this movement, and he was a primary inspiration, but many women also were among the earliest proponents for a radical change in society. The social changes mandated by the ultras included not only the immediate end of slavery, but also equality for women as well as African Americans. This progressive stance regarding equality meant women and blacks could, and did, serve in leadership capacities. These revolutionaries increasingly condemned organized religion and government for their failures to act in a timely fashion. Ultras often were vilified, even among antislavery communities, for their progressive stances, which to many contemporaries were quite radical.[13]

Colby and her neighbors were not immune to the effects of the changing times. Cherry Valley could not have been considered an urban environment by any definition, but it was still a vital participant in Ashtabula County's social and political culture, which was a microcosm of New England culture. The attitudes and actions of the county's citizenry before and during this period demonstrated this cultural connection as Ashtabula County reacted at a local level to unfolding national events. Like much of the rest of the North, the very vocal fight against slavery, which had characterized the 1830s, had receded into the background in the 1840s. Political and legislative acts in the 1850s brought the antislavery issue back to the forefront, especially in the Northern states like Ohio that directly bordered the South. The Fugitive Slave Act, in particular, was an extremely volatile issue in Ohio. Especially troubling to Northerners, the law empowered slave owners to enter free communities and claim supposed fugitive slaves without having to prove ownership in local courts. The Ashtabula County Anti-Slavery Society rose from a somewhat dormant state and became more militant in response. In December of 1850, in direct rebuttal to this law, their members defiantly stated, "sooner than submit to such odious laws we will see the Union dissolved." The county also experienced increased public acceptance as well as participation in the Underground Railroad movement in the 1850s. A partial explanation for this more positive attitude in regard to the Underground Railroad stemmed from the extremely negative response of Ohioans, as well as people in many other Northern communities, to what they viewed as the prospect of federal officers invading their cities.[14]

As Colby formed opinions from childhood into adulthood, she obviously was exposed to a certain level of progressive thought, which no doubt colored her views in regard to social issues. Ashtabula County had its share of vocal reformers. Ohio Congressman Joshua R. Giddings was from Ashtabula County and Colby socialized with members of his extended family. Giddings was an outspoken antislavery politician as well as a contributing editor to the *Ashtabula Sentinel,* so his views were well publicized. John Brown's place in history would be sealed with the 1859 raid on Harper's Ferry, but he was already well known locally for his fierce and unwavering resistance to slavery. He was connected to Ashtabula County through family, and many of the ferry-raid participants were from Ashtabula County. His son, John Brown Jr., had attended the Grand River Institute and even lived for a time in Cherry Valley. Colby was also acquainted socially with them. Betsey Mix Cowles, who served as the preceptress of the girls' department of GRI during Colby's attendance, was a well-known antislavery advocate and women's rights supporter. She was also an Ashtabula County native. Undoubtedly, Colby's time at the Grand River Institute, where she may have been exposed to radical speakers and ideas, had some lasting effect on her beliefs. As GRI's "Historical Sketch" noted: "It hardly needed the stirring eloquence of James Monroe, Stephen Foster, Parker Pillsbury, Abbey [sic] Kelley, and Wm. [William] Lloyd Garrison to create an intense interest in the impending struggle, yet these and other famous abolitionists came here and came to find a community, church, and school united in its [their] conviction of right."[15]

Nonetheless, Colby's influences were not all progressive. Despite GRI's boasts, although Ashtabula County citizens advocated the end of slavery as a general principle, the county was not a bastion for radical reformers. The citizens, for the most part, did not support the extreme, antireligious and antigovernment positions articulated by the ultra-abolitionists, nor was the county a center for progressive thought regarding women's rights. The majority viewed these ideas as radical. The county's prevailing social and political tenor shows itself in the local newspaper, the *Ashtabula Sentinel,* which began publishing in nearby Jefferson in January of 1853. As one of the first eight-page newspapers in the state, it served as an important source of political, social, and economic information. The paper and its editors were early advocates for the antislavery movement. Indicative of the prevailing tone of its citizenry, the paper took a very conventional approach to the issue of antislavery, with a heavy emphasis on the belief that solutions lay with elected officials and legislative mandates. Politically, the paper endorsed candidates from the Free-Soil Party and then the Republican Party when it emerged. In line with those views, sympathetic support was given to the temperance movement, but for the most part the paper ignored the "woman question." An 1878 history of Ashtabula County notes with pride that "the radical element had some force, but there was some conservatism mingled with it." It supported this conclusion by stating that although the speeches of ultraist reformers Abby Kelley, Stephen Foster, and Parker Pillsbury were met with respect, "their sentiments did not obtain." "The people" did not go along with the abolitionists' condemnation of the United States Constitution or their churches.[16]

Colby's influences were many and not always coherent. She came from a strict Calvinist background, received her education surrounded by progressive influences, and lived in a community that advocated freedom and accepted progressivism within acceptable boundaries and only when tempered with reason. Her sometimes inconsistent thoughts about her life, as not only a wife and mother, but also as a woman, reflected the effect of the diversity of these influences as she struggled to find constants that sustained her. Her published writings in the mid-1850s, in particular, provide a revealing glimpse into the thoughts of a woman whose life's view was still in flux and show evidence of the seeds of change that blossomed into the full-fledged struggle for a sense of personal identity evident in the five years before the Civil War. Regardless of her later progressive positions, Colby's published writings during the early and mid-1850s reflect acceptable community boundaries. Whether Colby wrote or published anything between her initial foray in 1851 and 1853 is unknown, but between 1853 and 1857 she published approximately forty pieces. She focused mainly on farming, family life, and nature, but occasionally addressed reform issues. Although sometimes inflammatory in tone, her approach to reform issues was not radical, and she addressed only antislavery and temperance, not women's rights. These pieces reflect her location in time and place, and her views were grounded in the conventional wisdom regarding a woman's place.

Ironically, Colby's public writing was in itself an act that put her beyond conventional thoughts about womanhood, despite the fact that the content of her published pieces during this time substantiated the idea of a true womanhood. Historical examination of the lives of many of the most prolific, nineteenth-century female writers demonstrates that irony to be endemic. While their actual lives frequently involved acting as the breadwinners and taking lead roles in their families or as single women, they consistently deferred respect or acknowledgment of that role, instead deflecting attention to their acts as mothers, sisters, aunts, or daughters, and representing themselves as "women of the home." To create culture was to presume a man's space, and for women raised in the culture of domesticity—in which women's domain was properly the home sphere—motherhood was deemed to be their natural and only truly worthy contribution to society. As one historian describes, the true woman's prescribed role as a mother in nineteenth-century, middle-class society was seen as the "preeminent social function carried on within woman's sphere." Prior to this time, all aspects of family leadership and guidance fell to the husband and father. Despite its new role in American culture, the abundance of literature glorifying the importance of a mother's love contributed to its rather quick elevation to premier status. Preparing children to assume successfully their parts in the expanding republic mandated that they be instilled with the necessary character traits of "propriety, diligence, [and] conscientiousness," and this task was deemed to be the very "essence of femininity."[17]

Catherine Beecher, an antebellum author and self-appointed sage for women, was a leading proponent of the idea of womanhood as a specialized and vital component to the republic. She endorsed a woman's subordinate role and partitioned her to the home sphere, but infused woman's domestic sphere with equal importance to men's public spheres. According to Beecher, women's apparent subordination to men was a choice necessary for society's success, much like the subservience necessary to make government work. Women merely needed to recognize the vital nature of this role within the home and rise to the occasion. Her vision of a woman's role in society was simple: "The success of democratic institutions . . . depends upon the intellectual and moral character of the mass of the people. . . . The formation of the moral and intellectual character of the young is committed mainly to the female hand. The mother writes the character of the future man . . . the wife sways the heart, whose energies may turn for good or for evil the destinies of a nation. . . . Let the women . . . be made virtuous and intelligent, and the man will certainly be the same. . . . Educate a woman, and the interests of a whole family are secured." Beecher's definition of the importance of the duty of mothers placed the fate of the world squarely on the shoulders of the United States' mothers. According to the mid-nineteenth-century ideals of Manifest Destiny, the future of the world depended on the United States. Since the future of the nation depended on the moral fiber of its citizens, and that moral character was shaped by mothers, accordingly, "to American women, more than to any others on earth, is committed the exalted privilege of extending over the world those blessed influences which are to renovate degraded man."[18] This designation, if incorporated into a woman's parenting philosophy, was one replete with cultural significance and subsequent societal accountability.

This prevailing attitude regarding motherhood obviously affected Colby. Although she wrote on other topics, the number of pieces in which she focused on family issues illustrates her concern about the role of motherhood. Over time, these essays show that her belief in what her role as mother and woman should be evolved. For the greater part of the mid-1850s, however, her advice falls squarely within the concept of republican motherhood. In an early essay, she called for mothers, "the nature of whose responsibilities would seem to demand a cultivated mind and enlightened judgment," to take the time to read. Colby posited that if a "thirst for knowledge" was created, then women will "reap the advantages arising from its gratification." The "advantage" she described was not the gain of a cultivated mind in itself, but rather, the direct effect on a woman's household.

> Their domestic duties will be performed with neatness and alacrity, while the mind is filled with pleasurable thoughts of the glad creation around them, and of the laws which preserve the harmony of all its operations. They will spend less time in preparing those rich and expensive articles of food, which are so pernicious to the system, but remain content with a plain, wholesome repast, which will nourish the body, without clogging the intellect or stupefying the soul. The time thus redeemed from unnecessary labor, would be sufficient in many families to perform *much* in the way of intellectual improvement . . . and a new and purer happiness would be the reward of their pleasant toil.[19]

In short, a mother whose mind was "cultivated" could be a better and more efficient "housekeeper," which meant a happier home. This theme was apparent in several essays written in the early 1850s.

The *Ohio Cultivator,* a semi-monthly newspaper published in Columbus, Ohio, was the recipient of many of Colby's pieces during the 1850s. The paper focused primarily on farming concerns, but the editor's wife was Oberlin graduate Josephine C. Bateham. She was in charge of the "Ladies [*sic*] Department," and she frequently ran articles on women's rights issues. The paper also featured women's rights writer, organizer, and activist Frances Dana Gage—"Aunt Fanny"—as an associate editor. Gage proved to be an important progressive role model for Colby in the coming years, but Colby's early contributions to this paper could not be described accurately as progressive. In one letter, Colby defended the *Ohio Cultivator*'s regular section, the "Ladies Department," against a man's query as to "what right have they [the women] there [in the newspa-per]?" Her argument, nonetheless, was prefaced on "traditional" assumptions regarding women's roles.

> Far be it from us to undervalue those accomplishments which render woman active and efficient in the kitchen or sick room, which enable her to perform with skill and dispatch the labor necessary to render her family comfortable, and her home the abode of neatness and order. But after looking "well to the ways of household" why may she not share with her husband the pleasure of his highest intellectual pursuit, and thus furnish her mind with food for profitable thought while her hands are engaged with laborious employments of the kitchen or dairy. This would enliven the hardest task, render life pleasanter, and preserve cheerfulness of mind among the thousand and one petty inconveniences, which prove so annoying to woman for want of something higher and nobler to occupy her thoughts.[20]

Although she zealously defended the rights of women to "furnish their minds" with not only her words, but her action as well, she also upheld the idea that woman's first duty lay with the household.

During this period when Colby publicly took a direct position regarding a woman's proper role, it was not to advocate equality as a public citizen. An 1854 essay demonstrates a view that could have been culled directly from Beecher's *Treatise:* "We doubt not that her presence and influence in the councils of our nation would have a purifying effect, yet her influence at home is the lever with which she may sway the destinies of the world. If the great mass of our sex fully understood their duty, and were prepared to fulfill it, how soon, how very soon would the moral aspects of the world be changed for the better."[21] A decade later, her comments regarding suffrage and women's roles would prove to be almost completely contrary to this 1854 essay, but her advocacy of the appropriate and necessary role of republican mother whose function was to train the next generation from within her home sphere is evident in many of her mid-century works.

True to this premise, although she had a daughter by this time, the male segment of the next generation received her most concentrated efforts. Toward that end, she recommended that mothers cultivate a love of reading in their boys as a means to keep them away from the tavern, store, and other unsavory places of temptation. "The fireside is the nursery of our future statesmen and rulers, and the parents are the educators. Home influences are powerful for good or evil." Although her message consistently advocated that mothers must act to "preserve their children from much temptation," the context made clear that by "children" she meant boys. Only very occasionally did she blur this focus on boys and speak to the future of girls as more than mothers. In an 1854 essay, she again spoke to a mother's duty to "strive by every means in her power to have her children prepared for their duties as American citizens." Although for the most part she again focused on the boys, she did address, albeit very briefly, the duty that daughters, as well as sons, may have in regard to future votes: "Every man has a voice (and the time may come when every woman will have a voice) in the choice of rulers." Further on she noted, "Her daughters it may be, will bear a part." Despite this small nod to women as potential full citizens, this rather mild rhetoric represents her most radical public stance regarding women's rights. She made no demand for the vote or even an assumption that women's expanded rights would, or should, happen.[22]

Colby also approached the subjects of antislavery and temperance from the view of motherhood. Her 1854 essay published in the local *Ashtabula Sentinel* confronted both the 1850 Fugitive Slave Law and the institution of slavery itself from the perspective of how each affected families, white and black. Colby employed the technique of personalizing issues numerous times over the years, and in this essay she used a childhood memory to make her point. She described a woman who had escaped slavery, settled in the north, married a free man, and started a family. They lived as welcome members of their community, "not withstanding the many oppressions which weigh down the free colored population of Ohio." Then the woman's former "master" appeared and attempted to take her back to bondage. Fortunately, neighbors rallied and the family was rescued and secreted away to freedom in Canada. According to Colby, she met the family as they spent their last night in the United States at an Ashtabula County Underground Railroad stop. This meeting, as well as the family's plight, "made a deep impression on [her] childish heart."[23]

This essay is obviously a condemnation of the 1850 Fugitive Slave Law and its provisions that, as interpreted by many Northerners, allowed slave hunters the right to "invade" Northern communities legally and "steal" former slaves back into bondage. Whether Colby's story is factual is of course unverifiable. Today, several communities in Ashtabula County are acknowledged as stops on the Underground Railroad, so her experience within that context was entirely possible. Regardless of the factual truth, she conveyed a truthful impression of the attitude many Northerners held regarding the law and its possible effects in their communities. The fact that the law sanctioned a stranger's assault on the integrity of their community was abhorrent to Colby as well as to the community at large. Many Northerners were increasingly suspicious and resentful of the laws that they perceived as a bow to the Southern elite. Fears regarding the potential effects of Slave Power in the federal government continued to grow.

Legalities and politics aside, Colby focused her essay on slavery as an inhuman institution, especially in regard to its ability to destroy families. A "cruel tyrant" legally could rip a child away from its slave mother at any moment. She framed her harsh words around the supposition that antislavery work for women properly was conducted within the confines of women's God-given sphere. In fact, it was a mother's duty. Her tone was emotional as she appealed to white mothers not to ignore the plight of those other mothers, whose hearts though they may beat "beneath a sable skin" were as "warm and pure" as their own. Colby's strong antislavery beliefs are evident, but she did not venture out of the sphere prescribed as appropriate for women: family and the future of the children. "Slavery must and will be abolished; if not in peace it must end in war and bloodshed, and our own cherished ones may be crushed in the overthrow. ... And narrow though our sphere may be, by using the power which God has given us we may labor effectually for its destruction." Despite this inflammatory rhetoric, she clearly advocated no action considered by society as overstepping female boundaries. Beyond her obvious disgust with the legality of slavery and fugitive slave laws, she did not venture into politics, or actively condemn the established institutions of church or state.[24]

Her initial public words on temperance, like these early expressions toward slavery, also focused on the traditional themes of home and family. In an 1854 essay titled, "The Daughter's Appeal," which appeared in the *Ashtabula Sentinel*, she emphasized the effects of the presence of a "drunkard" in a home: the broken promises, the lack of "common comforts," the uncontrollable flares of temper, as well as a multitude of other unnamed "degradations." She personalized this problem by using the life of a "real" family that lived in a nearby village as the vehicle for these observations. She described in detail the corrupted life of the mother and children, but she put the emphasis on the little girl who repeatedly entered an inn and begged her father to come home, only to be rebuffed.

When we see all this in our midst, it comes home to our hearts with an impression more deep and lasting than the well-wrought scenes of the moralist. An interest is awakened, and a corresponding desire is excited to do something for the relief, not only of those who are suffering for the sins of another, but for the degraded drunkard himself. When we see innocent women bearing up nobly under the sufferings inflicted upon them by the intemperance of those they love, we feel that our sex have an interest in the cause; that it is our duty to use the influence which men tell us is all powerful, for the suppression of the traffic which is filling our land with worse than widows and orphans.

In this essay, as well as in others on the subject, Colby pointed out that intemperance was not a problem only found in "big cities." Their local neighborhoods served as stages for scenes of decadence like this one. During this period, Colby's solution for intemperance was to eliminate the persons and places of business that "deal out a liquid poison to the weak and erring among our fellow man." Colby's early arguments show that she used alcohol's threat to the family to justify women's active involvement; her prescription, in which it was a woman's perceived "duty to use her influence" to stop alcohol's entrance into her home, was based on ideals of the proper female sphere.[25] Colby's disdain for the "rum-sellers" and "drunkards" remained a constant, but her belief in their ability to rehabilitate and women's responsibility in that rehabilitation process altered as time went by. She eventually changed her position on "women bearing up nobly." Interestingly, this essay exposes the dichotomy inherent in society's depiction of women's higher morality. According to this supposed wisdom, a woman is simultaneously a helpless "innocent" victim and also "all powerful." This dichotomy served as a foundation from which Colby's stance regarding women's obligations to intemperate husbands changed.

Despite the traditional republican mother/true woman tone present in Colby's publications, another factor points to at least a small measure of early defiance. Contrary to the themes consistent in her writing and more on point with the actual act of writing was in the use of her name. First, the fact that after her first publication, she used her own name, not a pseudonym, was unusual. Women's public pronouncements, even in print, often were not viewed in a favorable light. The use of pen names by women writers was so common that Colby felt compelled at one point to complain in an essay about their use. Second, Colby made a choice at some point that demonstrates that her attitude was more progressive than it appeared in print—she would always be known as "Celestia Rice Colby." This practice retained her birth name, Celestia Rice, along with her married name of Colby. She sometimes added a "Mrs." and occasionally used only her initials, as in "C.R. Colby," but she did not use what would have been the more customary "Mrs. Lewis Colby," or even merely Celestia Colby. Perhaps she was influenced by some of the more famous women of her time who retained the use of their given names to make a social statement, such as Elizabeth Cady Stanton or Abby Kelley Foster. Or perhaps it was in homage to her mother's great-grandmother, the storied "Irish gentlewoman of property," who refused to take her husband's name.

The fact that she wrote for public consumption combined with her name choice makes the assumption that she gave full credence to society's popular conceptions about women's roles less readily acceptable. The knowledge of her personal struggles with identity adds to this reticence, and by 1856, a change in Colby's public attitude was beginning to show itself. Her contributions to the reform newspaper, *The Anti-Slavery Bugle*, were an indication of this change. This newspaper was first published in 1845 as the official organ of the Ohio Anti-Slavery Society and then the Western Anti-Slavery Society, as it was later renamed. At that time, newspapers produced in a northeastern city could take from ten days to two weeks to reach the "West": Ohio, Indiana, Illinois, and Michigan. This newspaper, which was published in Salem, Ohio, was considered a vital link to possible new recruits for the abolition movement. Its publication was a chief concern of noted radical abolitionist Abby Kelley Foster, who was instrumental in obtaining subscribers and editors until its last issue in May of 1861. The paper covered a wide variety of issues, including women's rights, and although the paper's circulation was never huge, it was, as one historian describes, an "important new outlet for feminine protest in the West."[26]

The Anti-Slavery Bugle was considerably more radical than any other paper Colby had written for in the past. Two separate pieces, which were written in December of 1856, appeared in early 1857 issues. Although on the surface her initial contributions were relatively benign in tone, the fact that she was writing for this paper would have been considered stepping out of a proper woman's sphere. In one of these early contributions, she told the story of two sisters in which one sister marries into a Southern family. While Colby condemned slavery in this piece, she laid the blame on the "institution" and geography rather than vilifying the character of Southerners. She absolved her male protagonist from agency in his own lifestyle. "Circumstances, which are almost omnipotent in the formation of character, made him a slaveholder. . . . Reared under the influence of the system, taught from infancy that it was right . . . he saw no outrage . . . in thus holding scores of his fellow beings in bondage. . . . Had his birth place been among the rocks and hills of New England, his naturally kind heart would have made him the warm friend of freedom." In the traditional stance of many Northern churches, she condemned the sin, but did not name slaveholders as sinners. Her story ended in tragedy when the married sister was found guilty of teaching young slave children to read and subsequently sentenced to prison. The essay concluded with a call to praise those "nameless martyrs" who have "languished in prison or suffered an 'ignominious death' for no crime, save that of hating oppression and loving Liberty." Nonetheless, Colby did not take the next step to condemn any person or institution, other than slavery.[27]

The other contribution, an essay entitled, "Tobacco v. the Gospel," reported on a meeting of the Baptist Ladies [*sic*] Sewing circle who were "plying the needle, toiling to send the gospel to the benighted heathen of distant lands." Colby discussed the amount of the mission debt, and the sad fact that "very probably the amount of this worse than useless drug [tobacco] consumed by members of the church in one year would pay that debt." She ended the essay with this thought: "How inconsistent to spend thousands of dollars yearly in sending gospel to heathen lands, while the heathen at our doors are utterly neglected and permitted to perish for the bread of life while the door is closed against them by the laws of our country, which make it a *crime* to teach them to read." In this essay, she touched on several potentially controversial subjects, such as Ohio's Black Laws, the Church's inconsistent position on slavery, and ministers' potentially contradictory lifestyle choices, but did not openly condemn anyone or any institution. She also made clear her affiliation with the Baptist Church.[28]

Colby's private ideals, which are the focus of the next chapter, demonstrate that by late 1857 her private attitude had become quite progressive on many social issues. Despite this progressiveness, her publications in the years immediately prior to 1857 show her as a woman who apparently was living her life as society expected. For the most part, Colby's public and private actions were basically in line with her role as republican wife and mother: relatively ordinary in action and not particularly courageous in word. Her growing frustrations with the limits of that role only very occasionally seeped into her public rhetoric.

> It seems there are some even in this age of progress, who think the sum total of female perfection consists in her ability to minister to the animal wants of the human race, to wash and mend, and prepare their meals in due season. How to cook, wash, mend, &c., is *all* they think necessary for their wives and daughters to know, while they selfishly assume to themselves the proud distinction of mental superiority, seeming fearful lest the "weaker sex" should share even in the "crumbs" of science that fall from her "master's table," and thus become unfitting for the "sphere" *they* have assigned her, and neglect her kitchen duties.[29]

Although this complaint was anomalous when considered within the context of the majority of her writing to this point, it provides a ready preview to the struggles of the coming years. Up to late 1857, she had assumed the role expected of her, but she was about ready to challenge that designation. In the next five years, she attempted to change those role expectations. Battling with herself, as well as others, she struggled to incorporate more progressive social views into the context of her own life.

PART II

The Battle to Change Expectations

CHAPTER FOUR

October 1857–January 1858

"I sometimes think my whole being is changed"

In October 1857, Colby noted, "Nine years ago to day since I commenced 'housekeeping.' How many changes have been effect in the world since then, and many in my own heart; indeed I sometimes think my whole being is changed, whether for better or worse I may not decide."[1] After a lengthy hiatus, Colby resumed writing in her private journals on October 1, 1857, and the subsequent flurry of journal entries clearly display that Colby had indeed experienced "changes . . . in [her] whole being," which had numerous personal consequences. Unfortunately, these changes did not extend in any real way into her "outward life" as she termed it. Her daily duties as well as society's expectations remained static while her personal expectations, or hopes, altered in a dynamic way. The conflict between this "inner life" and the realities of her outward world grew more apparent as time went by. As a result, she experienced internal discord and external strife with her family and community. The struggle to find a satisfactory balance increasingly defined her life in the next few years.

Until this time, despite some discontentment with certain facets of her life, no clear or overwhelming evidence indicates that she expected or wanted a different role than the one societal norms reinforced. In the final months of 1857 and the beginning of 1858, Colby's apparent past acquiescence began to dissipate. By late 1857, her opinions on reform issues were becoming more and more radical, and her faith in established orthodox religion increasingly foundered. As her expectations for society grew ever more progressive, her expectations for her own desired life also evolved. Nevertheless, despite her obvious deep dissatisfaction with the course of her life, she was not always sure how to incorporate her changing ideas about her expected role into her everyday world. She felt she knew what was important to sustain a truly productive life, but lacked confidence in how to achieve those goals. Her first entry since 1854 reflected these thoughts, which unlike entries a decade earlier focused less on religious sustenance than on support of a more earthly nature; she simply desired time and "mental improvement." She remarked on her attendance at the Ashtabula County Fair.

> Yesterday I bid dull care adieu at an early hour and *enjoyed* the day. . . . Witnessed for the first time a sewing machine in operation and hope ere long to be myself comparatively free from the drudgery of the needle, and thus find more time for mental improvement. Visited a book store, but only took a long lingering look at the attractive volumes that crowded the shelves and coldly uttered the petition, "lead me not in to temptation," so necessary when such allurements meet the eye and too forcibly remind one of an empty purse. Well books are pleasant company even when silent and charm more than the miscalled conversation of many.

Unfortunately, based on her continued complaints over the years regarding the time required with the "needle," her optimistic hopes about the time-saving facets of a sewing machine were a bit unrealistic.[2]

Colby continued her entry with a discussion of the many attractions at the fair and noted disdainfully the display of patchwork bed quilts that were "suggestive of idle brains." She also discussed the lack of familiar faces and ruminated on the many past friends who were gone now—moved on to Texas, Kansas, or California—such as Celestia Bellow, who had "found a home on the soil of Kansas." Colby's reference to her friend's absence highlights a key factor affecting her satisfaction with her life. She felt that time to commune with like-minded companions constituted a vital component necessary for personal fulfillment, but sadly had discovered that the friendships she had cultivated during her schooldays were difficult to maintain. Scholarship examining the lives of rural antebellum women in New England demonstrates that this difficulty was common. As one historian notes, school represented "a time out of time" for most girls that was "at odds" with their lives. Young schoolgirls based their friendships on shared ideas about self-cultivation and intellect, but these identities were ill suited to rural life. Little connection existed between schooldays and adult life; consequently, few schoolgirl friendships survived the transition from girlhood to adulthood. Adult rural female connections more commonly were prefaced on the interconnection of shared responsibilities, not shared ideas about broader culture.[3] Colby, however, resisted this transition, and as 1857 drew to a close, one like-minded person—Annie Colby—served an important role in that resistance. Both the nature and the timing of their friendship suggest that it also served as a vital element in Colby's progressive evolution. Although other women influenced Colby's life during this period, Annie's friendship seemed to have the most profound effect on Colby's self-image. The dynamics of their relationship form an important pattern in which many other aspects of Colby's life are then interwoven.

Annie Colby's name began to appear regularly in Colby's personal writings upon the resumption of her regular journal entries in 1857. Annie was the daughter of Lewis's brother, David Colby Jr., and in 1857 was a single, twenty-year-old schoolteacher. Colby was thirty at this time, but, despite the difference in age, they had a developed a close friendship. In early October 1857, Colby sadly reported that Annie was "going west, and her absence will leave a vacancy in my mental enjoyments which others may not fill." Annie left the next week for her "winter quarters in Illinois," and Colby, for the first time, left her two oldest children overnight. They stayed at home with Lewis and the family so that Colby could accompany Annie on her roughly twenty-mile horse-and-buggy ride to Ashtabula where both women boarded a train. Colby then rode with Annie as far as Madison, Ohio. The reality of the extent of Colby's distance from any center of modern urbanization is obvious when her comments about this approximately fifteen-mile train ride are read. She noted that this ride on "the cars"—her first—was "first rate" and a "novelty indeed," and that much to the surprise of her seatmate, she had "never seen a car before." The woman's surprise was not unwarranted as the transportation revolution was well underway in the northeast United States. The rail line that extended roughly parallel across the northern edge of Ashtabula County remained its only line, but by this time, the northeast as well as most of the rest of Ohio was literally crisscrossed with railroad tracks. So, her seatmate's "perfectly astonished" reaction was reasonable as was her question of "what remote corner of creation" Colby inhabited.[4]

Colby returned home after her adventure, and her daily life continued much as it had before the trip. She keenly felt Annie's absence, however. The two women corresponded frequently, and Colby often noted in her journal that she had written or posted a letter to Annie or that she had received a letter from Annie. Colby corresponded with many other people, such as her sister in Illinois, various cousins and in-laws scattered about the northeast, and family friends who had moved away from the area, but Annie's letters were the most anticipated. Journal sharing was also common among close female friends during this time period, and Colby and Annie kept journals for each other that they then sent as letters. "For the last half hour I've been comparing dates in my

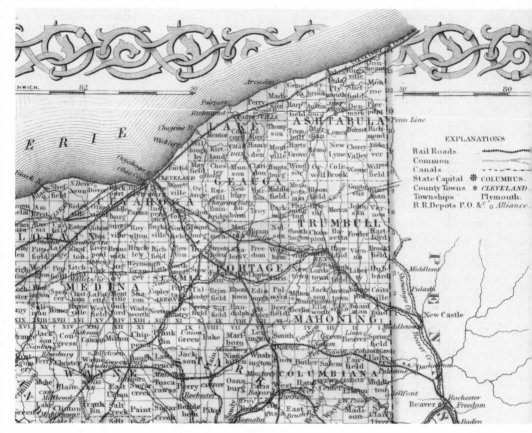

Ashtabula County sits in the far northeastern corner of Ohio and borders Lake Erie to the north and Pennsylvania to the west. This 1855 map also illustrates the county's lack of railroads and common roads as compared to the adjacent counties. *Map of Ohio* (New York: J. H. Colton, 1855).

journal and Annie's letter, also in the letter or journal which I've kept for her. It has been amusing and suggestive too, from similar entries made in the three under the same date, it would seem as if there was an invisible mental telegraph between us a sort of spiritual consciousness of each other's presence. Wonder what she is doing *now*, and of whom she is thinking? Wish I could impress her mind with a consciousness of my presence."[5] This "mental telegraph" or "spiritual consciousness," which was the level of connection Colby expected from her like-minded friends, was not a standard that was easily met.

The inability to find others who provided this level of support is a consistent theme present in Colby's private writings. This void made Annie's friendship that much more vital. "Oh for the presence of a kindred heart, who could understand me without words, and sympathize in silence." Colby deeply regretted that she was not able to find the support she desired closer to home. "I would not live solitary for every joy is heightened by being shared with a friend." She was frustrated by the absence of other friendships in her life, but her choices did little to advance possible friendships. Similar aesthetics rather than shared daily experiences were Colby's benchmark for friendship: someone who was of "kindred heart," not merely someone at hand. Consequently, instead of reaching out to neighbors, Colby sought out closer ties with those women whose lives exhibited experiences closer to what her ideals were. In that regard, she attempted to maintain connections with school friends whose lives had taken them to distant locales, and even offered her hand in friendship to strangers in an effort to build a network of support that included women whose life choices she admired. She consistently attempted to bond only with women whose surface lives had little in common with hers. This choice, as well as her expectations, complicated attempted friendships. During this time period, besides Annie, two names also appear frequently: Emily Sanborn and Jennie. Colby referred to Jennie only by her first name, and Emily lived for a time in North Dakota; available evidence then fades away, thus reconstructing a more complete picture of their lives is problematic. Emily Sanborn's fate is unknown, but Jennie, like Colby's school friends Vine and Cynthia, apparently died young. What is important for our purposes, however, is the role they played in Colby's life. Colby's letter of introduction to Emily Sanborn stated that her heart had "room enough to admit strangers as friends, if they can only whisper the watchword of kindred thoughts, hopes and aspirations." In addition, interpreting from the contextual framework in which their names appear in journal entries, these women, like Annie, were younger, unmarried or newly married, childless, and apparently worked outside the home.[6]

Colby's attempt to garner female support, even from a distance, was not in itself odd. Women commonly went to great lengths to maintain connection with other women, particularly family members separated by distance. As scholarship demonstrates, women maintained these vital, life-long relationships, even if they lived in different geographic locations, through visits and regular correspondence. These relationships functioned as support systems and sounding boards and were particularly crucial for those women physically isolated, separated from their families or, like Colby, emotionally isolated. Colby maintained many long-distance relationships and frequently noted sending, receiving, and anticipating letters to and from absent friends and family. Despite this apparent regularity, she still often noted correspondence quantity and quality with disappointment. In addition, even though Colby desired to maintain contact with like-minded women, her frustration with her own situation sometimes tainted her reactions to these friendships. Her reflections after receiving a letter from a school friend are of a bitter and envious nature. "Had letter from C.J. Peck last night. She seems blest with a contented mind just now, but I think contentment is hardly a virtue in her case. Had I half of her advantages I should think I ought to be contented. 'Access to two large libraries' while I am famishing for mental food. The society of 'twenty one teachers' who are, or ought to be educated, intelligent, and refined; and with whom she 'feels non acquainted,' while I have no society that interests, and am a stranger to all around me, and likely to ever remain so."[7] Colby's envy toward people who had access to cultural outlets beyond farm fairs and local markets was recurring, as was her attitude that she did not fit within her own cultural environment.

The rare face-to-face meeting with someone whom she felt could sustain her higher aspirations sparked dramatic attitude shifts. After listening to a group of visiting lecturers, Colby spoke with some of the attendees as well as several of the speakers. "Had a pleasant interview with M. [Maria] Child also. It is so seldom that I mingle thus with the outward world, that I often after a short interview of the kind, feel the pulse of thought bounding with a quicker flow, and hopes and aspirations which have nearly expired in the foul air they have been compelled to breath, have burned with new life." "M. Child" was Lydia Maria Child, and Colby's obvious admiration is especially noteworthy. Child was lecturing in Ohio with the American Anti-Slavery Society, but had begun her public life over twenty years prior as an author. She had written a very successful household hints book, *The Frugal Housewife,* which had been a mainstay for early New England homemakers. However, her book, *An Appeal in Favor of that Class of Americans called Africans,* had diminished her popularity with the mainstream public. Her public denouncement of slavery and defense of racial equality pushed her over the norms of acceptable female boundaries. She endured ridicule and the loss of income, but she stayed her course.[8] Child's ability to maintain her moral integrity, speak out in public, and write professionally represented a tangible manifestation of Colby's inner life. She provided an example of womanhood that Colby increasingly admired and envied.

Another speaker on this tour also sparked Colby's admiration and provides an additional indication of Colby's ideals regarding women's potential. "I had the pleasure of listening to a lecture on 'woman's rights' by Mrs. L. [Lucy] N. Coleman of . . . Rochester. . . . Mrs. Coleman staid with us two days and I enjoyed her society very much. And yet people call her vile, just because she does not believe all that they regard true." Lucy Coleman must have served as quite an example for Colby. She was a former evangelical who had turned her back on patriarchy to embrace abolitionism, women's rights, and spiritualism. In addition, she was being paid to inform the public, who as Colby noted, often vilified her for her message. The presence of Child and Coleman inspired Colby to think about how a woman's life could be different, but the inspiration was also tinged with the defeatist attitude that the "foul air" of her environment was a consistent barrier to any real change.[9]

Colby firmly believed that if her mother had lived that this "foul air" would be less of a hindrance to her happiness. Although she only could be a shadowy memory at best, Colby's mother was an ever-present model of perfect love. Even almost thirty years after her mother's death, Colby often revisited the subject of her absent mother, both publicly and privately. Her words provide strong evidence that Colby felt no one had stepped into the role of "mother," as she envisioned it. In her 1855 essay, which appeared in the periodical *The Instructor*, Colby wrote of how she missed the mother she never had, and in January of 1858 *The Anti-Slavery Bugle* published her poem, "My Mother," which lamented the heartache of never knowing her mother. The notations in her diary are in the same vein. After one of her children requested, in regard to Colby's journal writing, "write something about me ma," Colby noted, "The time may come when she will prize them as the only echo of her mother's heart. I have so often longed in vain to see a line or sentiment penned by my mother's hand that I could obtain a single old letter I should prize it as a treasure." Something as simple as a melody could also inspire deep emotion. "Heard Jennie sing a sad, sweet song this morning, 'What is home without a mother,' and the bitter flood within found vent in tears, for I could fully appreciate every line of it." Flavia Rice was buried in Andover, and Colby occasionally walked the several miles from Cherry Valley for solitary visits to the cemetery. After one such visit she noted, "I visited my mother's grave by moonlight, and longed, oh how earnestly to feel her warm caresses, but this bliss has never been mine."[10]

Colby's mother obviously was not available to offer loving acceptance or encouragement for her higher ideals and ambitions. Other potential candidates for this emotional nourishment could have included the women in her extended family, her neighbors, and friends. But beyond Annie, her immediate family displayed little regard for the things that Colby valued. The women in her community were involved in various levels of female-centered activities, such as sewing circles, charitable activities, visiting, health-related events like births as well as nursing the ill, but none of these activities met the standard of intellectual and emotional bonding Colby desired. This level of bonding had existed most recently and consistently at the Grand River Institute; consequently, Colby sometimes turned to those old school friends for emotional strength. Unfortunately, these women could supply only peripheral support because they lived in distant locales. In addition, as we have seen, Colby's envy of former school friends whose lives were spent in higher pursuits sometimes clouded her feelings. Despite this occasional ill will, her nostalgia about her school days is poignant.

She often recalled the "communion of like minds" she had shared in the past and desired for the present. Her time at the Grand River Institute represented a high point in her life, and the news that the women's wing of the school had succumbed to fire brought sadness and fond remembrance: "Have just learned the sad news that old GR Institution is in ashes. It affects me as would the death of a friend or perhaps in a less degree; yet it saddens my spirits. Some of the dearest memories of the past are linked with that spot, and the strongest ties of friendship which have blessed my path, and are blessing me still, were there bound in the sunny days of girlhood. How I have longed to revisit—even the silent rooms where we have sat together, and close my eyes, and let my heart travel back to the days of auld lang syne."[11] GRI assumed major relevance in her past because she had felt companionship and support during her schooldays. This relevance was all the more special because that aspect of her life was in her eyes now insufficient.

Colby's belief that the presence of kindred spirits would "more than double" her appreciation of life is borne out by recent scholarship. She longed for the types of friendships she had nurtured during her schooldays: friendships that were based on a shared sense of identity and deeply acknowledged mutual devotion. As some scholars point out, this rarefied type of relationship, which was so celebrated by contemporary writers, did exist among some urban, upper-middle-class women; however, rural women's bonds were forged more commonly by the reciprocity that existed between neighbors and kin: the interconnection of households, not the interconnection of souls. Nevertheless, whether urban or rural, women's private writings consistently support the important role that female bonds played in the maintenance of any endeavor, from the public arena of antislavery to the private one of everyday household life. So Colby's inability to sustain consistent support had potentially serious consequences. Her perception that her life offered insufficient avenues of support was founded on the early death of her mother, who in Colby's emotional memory served a pivotal role that, when severed, altered her development. The mother-daughter bond often formed the heart of the nineteenth-century female world of networks. The "highly integrated networks" of supportive women, which emanated from that bond, served various purposes that included, importantly, the development of a "sense of inner security and self-esteem."[12] Colby's inability to achieve contentment within her daily existence illustrates the possible effects of inadequate female bonding that began with the loss of her mother.

This lack of bonding continued into her adulthood and contributed to her disdain for many female-centered endeavors. Scholars show that supportive networks of women were most frequently "institutionalized in social conventions or rituals" that helped to reinforce the "essential integrity and dignity that grew out of women's shared experiences and mutual affection." Colby, however, resisted sharing time with women whose daily lives echoed the common elements of her life. Thus she failed to feel the "dignity" of these shared experiences. She privately complained about partaking in many of the social conventions of her community. She particularly disliked "visiting" in the traditional form in which women made "calls" on other women as a means of sharing, connecting, and fulfilling social obligation. For many women, these visits also served a more important purpose: physical and emotional support. Women depended on each other as they completed the many daily tasks that were particular to a woman's world. Contrary to that view, Colby viewed these social conventions as merely another task, and nothing indicates that she turned to those women with whom she "visited" for comfort or support. "It is Monday noon; I've finished washing and am going a visiting, not because I want to go, but from a sense of duty; wish I could make the duty pleasant, but I approach it with a feeling of fear, as the martyr does the stake, and the great question 'What *shall* I talk about' has been the query all day. But I must go. Well I have been a visiting, and spent the P.M. I was in the mood for writing when I went away, but now all those fleeting fancies have vanished, and I'm as dull as myself."[13] Colby participated in some of the rituals of the social norms of her community, but she rejected the formation of stronger or intimate ties with those women around her with whom she shared only similar, day-to-day experiences, not life views. Diary entries, like those above, as well as available correspondence, also exhibit that she displayed little hesitancy in speaking ill of her neighbors. She obviously felt no real connection existed with the neighbor women she often deemed "insipid."

Her rejection of these women made her dependence on those people with whom she did bond especially vital. The vital nature of this bond explains why Annie's absence was so keenly felt. Her extremely high standards also help to explain why Colby's efforts to find support for her evolving views occupied so much of her emotional life during this period. When her efforts to find human support fell short, she often turned to other means. Books began to play an increasingly important supportive role in Colby's life; however, even this

This and facing page: These October 1857 pages from Colby's journal are typical examples of her entries. In just three reflections, she touched on religion, friendship, books, morality, and her own recurring hopelessness. Used by permission Colby Collection, Illinois State University Archives, Illinois State University, Normal, Illinois.

inanimate means of support sometimes contributed to emotional stress. Colby struggled with issues of self-worth. The struggle for self-validation is especially evident in her feelings on the subject of her own level of education, which she felt was sadly lacking. Consequently, she constantly sought to educate herself through one of the only avenues open to her: reading.

18.

...oli. It is very interesting and instructive, and would well repay a second perusal. Yet it leaves a feeling of sadness on the mind, that the gifted authoress must pass from earth so suddenly in the midst of her usefulness; and that the last product of her genius, must perish with her ere its mission was accomplished. And then the old story of might triumphing over right, is sadly exemplified in her letters from Italy. "The world seems to go so strongly wrong! The bad side triumphs; the blood and tears of the generous flow in vain." She says, in a letter to her sister, written after the unfortunate termination of the revolution in Rome, "I should really like to lie down here and sleep my way into another sphere of existence, if I could take with me one or two who love me and need me, and was sure of a good haven for them on the other side." Is not this feeling natural to us in moods of desponding when hope fails and energy is gone, when wrong triumphs and injustice prevails?

Colby was not alone in this endeavor. During the antebellum period, a growing number of girls received some level of secondary education, and this education often led to a passion for books. These girls then became women who relied on reading as one of the few ways to further educate themselves. In addition, historical research shows that women used their interaction with books to help fashion their own sense of identity. Reading operated as a path that could connect a woman to the outward world of print culture, libraries, and literary societies; however, it also offered a path inward, where a woman could rely on books for escape or relief from the external world. Both paths provided women opportunities to experiment with different ways of thinking and communicating, ultimately intersecting with other factors to help develop their sense of being. Colby used books as solace and companionship increasingly as time passed, but the interaction with the outward—the sharing of ideas as well as the passion for books—also was important to this process, and Colby consistently failed to find satisfactory outlets for that path.[14] Consequently, her reading all too often was a solitary endeavor that instead of reinforcing or supplementing her education left her feeling inadequate.

She frequently bemoaned that her "ignorance" adversely affected her ability to always understand fully what she read, and her comments sometimes hinted at her unfulfilled desires to widen her horizons. Despite her claims of "ignorance," her reading list was quite varied and included all manner of choices from newspaper romance stories to classic literature. Her choices often indicated not only her desire to learn, but also her growing socially progressive attitude, with books on history, travel, natural science, and philosophy. Her numerous subscriptions over the years included Horace Greeley's progressive *New York Tribune* and well-respected periodicals such as the *Atlantic Monthly* and *Harpers*. She expressed her feelings about much of this reading in her journal. In October of 1857, she read two books focused on events in Europe—Madame Ossoli's [Margaret Fuller's] *Thoughts in Europe* and Bayard Taylor's *Letters from Northern Europe*. Colby's comments demonstrate her feelings of intellectual inadequacy as well as a desire to expand her horizons. "I am so ignorant of the science, art, and literature of which they treat, that I feel that I cannot half appreciate the author. Then my heart throbs wildly, with the vain and fruitless wish to travel in foreign lands, and see the scenes of beauty myself, to look upon those works of art and revel among the ancient palaces and ivy crowned ruins of the old world, and yet even there ignorance like a friend of darkness would rot one of my pleasures."[15]

Madame Ossoli was the married name of famed transcendentalist and women's rights pioneer Margaret Fuller. Fuller Ossoli died in 1850, and this particular book was published posthumously in 1856. In Fuller, Colby found another woman whom she especially respected. Fuller was part of the intellectual community that embraced transcendentalism and forged the utopian experiment, Brook Farm. In addition, she had served as the editor for the transcendental journal *The Dial* in the early 1840s and then as a writer for the *New York Tribune*. Her 1845 book, *Woman in the Nineteenth Century*, was one of the first fully articulated polemics on the subject of male/female relationships that called for equality. After its publication, she traveled to Europe as a correspondent for the *Tribune*, where she eventually married an Italian count and wrote an account of the ongoing Italian unification movement—the Risorgimento. Unfortunately, Fuller and her manuscript, as well as her husband and child, were lost in 1850 when their ship sank while returning to America. Colby's admiration was obvious in her reflections regarding the loss of such a talented woman. "It leaves a feeling of sadness in the mind, that the gifted authoress must pass from earth so suddenly in the midst of her usefulness; and that the last product of her genius must perish with her."[16]

Her opinion about another author was a bit more ambiguous. According to Colby, the purpose of Catherine Maria Sedgwick's new work of fiction, *Married or Single?* was "to show that single blessedness is preferable to double wretchedness, and show that the lot of an 'old maid' may be both useful and happy." Sedgwick had gained popularity in the 1820s and 1830s as a domestic novel author. As a former Calvinist, she had shed its limiting doctrines and emerged as an active reformer. Although never married herself, her earlier books clearly romanticized the idea of wedded bliss. Contrary to that notion, this 1857 book, which attempted to discredit stereotypes about "old maids," can be read as a validation of a sort for her personal choice not to marry. Colby's discussion focused not only on her assessment of the merits of the book, but also its applications to her own life. "There are many good things in the book, and yet on the whole it is not such a work as I had anticipated and I think the preface is the best of it. Yet blended with the thread of the story are many excellent moral reflections. To one like me, prone to pine over adverse circumstances this one thought, could I always remember it when attacked with a fit of 'the blues,' would be a blessing. 'It does not seem to me that the *facts* of our life are important, but the *character* that is formed from them. The herb is worthless after the essence is distilled.'" These words were a direct challenge to the notion that the "facts" or the circumstances of one's life necessarily dictated the limits of personal achievement. She obviously wanted to believe that character could rise over presupposed destiny. This bravado, however, was consistently countered by negative depictions of her own circumstances. "Weary and sick to night—tired of the din of voices, and longing for rest for the body."[17] Complaints such as this were common and show scant indication that she felt any level of character building attached to her workload.

Her private words often centered on her doubt regarding her ability to affect change in her own life:

The little ones are all asleep at last, and the eve is before me for labor or writing, yet my heart throbs with wild unrest and unfits me for enjoyment of either. There is a secret page in every heart, known only to the All-Seeing. I seldom glance at that sealed book, but at times it will be heard and I may not silence its voice. Ignorance has been the curse of my life, and I fear the effects of my mistakes will weave a sombre thread through the warp of my whole existence. But if my little ones may be better prepared for the duties of life, and be qualified to act wisely, and intelligently, I shall be content.

Perhaps because she felt little regard for her own accomplishments she frequently pinned her hopes for the future to her children. This attitude was consistent with the prevailing notion of the day that mothers, as "America's female agents of socialization," were responsible for the task of molding a new generation.[18] However, Colby desired that her life have a personal meaning that incorporated more than being the "mother" of the next generation, so her frequent returns to this subject serve as an apt demonstration of her frustration with the confining nature of her own future.

The dichotomies between her subscribed role and everyday responsibilities as a mother and her desired role as a woman were not the only dichotomies beginning to show in the fall of 1857. Her political and religious views also veered from community norms. In the week after Annie left for Illinois, Colby heard a lecture that inspired the following journal entry. In it, her recurring feelings of personal inadequacy are evident, but a glimpse of her still private views on antislavery politics, religion, and women's roles are also revealed. Within a few short months, these private views on politics and religion will become her public views.

> Yesterday I went to hear S.S. & Abby K. Foster [Stephen S. Foster and Abby Kelley Foster] and others lecture on the anti-slavery question. I admire the moral heroism which they exhibit in the bold and fearless manner in which they utter unpopular truths. Their names have long been cast out as evil by the over righteous pharisees of the present day, but I believe them to be earnest seekers after truth, and bold and fearless in its utterance. Years ago, when I first listened to them, I did not like them. They were called "infidels," and that seemed a *terrible epitaph then.* But such men and women have given dignity and beauty to that word. Looking through the glass of prejudice which my early training had inspired, I thought Abby Kelly was entirely "out of her sphere" but it seems not thus now. Long may she live to fill the sphere which she now occupies, and which she fills so well and so fearlessly. The world needs her labors in this sphere, and I would that there were many women fitted for the same task. To me it seems that the position of the "Come outers" or disunionist is the only consistent position for an antislavery person to take.[19]

Abby Kelley had begun to lecture on the slavery issue in the 1830s, but as a woman, she represented more than merely an antislavery lecturer, not only to Colby, but also to the reform movement and society in general. Her radical reform stances as well as her belief that her gender, marriage, and subsequent motherhood should not limit her work had made her a lightning rod of sorts for mainstream society's complaints about reformers' morality.

Within the reform community, Kelley's election into a leadership position in the American Anti-Slavery Society had put her in the center of the 1840 controversy that ended with the split of the movement into two main factions. In the above entry, Colby ideologically placed herself firmly with the more radical of those factions: the ultras. She endorsed a woman's right to have an active role in the antislavery fight, questioned orthodox religious training, and supported the idea of "coming out." These positions were the radical limits of the ultraist wing of the abolitionists' movement. To "come out" was to disavow allegiance to those religious and civil institutions that did not call for immediate abolition. Within governmental context, this idea manifested as a call for the Free States to break from their union with the slave states. Within a religious context, it meant breaking ties with the mainstream orthodox denominations that had not broken with their slave-holding Southern partners. Her endorsement of coming out as it applied to religion likely would have had more immediate personal repercussions. As her references to "over righteous pharisees" and the "glass of prejudice" show, Colby was experiencing serious doubts regarding her religious foundations. These questions and doubts directly affected her private life.

Received a letter tonight from Orrin [likely Orrin Colby, who was Lewis's brother as well as a teacher], and opened it with some curiosity. He rests in perfect peace in his belief or rather unbelief. Shall *I* ever attain this repose? Or shall I ever wearily and painfully ponder over the question "*What* is Truth?" One thing seems certain, I can never again rest my soul in perfect peace in the belief of the gospel plan of salvation. For myself I can endure the torture of these endless doubts, but *how* shall I teach my children? Thus far, I have ignored the whole subject, lest I should give them a stone for bread, and instill error for truth. But this will not always satisfy them. Shall I leave their minds unbiased and free, or as the orthodox people would call it, in a "state of heathenish darkness"? Or shall I teach them a faith I do not believe. Or shall I instil doubts into their minds, even those doubts that agitate my own soul. What can I do. I know not.[20]

This entry leaves little doubt as to her crisis in orthodox faith. It also shows that her doubt left her, and us, more questions than answers.

As previously noted, Colby's earlier evangelism can be seen as a part of a rite of passage from which she drifted away when it no longer served a purpose. This diminishing religious fervor as well as spiritual questioning had been evident as early as 1853; however, the direction this drift was going to take was not immediately obvious. At that time, she did not appear to be returning to mainstream orthodoxy, but she also showed no clear indication that she was rebuking orthodox Protestantism. She had questioned her own spiritual weakness, not necessarily religious practice or teachings. In 1852, Colby was firm in her belief in the absolute truth of biblical teaching, but by 1857 she was comfortable claiming "unbelief" in the "gospel plan of salvation." What precipitated this dramatic shift and when did it consciously surface?

If an assumption is made that this shift occurred over time and not abruptly, then various factors likely contributed. Her self-perceived status as a "marginalized" woman might be reason enough for not simply "aggregating" and becoming an enthusiastic supporter of orthodoxy. However, some less theoretical reasons likely contributed to her choice to challenge the teachings of orthodoxy rather than simply condemn her weakness of faith. Leading up to this point, she had been exposed to numerous influences: the emotional effects of the death of her first child, the expansion of thought precipitated by reading literature and hearing progressive speakers, the frustration linked to orthodox churches' apparent lack of concern and action regarding slavery, and the realization of the inequality of women's traditionally allowed church roles. Colby's early childhood religious experiences also connected orthodox religion with fear, a lack of control, and ignorance, which in adulthood possibly contributed to her initial embrace of evangelism. Then, as Colby's evangelistic fever "burned out," negative attitudes toward Calvinism, which spawned the disdain and distrust of orthodox Protestantism, combined with positive images of the more progressive attitude that characterized her school experience, provided a broader context that allowed the above-mentioned influences to take root.

It is not entirely evident that her "unbelief" occurred as a gradual loosening of religious bonds, but years of exposure to various levels of radical thought and her personal experiences certainly could have laid a foundation of dissatisfaction. In addition, although no clear signs of this level of disbelief appear before 1857, certain clues lend credence to the notion that her religious doubts had been deepening since her initial spiritual crisis in 1853. When writing on the subject of faith in December 1857, she noted, "Thus far, I have ignored the whole subject," which implies that she had some prior thoughts on the subject.

In October 1857, after attending a church service, Colby discussed the subject of religion in her journal, and this entry also sheds some light. She critiqued the sermon, which "as usual" was nothing more than "an exhortation to believe," and questioned various aspects of people's adherence to religious dogma. "If people believe as they profess their conduct is strangely inconsistent. Do they believe? Once I had faith. . . . Experience and observation have both taught me the falsity of that promise. I staid in class meeting yesterday for the first time in nearly six years. I made a formal request that my name be erased from the class book." She noted, "I do not wish to stand connected with any church, but it is not easy to get out of one." One option was to be expelled for "bad conduct," but she observed that she would "hate to commit a crime that would arouse the ire of those who can fellowship drunkenness and dishonesty and other evils."[21] Her language, such as "once I had faith" and "experience and observation," easily lends itself to the interpretation that her private doubts went back as far as her crisis of faith in the early 1850s. Her public acknowledgment regarding this lack of faith may have been the new occurrence.

A reexamination of her 1856 essay, "Tobacco v. Gospel," written for *The Anti-Slavery Bugle,* adds another layer of evidence for this interpretation. She wrote this essay only ten months prior to her request to be removed from church membership. Despite her clear disgust with the church in October 1857, this December 1856 work failed to indicate any blatantly negative feelings regarding the church. In fact, it seemed to reflect positively on religion's role in bringing Christianity to "heathens," apparently only calling into question why more energy was not devoted to "our own native born," rather than "those in foreign climes." If this essay is read only within the context of her other publications to this point, then it can be construed merely as a call for Christians to minister to the needy of their own country. Deeper and more radical intent emerges if her subsequent private writings are also considered. Interestingly, this piece does not list her full name as the author. It merely states "By Cele," so perhaps she was uncomfortable with the possible, more radical, interpretation as it represents one of the only known incidences of the use of something other than her full name since her first publication in 1851.

The closer reading of the essay, within the wider context that the knowledge of her private religious doubts provides, reveals that it also can be easily interpreted as an oblique indictment of the church. "In the name of consistency, let us not deprive our own native born people. . . . Talk not of the Lord's 'opening a door' for the gospel to enter, while we as a nation, are shutting up three millions of people in heathenish darkness, denying them the dearest rights of humanity, and doing this in the name of religion and morality and, strange inconsistency, of the present evil times, calling the whole a missionary operation and calling God and the bible to prove its justice."[22] She condemned the church's complicancy in perpetuating slavery, but in an indirect way; she softened her accusation by calling it a byproduct of the "present evil times" in much the same way she had made allowances for the slave-owning husband in her story written during the same period about the two sisters. This essay represents a trend that is apparent when Colby's public works are considered within the context of her private life. Her body of work from the time of Plummer's death in late 1853 through late 1857 shows that this period served as one of quiet but altogether progressive evolution in private opinions on many issues.

In late 1857, this quiet evolution surfaced publicly. First, she revealed her progressive thoughts in a somewhat oblique and personal context, and then, as the next chapter examines, on a much wider public scale. Those small personal revelations were no small step for a woman in her place and time, and it is no wonder that she struggled with how to proceed. Although she denounced her church membership, she continued to attend services of varied denominations, both orthodox and other. Clearly, she was attempting to find a spiritual foundation for her burgeoning progressive beliefs; however, her private life also lacked key factors that may have facilitated a complete break with orthodoxy. She did not have the consistent support of those who were like-minded; she suffered, as well, from a faltering ego, which likely diminished potential independence regarding simple, everyday, family- and community-sanctioned acts. Pressure from within her family and community, her own desire to know the "truth," as well as a lifetime of socialization contributed to the inconsistency sometimes apparent in her words and actions regarding religion. In addition, regardless of the possible effects her religious decisions had in her own life, this subject was granted an even greater importance by her belief that her children's futures were at stake. These factors partially explain why, although she exhibited the requisite doubt and anger toward orthodox religion that might have led to a complete break, she also seemed hesitant to make that final move.

Although she did not completely rebuke orthodoxy in practice, Colby's search for alternative avenues for spiritual contentment led her to examine the tenets of other faiths such as Mohammedanism, Universalism, and Spiritualism. By early 1858, her public lack of adherence to any one orthodox group, her emerging public doubt regarding biblical authority, and her unorthodox interests began to affect her interactions with her community and family. In a time, as well as a place, when organized religion served as a vital connector in people's lives, especially women's, Colby's sometimes unsettling religious stances put her on the outside of the mainstream of her circle of available connections.

The possible effects of Colby's public questioning of religious authority should not be underestimated. The importance of church in the lives and activities of nineteenth-century women has been well documented. Church affiliation played an important role, socially, as well as spiritually. Church membership provided clarification, or reinforcement, of status and held importance for those people who desired upward mobility. In the nineteenth century, membership in the emerging and increasingly important middle class was not only defined simply in economic terms, but also in cultural and ideological terms. The traits glorified by orthodox religion—morality, self-control, and domesticity—were important factors that helped to define successful membership within the middle class.[23]

These traits defined acceptable behavior, especially female behavior, and increasingly Colby struggled with the rules of conduct that sought to confine women in domestic roles. Despite the influence of the Second Great Awakening, mainstream orthodox church structure was still a highly patriarchal one, and male ministers remained firmly ensconced as the authority figures. This patriarchal arrangement allowed women to take on greater roles within the church and still be viewed by mainstream society as within acceptable boundaries because these new responsibilities were primarily benevolent and supportive in nature. As Colby's attitude about society's strictures became more cynical, her intellectual belief and adherence to patriarchal church authority lessened. Scholarship consistently demonstrates that class, denomination, and region affected how women incorporated possible opportunities for expanded roles. Most women, even those involved in reform efforts, were content to accept secondary and non-leadership roles in church-sponsored endeavors. In almost all cases, if a woman desired a role in which she exercised a greater degree of autonomy, then she ran the risk of being perceived as overstepping her boundaries. Few women were willing to step over that boundary and cut the ties to organized religion. Church represented ties that were too important—socially and spiritually—for most women to break. Only the most radical women turned to other like-minded reformers, male and female, rather than the church when organized religion placed oppressively stringent boundaries on their efforts.[24]

Despite her doubts, Colby did not completely break with the church; nevertheless, her family and community soon were aware of her doubts and questions, and she met a considerable lack of support. This lack of empathy regarding her search for spiritual truth affected their interactions and relationships. In December 1857, after a visit with "sister E." [sister-in-law Emily Colby] in which they engaged in a "long talk over the Bible and the evidences of its divine authority," Colby expressed sad disbelief. "Wish I could exercise faith as she can, but it is impossible. I think if the Bible is true, she must have been born one of the elect, and faith given to her accordingly. But some strange ideas seems to have mingled with it. For instance, she asked me what idea of God we could have aside from the Bible? Surely one must be blind and deaf, not to see and hear evidence of His existence and power all around them." Ironically, almost a decade earlier, Colby had decried her friend Vine's belief in a natural religion over a biblical faith, but now she felt that the proof of God's revelation was not in a book, but in the natural world. Emily was not convinced and continued to try to put Colby back on the right path. Toward this end, she gave Colby a book, *Evidences of Christianity*, in hopes of turning her from the "errors of her ways." Colby promised Emily, as well as herself, that she would give the arguments in *Evidences of Christianity* "careful investigation." She did; however, her reaction was not the one that Emily had hoped. Colby concluded that the book's arguments could be "equally applicable to prove the divine origin of Mohammedanism."[25]

As early as January 1858, Colby's doubts affected other family relationships: "Received three letters to night, one from Tho. Brown, one from Cordelia and one from Annie. All interesting though C. [Cordelia] does not understand me now as she used to when we were one in spirit. Annie has the key to at least a part of my heart and knows how to interpret my errors of the head better than others do." This entry aptly illustrates the level of personal and emotional disruption that her religious doubts could cause: she placed Annie above her cherished sister, Cordelia, because her sister was troubled by Colby's changing attitudes. Her father also registered unhappiness at her attitude, and in particular the influences that this change brought into her life. She lent him a book that she referred to as "Wright's autobiography." Later journal references indicate that Colby likely was referring to progressive minister and activist Henry Wright. Wright was, as one historian describes, "vehemently anticlerical." He had turned away from Calvinism and was viewed as an infidel by much of mainstream society. Her father returned the book with a strong reaction:

> He said he had read but a few pages in it, and yet he denounced it in no measured terms, and seemed almost shocked that we should keep such a book in the house. Said all sorts of hard things against the author, and some against those who are so weak as to be lead away by such trash. Well I suppose I am the keeper of my own conscience and that *my own reason*, and not that another be my guide. Even infidels have a "cross" to bear if they are true to themselves, and act in accordance with their own ideas of right. . . . And while I cannot "believe" merely to please any one, however near the ties of relationship, still my mind shall be open to conviction.[26]

Perhaps the last line provides the most important clue as to not only her hesitancy to completely break with the church, but also to other struggles in her life. Despite her intellectual convictions, she did not wish to completely alienate those people within her family circle. She longed for a sense of belonging, community, and support. Nevertheless, throughout the fall and winter of 1857, Colby's discontent brewed. Her private reflections increasingly noted her impatience with the status of her personal private life as well as disgust with many facets of the more public social interactions within her own community. Up to this time, her progressive leanings had been apparent only to a small and primarily private family and community context. That context, however, was about to change.

CHAPTER FIVE

December 1857–May 1858

"Yet I live a life they know not of"

ON DECEMBER 19, 1857, Colby noted, "It seems impossible that I can be thirty years old and yet it is. Yet once a person of that age seemed old to me and passed the time of high and lofty aspirations . . . passed from the *Ideal* to the Real. Doubtless *I* appear thus to many, yet I live a life they know not of."[1] As Colby entered her thirties, she was well aware of the specter of passing time and its potential effect on reaching her "lofty aspirations." This internal consciousness of age was an important underlying foundation for her path toward public radicalism. However, the speakers touring with the American Anti-Slavery Society (AASS) may have provided the final external brick for this road. Despite her hesitancy to break from the church and her desire for community, she was increasingly angered by the attempt of churches as well as her community to stand aside from anything controversial. The December 1857 appearance of the radical AASS was one of those controversial occasions.

Lucy Coleman's presentation on women's rights provided fodder for Colby's private indignation. "We were *packed* into the schoolhouse which was not half large enough to hold those who wished to hear; just because the church wisely 'voted not to admit lecturers.' These *Holy Houses* that are too good and too pure for the use of humanity—I've no fellowship for." In addition to Lucy Coleman, antislavery lecturer Joseph Howland spoke. His speech so inspired Colby that she went home and wrote something of her own on the subject. In her journal she noted, "I've written a long letter to the Bugle and sent it out on the spur of the moment. Wonder if it will get published. It would almost frighten me to read it in print, and certainly shock some good people."[2] Her letter to *The*

Anti-Slavery Bugle, which certainly did "shock" some people, represented only the first of many increasingly radicalized opinions she placed into the public forum. In the months after this December 1857 AASS lecture tour, she boldly and publicly articulated a progressive view of humanity in which true equality was the status meant for all humankind, not just white mankind. Ironically, while Colby publicly represented herself as a strong-willed advocate of freedom for all people, simultaneously she struggled to achieve a sense of autonomy in her own life.

Until late 1857, Colby's progressive evolution was primarily a private one, in the context that her changing stances were evident only to those within her immediate personal community. As 1857 closed, her efforts escalated to bring her ideal inner life, or the life "they know not," into her outward world as well as make it a societal reality. Her choice to take her opinions into wider public view was grounded on her personal evolution, but it was also a function of an extremely volatile political, social, and economic context. In addition, Colby's opportunity—as an ordinary woman—to have a venue in which she could move into a wider public arena reflected the nature of the newspaper business at this time. The sheer number, as well as range, of newspapers available had exploded during the last several decades and provided venues for the expression of opinions by those individuals previously unheard, including women. Newspapers of the antebellum period perhaps could be more accurately viewed as forums for particular agendas and political rhetoric, rather than papers for conveying simply news. Even the commercial and penny press, which often claimed to be politically neutral, seldom were. The media did not view unbiased or balanced coverage of issues as a requisite qualification for responsible journalism. The 1850 census reported that only 5 percent of newspapers were actually independent of a political party. In addition, many nonparty newspapers funded by private sources and public subscriptions, which focused on antislavery, temperance, and women's issues, also appeared in this period.[3] In the 1850s, this increasingly opinionated information sector, which had been emerging since the 1830s, intersected with growing national volatility.

The 1850s opened with the controversial Compromise of 1850, and sectional and ideological differences escalated as the decade unfolded. Politically, Northern unrest contributed to the founding of the Republican Party. The newly minted Republican Party opposed the extension of slavery in the territories, but took no official party position on abolition, the rights of free blacks, or the odious Black Laws. Their slavery anti-extension position was driven more by economic and political underpinnings than moral ones: the rights of white men were primary, not the rights of slaves. Despite their somewhat uninspiring stand on the slavery issue, more and more antislavery proponents saw them as a viable choice. The Republicans' 1856 presidential candidate John Fremont lost to Democrat James Buchanan; nevertheless, the Republican Party gained ground in Congress. The slavery dispute in Kansas, as a result of the Kansas-Nebraska Act, was an important political backdrop in this election. This 1854 act had placed the responsibility for the decision of whether Kansas would eventually enter the Union as a free state or a slave state on its settlers, which resulted in violent clashes as Free-Soilers and slave owners flooded the territory and vied for power. News of increasing levels and incidents of violence coming out of "Bleeding Kansas" prompted hot political debates on the steps necessary to stop the bloodshed.

This political debate soon took a nasty turn. Abolitionist senator Charles Sumner was attacked and beaten with a cane while on the Senate floor one day in 1854, proving that violence was not limited to the Wild West. Unfortunately, the volatility was not due to fade away anytime soon, as two days after Buchanan's inauguration in 1857, the Supreme Court handed down the infamous *Dred Scott* decision, in which black Americans were denied not only access to "any rights which the white man was bound to respect," but also to citizenship. This decision fed into the growing fear in the North of so-called Slave Power and its control over the federal government. On the heels of all this agitation, an August 1857 insurance company failure precipitated the Panic of 1857, which by October was a full-blown national depression that contributed to the antislavery debate as it fed into the increasing controversy over free labor and slave labor coexisting in the national economy.

These events and issues were not merely subjective fodder affecting distant national political candidates; they were also felt on the local level. Colby's October 1857 entry regarding her friend Celestia Bellow's move to Kansas reflected this interconnection. Colby noted, "Such women are a blessing to any land. Educated, energetic and progressive, she will exert a salutary influence in any society; but in a new country where society is not yet settled down into the trammels of a narrow minded conservatism, her power for good will be far greater, and she cannot fail to leave her mark upon the early strata of society, whose formation will affect the future destiny of Kansas." Colby's reference to the "future destiny of Kansas" displays her awareness of the importance of "Bleeding Kansas" in the greater context of the antislavery fight. The bloodshed in Kansas also was of particular interest to Ashtabula County residents because of John Brown's involvement. Violence occurred on both sides, but Brown's alleged part in the 1856 deaths of five proslavery settlers was the beginning of his controversial place in national history. As might be expected in an area sympathetic to the slave and home to members of the Brown family, Ashtabula County appeared to support John Brown Sr. The local newspaper referred to him as the "Ethan Allan of Kansas" and printed and endorsed an April 1857 letter from Brown asking for money to fight slavery.[4] But this conditional support of Brown did not mean that Ashtabula County citizens were primed to raise their level of accepted activism to such extents.

Locally, radical abolitionist-speaking agents, such as Abby Kelley Foster, Stephen Foster, Parker Pillsbury, Joseph Howland, and Lucy Coleman brought their brand of radicalism to the Western Reserve counties in the autumn and early winter of 1857. During this tour, these reformers met in Cleveland in late October 1857. The statements coming out of their talks, which included calls for the destruction of the Union and national government, received broad press coverage. Although many northeastern Ohioans were disgruntled with the political system that had thus far failed to even repeal the Black Laws, this extremely militant stance was highly unpopular. Even some of the more conservative of the radical abolitionists were hesitant to go so far as these ultras.[5] Ashtabula County's attitudes mirrored northeast Ohio's as well as most of the northeastern United States. Most citizens opposed slavery, but hoped a peaceful legislative solution could be reached. They disagreed with the extreme rhetoric and proposed actions of the radical abolitionists, whom many Northerners viewed as potentially dangerous dissidents. Instead, they favored benevolent antislavery societies and supported politicians who kept their interests primary to the slaves' interests. Within this framework, socially acceptable antislavery work was readily available for women who desired to act on benevolent urges.

Recent scholarship disputes some prior ideas that women disappeared from the reform fray when the antislavery fight turned more political. Current scholarship shows women's antislavery work did not falter in the 1850s. Instead, the rapidly shifting social and political context offered women a chance to alter and redefine strategies. As one historian notes, the 1850s was a decade where women not only continued their reform efforts, but also experienced one of "the most profound and wrenching shifts of its history." Colby actually would have had various socially acceptable avenues of reform available. Another historian observes that "a stalwart core of women" continued antislavery work even through lack of success and internal divisions. In regard to these so-called ordinary women, like Colby, this historian confirms that "whether as members of societies or sewing circles, secular or religious in orientation, black or white . . . and we have no way of knowing how many, [they] never dropped out of abolition. They were not professional reformers. . . . They did not spend most of their time working for the cause. Rather these women wove their commitment into the fabric of annual routines."[6] Many of these ordinary women continued their work without arousing the ire of their communities because they kept their activity within acceptable female boundaries.

Colby's publications over the next few years show that, instead of these avenues, she chose to embrace a more radical approach. Her role models for this brand of reform would have been fewer, but they did exist. Abby Kelley Foster served as one of the most vocal of these activists, but other women also could be classified as professional reformers. Women like L. Maria Child, Lucy Stone, Lucy Coleman, Sally Holley, and Betsy Mix Cowles devoted considerable time and effort to the cause of abolition. Because these women's activities were more public, proactive, and confrontational—thus removing them from acceptable societal norms—they were less well received by mainstream society. In addition, whether or not they made verbal statements endorsing women's rights, their actions spoke volumes.[7]

Economic and societal status in many ways determined what direction women chose to take their reform efforts. Historians commonly find that women who were members of the "higher" classes frequently chose to engage in benevolent activities. These women assumed that different social roles were assigned and relatively fixed—male/female, black/white, rich/poor—because this social order had been their primary experience over several generations. As members of the "higher" class, they assumed a "duty" to help those whom they deemed worthy in the lower classes until they could either fend for themselves or the state stepped in. Members of the rather volatile and constantly aspiring middle classes frequently had firsthand experience with social and economic mobility. This awareness of the dangerous consequences of vice and the loss of self-control guided them to strive to educate and rehabilitate, rather than condescend. These women relied primarily on the existing framework of local church and state organizations in their attempts to raise the "fallen" so that he or she could assume a functioning role in society.[8]

Women who sought a more public and proactive role in reform often fell into separate and less easily defined groups in regard to class. Ultras often felt that their economic and/or social status was marginal. For men, in particular, this marginal status could be a consequence of their views as well as a foundation. However, for women, their own perceptions of a socially marginalized status more commonly grounded their views. Colby considered herself in the latter category: she felt socially marginalized. Ironically, her birth family and the family she married into were some of the area's earliest pioneers as well as successful land and business owners. Hence, if Colby did experience social and economic marginality, then this status likely did not arise from a preexisting inferior status within her own community. Instead, any community disdain she experienced was likely a consequence of her radical views. However, Colby's personal perception of social marginality was not merely a byproduct of her neighbors' disdain. It was founded on something much more profound; she felt that as a woman she occupied a secondary place in a wider cultural context. Her recognition and disdain for this placement made the ultras' ideas about societal goals attractive. Ultras envisioned the "formation of democratic and egalitarian social, political, and economic relations," and as such they received little support from mainstream society and their existing organizations, such as churches. Consequently, ultras operated in a more fluid, event-oriented, decentralized way. Out of necessity, their strongest ties were frequently to "family, friends, and fellow reformers."[9]

Unfortunately for Colby and despite her attraction to their ideals, her daily life rarely brought her in contact with these like-minded among her family or friends who could offer support. Despite this lack of consistent support, as well as the potential for negative personal consequences, a flurry of publications written in early 1858—at least six in six weeks—demonstrate that Colby chose to take her private views, which aligned her with the ultra minority, public. The perception, or in many cases the reality, of their marginal social status often contributed to ultraist women's willingness to brave the scorn of mainstream society. Although many Northern women advocated the end to slavery, the majority of them, if faced with a decision on an action that would push them across the boundary of acceptable female behavior, chose not to engender public censure. Instead, they worked within their perceived sphere through established avenues of reform, such as churches and benevolent societies. Colby's early 1850s' writings had placed her within this socially acceptable category emphasizing women's place as a higher moral agent, which through loving influence could right the wrongs of the world. Colby's writing after the mid-1850s, however, often placed her beyond that sentimental framework. Her willingness to claim positions that may have garnered local criticism set her apart from those women involved in socially acceptable reform efforts.[10]

Any lingering doubts that Colby's immediate community harbored regarding her stance on the church and slavery were eliminated with the aforementioned January 1858 letter that she feared might "shock some good people." In it, she held little back in her condemnation of orthodox churches.

> We have had the pleasure of listening to a genuine Anti-Slavery gospel to day, which was very interesting, even though denounced by good orthodox people as only *Infidelity* in *disguise*. If this *be* infidelity, and if in order to maintain our standing in the church we must ignore this great

question of human rights, and pass by on the other side, and join hands
with the slave holder, then let us at once, and boldly too, bear the stigma
of reproach for the sake of this unpopular truth, and take our position
with the so-called infidels. . . . Strange that a person who should be sus-
pected of infidelity, merely for expressing sympathy for the oppressed and
downtrodden slave; strange that our churches, with but few exceptions,
are closed against those who would plead his (the slave) cause—stranger
still, that our priests, and church members, our lawyers and politicians
should alike talk so gravely of the *rights of the slaveholders.*

She maligned churches that did not condemn slavery openly as standing with
the "devil." Colby then turned to politics and the hypocrisy of the "glorious constitution." She wrote, "And can we of the North still our conscience by saying
that 'we have no right to meddle with slavery in the states, no right to exclude
it from the Territories, that the Constitution guarantees to the slaveholder the
right of property in his fellow beings, and we have no right or power to inter-
fere;' and with this quietus upon our souls, go on voting with the democrats,
know-nothings, or 'black republicans,' (black enough politically, aint they,) el-
evating this, that or the other candidate to the presidency, all to 'save the Union,'
when the Union is not *worth* saving."[11] With this essay, Colby stepped decisively
out of the kitchen and in front of the ballot box. Despite the rising popularity
among many antislavery proponents for the Republicans, she obviously doubted the legitimacy of any group that claimed to work within the system. Statements that condemned church and state as significant contributors in slavery's
continued legality were not popular. In addition, although sectional divides
were growing, the vast majority of people in the North did not support the idea
of "disunion" and did feel the Union worth saving.

The general public's extremely negative reaction to the radical ideas that
came out of the October 1857 meeting of ultras in Cleveland proved that a fear
of social retribution for taking such a radical stance was a legitimate concern.
Nevertheless, Colby condemned the moral and political hypocrisy of those
people whom she perceived as refusing to stand for a change. Beyond con-
demning slavery, she also made a statement for racial equality with her admo-
nition that the situation could be reversed. "Wonder if these sagacious moral-
ists would pay equal respect to the 'majesty of law,' if it reduced *them* and *their
dear ones* to the degradation of slavery. If the order of things could be reversed,
and they could wear the fetters they are willing to fasten on others, and bear the
heavy burdens they are willing to lay upon other men's shoulders, should we
hear them proclaim the duty of a people to reverence and obey the unjust and

impious enactments of the tyrants in power." This brash statement assumes no natural inferiority or superiority that would render the reverse any more unnatural than the current state of affairs. Her demand was not calling merely for women's moral indignation regarding slavery, but for a radical revolution. She closed this letter with a fallaciously sincere nod to the notion of a proper woman's sphere. "[T]hey say women can't reason well if they leave their sphere, and overstep the bounds of their kitchen, and I thank God that I can't see light in darkness, recognize a legal or constitutional right, in a moral wrong, and above all that I'm not a voter, though a firm 'woman's rights man.' May I so train my son that he may not *dare* to bow to party sound, or take the oath of allegiance to a slave-holding government."[12] This statement represents a direct assault on the popular notion of a republican mother's responsibility as Colby announced her intent to use her assigned "sphere" to teach her son that he owed his country no allegiance as long as it supported slavery.

Both church and state's complicity in upholding the institution of slavery consistently appeared in her public writings as she addressed not only the moral issues of slavery but also the political issues. A January 1858 essay written several weeks after the above strongly condemned the Republican Party and its continued compromises with slaveholders.

> From their birth as a party, their whole course has been *downward,* a continued backsliding from beginning to end. If we trace their course from their first organization till the present, and note their oft repeated compromises with the slave power, we shall be led to inquire if there is a still lower deep to which they can sink, without abandoning their baseless claim to Anti-Slavery principles. Their rallying cry of Liberty . . . has been successively changed, till now they are anxious to make the world understand that they are not "abolitionists," that they have no desire to meddle with slavery where it is, and meekly and humbly ask in self-defense that there be "no more slave states."

She also noted that "yet there are many noble men in that party whose position is almost an enigma, men who are leaders, and we fain believe sincere." This statement should not be read as a benevolent endorsement of the "Party's" possibilities. More likely she intended it as an acknowledgment of Ashtabula County abolitionist and politician Joshua R. Giddings and those few others like him who at least attempted to make legislative changes. "Could these men lead the mass of their party up to their own standard, the platform of party would not be so often lowered to accommodate the weak and feeble ones."[13]

She continued her assault on the ineffective leadership in her state as she made another assumption of equality with her condemnation of the Ohio Black Law that segregated education. "Our state would not be disgraced as now, by a 'school law' that does not recognize the right of every child without regard to color to the same educational privileges." Her disgust then widened beyond the shortcomings of her local politicians to moral outrage at the state of affairs in general. "In short, the entire North would not be daily and hourly reduced to practice a sentiment that shocks their virtuous sensibilities and aroused their indignation, when for the first time they saw it clothed in the language of Taney's decision—'Colored men have no rights which white men are bound to respect.' Well it does look odious in words; but words are harmless if we do not give them life and power by viler acts, and more odious deeds."[14] "Taney's decision," as she referred to it, was the 1857 Supreme Court's *Dred Scott* ruling. She implied that the Court's power was not absolute; it could be tempered perhaps by those "noble" politicians, or even voided by the people's renunciation.

Her condemnation of church and state for their part in the perpetuation of slavery was absolute. She denounced political efforts and "so-called" antislavery politicians who "trim their sails to catch the favoring gales of public sentiment" and whose "official acts proved that *liberty to the slave* was not, as *is* not their aim or desire." She damned religious leaders from the North and South who refused to condemn slavery as a sin and was particularly harsh on Northern churches. Her facetiously titled essay, "The Unpardonable Sin," spoke directly to their hypocrisy. "But this obliquity of the moral vision that sees a greater criminal in the devotee of pleasure than in the brutal slaveholders, is not confined to the latitude of Alabama. There are those in free Ohio (?) who advocate the same sentiment. Less than two years ago, I heard a 'minister of the Gospel,' who was troubled with the exhibitions of rowdyism during public worship, say that such acts as he had seen while preaching (and he specified shuffling cards in the gallery and dancing before the door of the church) was *worse than the acts of slaveholders!"*[15]

Colby did not limit her complaints to institutions and attacked societal norms as well, specifically ideas about what was proper conduct for a woman. She also made harsh statements regarding people's tendency to avoid controversy for fear of social reprisals. In another early 1858 essay, she condemned this fear of reprisal as a reason for keeping silent. She publicly challenged the notion that people should self-censure their acts or words to avoid the condemnation of fellow citizens. She chastised those "slaves of public opinion" who obey the "law of society" no matter what their true opinions. She harshly derided those members of society who vilified anyone who dared to challenge these so-called laws of society. As an example, she focused on the disparagement of women who were accused of leaving their sphere:

> For instance, if a woman (no matter how great her qualifications of mind and heart) should dare to address a public assembly on the great moral questions of the day, which interest her *in spite of her sex,* she is met at the threshhold of every consecrated house with the inspired assurance that woman should "not speak in the church"; that she must not teach, but learn in silence, and if doubts perplex, she must meekly "ask her husband at home," if she has one. Her reputation is set up as a target for the vicious to shoot at; her purity is called into question, and all the low slang in the vocabulary of vice is leveled at her, not only by the vicious and foolish, but by those who pride themselves on their respectability and good standing in [the] community. If she accepts as a co-worker and fellow laborer in the cause of humanity, one of the opposite sex, and travel with him in the same car or stage-coach, instantly the sensibilities of all "good society" are shocked beyond the power of expression, and no terms can be found strong enough to express the concentrated indignation and contempt which that immaculate body feels for her. Churches and school-houses are closed and barricaded by public opinion; and if any reckless individual is so daring and foolhardy as to "run after" these fanatics or express sympathy for them and their opinions, a portion of the same righteous indignation is meted out to every offender against the majesty of this unwritten law.[16]

This essay was not merely hyperbole. Although during this period the abolitionists' antislavery message was beginning to meet a slightly more receptive audience in northeastern Ohio, women lecturers still were subjected to considerable derision. When the abolition message was mixed with women's rights, if only in the form of a female speaker, the message itself was often ignored in favor of vilifying the messenger. American Anti-Slavery Society speaker Joseph Howland, who visited Ashtabula County several times, noted of his experience in northern Ohio that the abolitionists were often branded as "Free-lovers, infidels, and last and mightiest, Abby Kelleyites."[17] The latter was no slight insult. Abby Kelley Foster represented quintessential female immorality in the eyes of many.

In the early months of 1858, Colby took advantage of numerous opportunities to hear those previously mentioned AASS speakers who were touring northeastern Ohio. Several times, she traveled the approximately twenty miles to Monroe to attend lectures given by AASS agent Andrew T. Foss. According to Colby, "Mr.

A.T. Foss had been a priest for twenty-five years, but is a so-called infidel now." Hearing his take on the slavery issue prompted her to write several items for *The Anti-Slavery Bugle,* including a particularly strong-worded letter to the editor. In this letter, she cheered the right of "freedom of speech" that made these meetings possible, but she complained bitterly about the "usual negative opposition" that resulted in the venue of "far too small" schoolhouses. She then addressed Foss's controversial interpretations, and her rhetoric was even more inflammatory than just a month prior. She again condemned organized religion, but in agreement with Foss, she also turned on the base of Christianity itself—the Bible. "Mr. Foss took a religious or as the orthodox would call it, the anti-religious view of [the] slavery question and labored to show that American Slavery with all its horrid cruelties is sanctioned by the Bible, and has grown up in harmonious relations with the religion of the land. . . . Mr. F. showed conclusively that the slave had nothing to hope from the efforts of church or state in behalf of emancipation, both being leagued with oppressor and working in the same harness to strengthen and uphold the peculiar institution." She discussed the fact that Foss's position was obviously met with shock, especially from "true believers." Based on the proof Foss presented, Colby claimed, "Yet I can see no course of reasoning by which to escape from this unwelcome conclusion." In reality, despite her claim that "the public mind is awakening on this subject and no system or creed can stand its scrutinizing investigation unles it is true to the highest interests of humanity," her analysis of the issue produced conclusions not readily reached by others interested in the antislavery movement; most female reformers, in particular, not only maintained ties with religious organizations, but also worked within some type of religious framework in their reform efforts.[18]

This inflammatory letter was the last of an outburst of radical reform letters and essays written from December 1857 through February of 1858. Colby's private journals show this progressive leap was part of a progressive evolution; it did not simply explode from nowhere in 1858. It had been brewing for some time, but these proactive and very public steps represented a definite escalation. This escalation coincided closely with Annie's departure and Colby's attendance at the Abby Kelley Foster lecture, which was the first of multiple appearances by radical speakers, many of whom were women. Colby's newfound public bravado likely was inspired in part by these women. Annie's friendship and subsequent departure left an obvious void, and Abby Kelley Foster was well known for her inspirational effects. From the time of Foster's October 1857 appearance into the spring of 1858, Colby's attempts to claim a different role in her own life escalated. Her public and ultraist opinions regarding abolition and the concurrent implications regarding women's roles represented an extremely

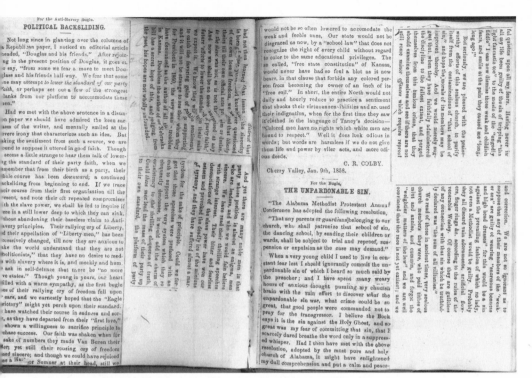

These pages from one of Colby's scrapbooks, c. 1858, show a typical layout. She clipped her essays out of the newspapers and then pasted them over used account books—using every available space on each page. Used by permission Colby Collection, Illinois State University Archives, Illinois State University, Normal, Illinois.

progressive mindset. If that attitude could be applied subsequently in her actual daily life, then real change would result. An examination of her daily life during this period demonstrates that she did attempt to incorporate progressive ideals into her day-to-day existence, often with the same sort of energy as seen in her writing. Unfortunately, the results were not as successful as she desired.

Her ability even to strive for a change was impacted to a degree by the fact that by late 1857, Colby's children were no longer infants. The youngest, Rose, was well over a year old, and the oldest, Vine, almost six years old. Although they still required diligent attention, their ages, as well as Colby's probable end to nursing, made them all much more mobile. This meant she had more freedom of movement both with and without the children, and of this she took advantage. Sometimes her trips were work related in which her children shared the day. "Rode down to Wayne this afternoon to get my carpet yarn &c. Took all the children along, had a pleasant ride. Run in debt a little on the credit of C. R. Colby. I believe in a woman's right to pay her own debts, and it always goes contrary to my feelings of independence to say 'charge this to my husband.' The amount of my indebtedness is three dollars and seventy cents. But I must go to work though my fingers are itching to use the pen."[19] Interestingly, this one succinct entry displays her desire for further independence from society's ideas about "woman's work" as well as the inaccurate view regarding women's capacity to engage in the "male" world of the market economy.

She also was able to continue to travel to various locations, such as Wayne, Monroe, and Andover, to hear speakers who focused on subjects in which she was interested, including abolition, temperance, literature, and education. She often noted in her journal that she spoke briefly with some of these speakers. In addition, Lucy Coleman, Andrew T. Foss, and Joseph Howland each spent at least one night at the Colbys' home. She enjoyed these evenings immensely. Foss was a guest several times and she greatly admired him. She noted, "Never before did I hear the echo of my own thoughts on this point [orthodox religion's culpability in sustaining slavery] so fearlessly expressed." She also thought that "his conversation was interesting and instructive." She especially enjoyed his book recommendations because she constantly desired worthy reading material. Beyond acting as passive audience members, she and Lewis also tried to attend regular meetings of available cultural organizations, such as temperance and literary societies. The fact that many of these groups were made up of both men and women was a common occurrence in the rural North. This mixing, however, generally did not equate to any ideas about gender equity. Societal conventions still ruled as women were expected to take subservient roles. In Colby's everyday life, these norms also affected attendance. Unfortunately for Colby, Lewis was able to partake in these activities more consistently than she because, even given the children's greater mobility, it was not always a practical option for her to attend. If someone needed to stay with the children, it was invariably deemed her responsibility.[20]

Despite the obstacles that existed during this period, Colby made a great effort each month to attend the meetings of one group in particular: the Progressive Friends. A small group of ultraists had founded the Progressive Friends in New York in 1848 under the name of the Congregational Friends, with the goal to provide a social and religious organization that allowed for attention to the "Divine Light, in its present and progressive unfolding of truth and duty." The organization's 1854 name change to Friends of Human Progress represented an effort to reduce a "sectarian feeling" and thus distance the group from not only its Quaker roots, but also from orthodox religions in general, which the membership felt had failed in their duties to all society. The Progressive Friends, as they were commonly called, offered Northern progressives a definitive alter-

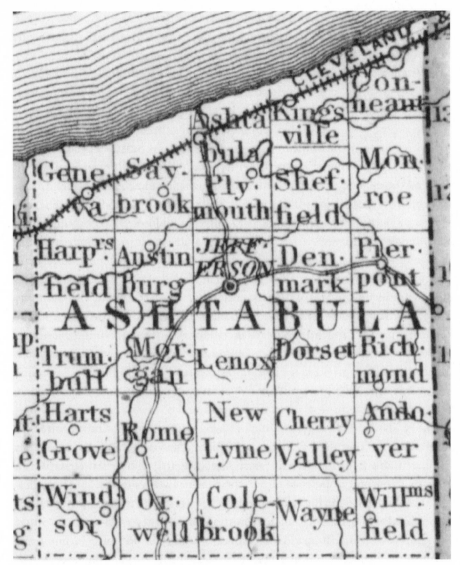

Although Ashtabula County had only two intersecting common roads, which at their closest points were ten miles away from Cherry Valley, Colby frequently visited Andover, Wayne, and Monroe—traveling by foot, horse, and buggy over undeveloped terrain—as well as trekking several times the approximately twenty miles to the train station in Ashtabula. *Map of Ohio* (New York: J. H. Colton, 1855).

native to traditional Christianity in that they were a group devoted to "equality in the human family, without limitation to sex, or complexion, or national peculiarities." This group represented a possible answer to the spiritual needs of ultras. An 1859 annual meeting of the New York Friends of Human Progress demonstrated the extent of their distrust for traditional institutions when the female members drafted a document that stated that religion and government were proslavery and antiwomen, calling government an "abomination" and religion "superstitious, idolatrous, and [full of] atrocious absurdities." Colby appreciated to a great degree the intellectual and spiritual outlet, as well as a measure of gender equality, that the Progressive Friends' monthly meetings provided.[21]

The Progressive Friends' belief in equality transferred into action in many ways. Colby noted one of the most appreciated ways in February of 1858. "Went to Wayne to attend the monthly conference meeting of the Progressive Friends. Took all the children along. 'Liberty Hall' in which we met is furnished with a nursery, containing cribs and a cradle, so that the mothers can be relieved from holding a sleeping child." This early example of child daycare allowed her to note, "I enjoyed myself well." It also meant that she could attend meetings that she might have otherwise missed. The Progressive Friends offered another outlet for enjoyment that was rather unorthodox for its time: dances. The Colbys made several appearances at these social events, which prompted Colby to note somewhat irreverently that she did not feel guilty about her attendance or for her rather unsuccessful attempts to dance. This expression of guiltlessness was, no doubt, a challenge to her previously held orthodox religious beliefs, which named dancing as grounds for involuntary removal from the Baptist class. She even laughed at her efforts and noted, "Thirty years old and learning to dance. Strange that when in my youth I never indulged."[22]

She enjoyed these many activities, but her private words demonstrate that Annie Colby's continued absence represented a constant void in her life that reading, writing, meetings, and dances inadequately filled. "Have written a sheet to Annie and dispatched two of them. How I wish she was here now. Her presence would soothe the wild throbbings of my heart, or perchance increase the restless longing that has taken possession of my soul. I'm in a strange mood to night. How strange it would look on paper were I to trace the deep emotions of my heart. But I will not do it. Hush, restless spirit be still. That pure dream is not for thee." Colby's desire to see Annie also did not abate with time. "Have been 'longing' for a letter from Annie, and have got it too, but it has not *eased the pain*. Wish I could *see her*. The sound of her voice might do me good."[23]

Despite the presence of some positive influences, her "longing" for Annie indicates that she was not entirely satisfied with the state of her everyday life. Her unresolved issues regarding religion were another indication. Contrary to her public and uncompromising bravado against the church, her private thoughts about spiritual issues revealed ambiguity. On one hand, when her essay that she feared would "offend some good people" appeared in print, she noted in her journal, "I believe it is not so very wicked after all." On the other hand, however, only a week later after sending yet another controversial essay to the newspaper, she confessed doubts. "I fear it [the essay, "The Unpardonable Sin"] will be considered almost unpardonably wicked. I believe I'm growing wicked in belief at least, though I don't feel the need of all these restraints of church and state to keep me from crime." Her socialization, which said the church was one of the community's, as well as an individual's, most important social and spiritual institutions, haunted any effort she made to completely abandon it. "Would that I might pierce the mystery 'beyond the vail' and know the destiny of the thing we call *mind*. Will all its aspirations *ever* be satisfied? Shall I ever *know the Truth* and find rest and peace in that knowledge divine? Have I strayed from the only fountain of light, and am I given over to believe a lie, or am I following a dim uncertain light that shall lead onward and upward to endless day? I cannot solve the doubts that perplex me." Nevertheless, Colby's public words continued to show a disregard for reverence to a specific church or religion, even while she struggled with her personal spirituality. In January 1858, she encouraged readers not to follow religious leaders blindly. "Away with any and every religion that makes us deaf and blind to the suffering of humanity, and let us have hearts to feel for the slave as bound with him."[24]

Despite the unapologetic progressive inferences regarding women's roles present in her antislavery rhetoric as well as the implications inherent in her allegiance with the ultraist camp, Colby's writings during this period actually reveal a fair amount of ambiguity about women's roles. On the surface, her public support for those women who speak out seems straightforward, but these statements can be interpreted in a way that indicates that she—personally—was less than fully invested in equality for women. When she condemned society's attitude regarding women in public antislavery roles, she focused on another anonymous woman—who was quite possibly Abby Kelley Foster—whose "qualifications of mind and heart" gave her the right to speak on "the great moral question of the day" without condemnation. She did not venture into women's rights in a broad sense, and ironically, although she condemned those who silenced themselves for fear of public opinion, she wrote the essay in the generic third person and not from a personal perspective. It is possible to read too much into this apparent hesitancy; it may be merely a literary style choice. Nevertheless, she did not address the subject of women's rights as a distinct and separate issue for some time; considering the radical tone of much of her work, this choice seems deliberate.

Several intersecting and underlying reasons likely came into play. Colby clearly struggled with how to incorporate progressive ideas about women's roles into her life. This struggle probably affected her ability to put forth cohesive and personal public arguments. She also sincerely cared about the slavery issue, and unlike condemnation of the church's role, advocating for women's rights added no clear and positive good to the fight at this time. Even in the more socially progressive northeast, radical positions on antislavery still often were viewed in a more positive light than women's rights. Given her understanding of the volatility of the subject and the tendency for women's rights rhetoric to shift focus away from slavery, her choice may have reflected her desire to remain focused on antislavery issues. Possibly, she also feared censure. Colby made several entries over the next few years in which she alluded to having private conversations about women's issues while simultaneously taking care to watch for unsupportive ears. Although considering her other controversial public views, that assumption as a singular overriding reason seems unlikely. Despite the fact that she did not focus on women's rights directly until the Civil War began, she wrote extensively about women's rights issues, such as temperance and female educational opportunities, without openly endorsing "woman's rights." These works display a progressive shift in her public attitude that lends support to the notion that her personal beliefs also evolved. The increasing frustration she felt as those evolving ideas about women's roles collided with the reality of her day-to-day life also supports this interpretation.

This distance between her personal ideal for fulfillment and the reality of her life became more obvious as time passed. Her intermittent attempts to find a compromise between the real and the ideal resulted in little actual change. Reality was work. "How sweet is sympathy. Tonight as I was *so tired* I could hardly go—aching in every limb, Rose a crying, Branch a hooting and shouting with all his might, and I a little out of patience with the world in general and myself and surroundings in particular, little Vine came into the other room and as I was stooping to raise my dishwater from the stove she threw her arms around my neck and kissing me, sweetly whispered 'Ma I'm sorry for you.' The little act of kindness and sympathy from my precious child soothed me and gave new vigor to my weary frame." She contemplated, mostly without hope, a different life. "Shall I ever have books and leisure. Oh I want to live for ever, not as now!" This tone permeates much of her private thoughts, and this frustration translated into delayed hopes for her children's better futures, who, as the above illustrates, were sometimes the only bright spot in a barren day. "There are thoughts busy within that *must be still*, and I must toil and fill my lowly destiny. But if I may only fit my children for a *higher nobler one* I'll be content."[25]

Colby also realized that her responsibilities, which society deemed a "woman's duty," were the weight that kept her from other loftier goals, and she privately questioned why these duties must be solely a woman's. "The same and kindred circumstances are the iron chain of destiny to many aspiring souls. How many bright fancies and glowing thoughts have been buried in oblivion, that the body might be fed and clothed, and that the world might say she has not neglected her duties. And *are* our household duties always the first and, *highest* and only duties a woman owes her family? I believe not always."[26] Although she privately questioned societal norms, she continued to perform her duties even as they wore her down and kept her from pursuing her "bright fancy." The above entry was inspired by a newspaper story titled, "Why Aunt Kitty never became an Authoress," which touched a nerve because Colby's loftiest personal goal was to become an "authoress" and write a novel. This dream at times appeared fleeting.

Colby desired something "more," but her responsibilities kept her from claiming it. The difference between the deference and futility that often overrode her private words and the defiance of her public words is striking. Colby's words of hope for her children and demands for society were consistently balanced with negative comment about her own place and purpose. She was immersed in a struggle to bring together the divergent facets of her inner desires and the outward world. Over the next few years, her emotions regarding this struggle fluctuated, as did her expectations for the future. In the spring of 1858, she maintained some level of optimism. "My heart is in a pensive mood—longing as ever for the unattainable! Shall I *ever realize* the restless yearning of my soul? Could I know the bright fruition of my purest dream were ever to be a reality, I could plod onward hopefully and labor and wait patiently."[27] As the days and months unfolded, reality continued to fall short of her "purest dream." This failing became even more obvious to Colby when she took a trip across country to visit Annie in Illinois that gave her a glimpse of what life might be.

CHAPTER SIX

June 1858–December 1858

"Eleven years ago to day since I took upon myself the cares of a housekeeper"

IN JUNE OF 1858, Colby and her six-year-old daughter, Vine, traveled to Illinois. The logistics of this trip serve as an apt reminder that despite the "transportation revolution," traveling the distance between Ohio and Illinois in the mid-nineteenth century represented a significant undertaking. Several modes of transportation and a considerable outlay of time were needed to complete the journey. First, an early morning horse-and-buggy ride brought them the approximately twenty miles to Ashtabula, Ohio. They would not have reached a "common road" until Jefferson, Ohio, so the first ten miles of this segment likely were traveled on what was basically a path worn down by years of traffic. In Ashtabula, they caught the train at noon that started them west on their lengthy, cross-country trek to Chicago. The rail company advertised the time for the segment between Ashtabula and Cleveland, a distance of approximately sixty miles, as two hours and fifteen minutes. The additional 350-plus miles to Chicago meant another fourteen hours' travel time at a minimum, which with stops and layovers likely translated into more than one day. In Chicago, they took another rail line west to Geneva, Illinois, where they disembarked and walked "over the prairie along the track for five miles" before finally arriving at Colby's sister Cordelia's home.[1]

Colby and her daughter stayed a week with Cordelia, and the visit elicited mixed emotions in Colby. "She [Cordelia] has many severe trials to bear . . . and it is sad to think that these trials are the result of an unenlightened conscience. . . . I do not dare to speak all my thoughts to her freely." It is unclear to what "trials" Colby referred, but her inability to speak candidly to her closest sibling spoke volumes about the effect of Colby's changing sensibilities. It was with a sad heart but eager anticipation that Colby and her daughter left for Freeport, Illinois, where Annie was waiting for them. They departed early in the morning, and although most of the sixty-odd-mile trip was conducted over rail lines, it still took most of the day.

> Left my dear sister this morning, after a pleasant visit of a week. She was very reluctant to let me go to day, and plead only for twenty four hours more, but I had sent word to Annie to meet me at Freeport and could not well avoid going, though I would gladly have staid till now if the time were only at my command. All day long my heart has been alternately traveling back to her, and longing to gild with sunshine her weary pathway; and then flitting away to Annie, who is truly a sister to me in all but the name. . . . I left her [Cordelia] early this morning and saw her watch me from the window till a gentle swell of the prairie hid her from my view, perhaps forever. . . . I did not reach Freeport till 4 o'clock. Almost the first face that met my searching gaze was Annie's, and her glance was like sunlight to my soul.[2]

Colby's affection for Annie is obvious. She even felt the need to legitimize her feelings for Annie, who she claimed was "truly a sister . . . in all but name," as she clearly relished the thought of their time together.

Their time together confirmed Colby's hopes. She and Annie spent long hours talking and sharing thoughts. "Annie and I went to bed, but talked on till to our surprise the birds began their early vespers and day dawned. Then Annie dropped the curtain, shut out the day light and we slept for an hour till called to breakfast. But more precious to me are such hours of heart communion than all the enjoyment of slumber can be. Sleep may refresh the weary frame and give it new vigor, but from such converse the soul gathers strength and energy, and courage for the battle of life, and is refreshed for the weary journey." Colby's joy at this opportunity to spend time with others whom she felt were like-minded was the common thread in her private writing during this visit. The ten-day visit among kindred spirits gave Colby a "sense of joyous freedom as [she] seldom felt before."[3]

The feeling of joy was part and parcel of the overarching theme of her thoughts about this trip: the notion of "freedom." The trip gave Colby a glimpse of what life could be like. "Then there is a sense of *solitude* here. From this window no house is visible, nothing but a broad green meadow stretching away to embrace the sky! The feeling that it inspires in my heart is sense of freedom

from all human restraints, and a desire to live with kindred hearts—a chosen few—in such a sweet solitude forever. To read with them, and 'dream such
dreams as make life worth living,' to roam, all free from care over the fields,
and live simply and happily as a true child of nature." She did not associate this
feeling with her home. Home was not a place where she felt free to pursue her
higher aspirations. "There are *other pages* I long to write, and feel power within
me born to give utterance to these, but have not the courage to lift the vail, lest
some careless eyes should read more than is intended and malignant tongues
give to the airy phantoms of my brain." Instead, home meant responsibility
and the lack of support. Her outward world was not an atmosphere conducive
to writing those "other pages," which was likely a reference to her unfinished
novel. This visit made that knowledge even more bittersweet because she saw
the possibilities of leading a life in the outward world that did not clash with
her inner desires. "I shall look upon these fair scenes and feel their enlarging
influence, and then return to my daily task feeling stronger perhaps yet still
with the restless aspirations within all unsatisfied."[4]

Beyond providing Colby a glimpse of a different type of life, this trip also
offered a chance to tour some of the rapidly changing districts around northern Illinois. Numerous relocated family members and friends were in Illinois,
so she planned several stops besides rural Geneva and Freeport. She visited St.
Charles and the Fox River, LaSalle, and Ottawa. The trip from LaSalle to Ottawa
offered an especially interesting experience. Colby and Annie "paid fifty cents
for a passage on a freight train . . . a distance of sixteen miles." She noted that
despite the assumed discomfort they "had a very comfortable ride however,
and our traveling companions (all men on board except Annie and I) were all
civil and some very kind." Despite her obvious interest in what the city offered,
this visit to "the smoky atmosphere of Ottawa" reinforced Colby's ideas about
the inherent superiority of the country to the city. "[W]ho could hesitate to
choose the quiet beauty of a home on the prairies for a residence in a smoky
town." Colby's sentiments verbally painted an illustration for the commonly
accepted understanding of the difference between the city and the country. Urban life was dynamic but possibly corrupting, whereas rural life was static but
pure. Neither portrait was entirely true, but each was firmly ensconced in the
collective imagination. The idealized and sentimentalized portrait of genteel
country life, which rural dwellers perpetuated, allowed those dwellers to set
themselves apart—and morally above—the dirty atmosphere of city life.[5]

After a two-day stay at the home of a friend outside of Ottawa, Annie left
for her home, as did Colby and her daughter. The train ride, which began in
Ottawa, Illinois, ended three days later in Kingsville, Ohio, where Lewis waited.

Their experience at the train station provides not only a colorful example of the realities of antebellum travel, but also another metaphor for the transition from city to country. Colby noted that she and Vine were "so covered with dust and cinders that he [Lewis] hardly knew us and I guess I was a little ashamed of our filth." They were twenty miles or so from Cherry Valley, and due to the exhaustion of the horses they stopped about halfway home and spent the night in Monroe. The next day they returned to Cherry Valley and life immediately returned to status quo.[6]

Status quo in the Colby household was considerably different from the environment that had inspired Colby in Illinois. Annie was a single woman working as a teacher and living within an extended family in which she was not the matriarch. Colby's reality was that she was the "housekeeper"—a married working woman in a farm family with three small children. The inspirational effects of the trip almost immediately ran into reality. Only a few days after her return, she noted, "Since the necessary task of the dairy were finished I've tended Rose and scribbled some. . . . I've mapped out lots of work for this pen to do, but it will be strange if it's ever done. Time is so scarce with me and there is a prospect that may still [be] more scarce, that I can only muse and dream impossibilities." This entry and its notation of time being "more scarce" also may be a reference to the possible fifth pregnancy. If it is, then it is the only one that appears in her journals, so in reality it is impossible to tell for sure. It is equally possible that the entry is referring to something work related, such as a contract for extra cheese. The cheese industry experienced increasing competition as the 1850s unfolded, and cheese prices sharply dropped between 1856 and 1858, both of which likely affected her workload. No matter the underlying cause, a week later, her attitude had denigrated to one of weary acceptance of her duties coupled with personal disparagement regarding her contributions. "Have done nothing of any account. Made cheese and finished my dairy work, got Rose asleep and sat down with my pen but the thoughts that kept bubbling up when bending over the cheese vat, would not come. So I could not write. . . . So the day has passed. I have read none, wrote but two pages; the rest has been work, work. But it is one of the days of my life, and has passed as most of my days do; yet it saddens me to think it is gone, and that thus the succeeding ones will go and leave no worthy trace behind."[7]

Colby had felt inspired to make a plan for her life that included her writing, but quickly realized that her responsibility to the outward world was in opposition to her aspirations. If her newfound inspiration was to come to anything, she needed to make changes in both her internal thoughts about her life and her external interactions within her household. In short, any real changes in her life necessitated that she not only incorporate a different style of domesticity into her everyday life, but also make a break from societal expectations regarding home and family. Colby actually had discussed issues of women's rights with Annie as well as her brother-in-law Rowell Colby while in Illinois, but even in that more accepting atmosphere she felt unsure about the advisability to be too forthcoming.[8] Given her understanding of society's general attitude regarding women, these changes would not be easy ones, and she had few real role models to imitate, even in the world of the most radical of reformers. As we have seen, ultraist women were most likely to challenge societal norms and live unconventional lives, but even many of them hesitated to completely defy convention, especially after marriage and motherhood.

One of the earliest and most celebrated abolition and women's rights proponents, Angelina Grimke, retreated almost completely from public life after she married fellow radical reformer, Theodore Weld. William Lloyd Garrison's wife, Helen, was firmly ensconced in her role of supportive and private wife. Of course, some women did defy convention, but their examples likely offered as much apprehension as inspiration. Abby Kelley Foster and Lucy Stone challenged societal norms by maintaining a public presence while also acting as mothers and wives. The general public's reactions to them illustrate the decidedly negative effect of their exposure, as they were consistently vilified and called immoral and unfit mothers. In reality, these two women also struggled with how to balance their public service with motherhood, in particular; however, in both cases their decisions were made easier by support in the form of hired help, a circle of friends and family, and most importantly the backing of their husbands.[9]

As previously noted, Colby's circle of family and potential female friends showed minimal support for her progressive ideas, and the level of Lewis's support seems to have been ephemeral. His participation in groups like the Progressive Friends indicates a progressive mindset, but little evidence points to his active support of Colby's attempts to change the most debilitating facets of her daily circumstances, in particular her housekeeping duties. As for Colby's access to other forms of help, her location worked against that solution. Rural housekeeping meant more work and fewer resources, including any kind of regular hired help. Generally, rural women relied on kin and neighbors for help with only the occasional addition of a "hired girl." Colby's experience confirms this generalization, as either their financial situation or a lack of available qualified candidates, or both, kept them from obtaining and keeping regular household help. Colby made only one reference to having outside help during this period and it was short lived. "Ann went away a week ago . . . and of course

I had more to do." A community the size of Cherry Valley supplied only a minimal pool of potential workers, and census reports indicate that young men hired out as farm help more frequently than young women as household help. Colby also occasionally commented on her lack of funds, particularly after the October 1857 bank failure precipitated a national economic "bust."[10] In short, resources that may have aided Colby's efforts to actively step out from her role as the "housekeeper" were rather paltry.

Despite this shortcoming, in the months after her return from Illinois, Colby attempted to widen her sense of usefulness by acting more often on her progressive thoughts. Although she continued to attend monthly meetings of the Progressive Friends and the Temperance Society, she also took more hands-on steps. She made her opinions better known to unsympathetic family members and her immediate community. She engaged in more one-on-one conversations with specific goals in mind, such as confronting a local storeowner "in reference to selling liquor." She also took opportunities to speak in public; she officiated at a Temperance Society meeting, and although it required "desperate effort," she "for the first time read an essay in public."[11] Despite these attempts and the satisfaction they brought, her private words still show that her decidedly negative attitude about her circumstances prevailed.

Over a year after her inspiring Illinois trip, her attitude indicated that no real change in circumstance had occurred. Colby noted in her journal, "Eleven years to day since I took upon myself the cares of a housekeeper, or as the phrase is 'commenced housekeeping.' Weary years have they been in some respect, for Care and Toil have been my constant companions." Her use and setting off of the term "housekeeping" implies the fact that she was well aware that her duty was dictated in part by certain societal expectations. These societal norms, which not only prescribed her duties, but also granted them little real monetary value, affected the way that Colby thought of herself, as did her own thoughts as to what constituted value. Society valued money; Colby valued a pursuit of higher goals. Hence, the self-defeating attitude because even though her days were laborious, if she had not received a wage or had not written anything, then by either definition she "had done nothing of any account."[12]

For Colby to say that her days were filled with "nothing of any account" discounted an immense amount of labor and value. As previously noted, the perception existed that nineteenth-century housekeeping was devoid of labor, but, as is examined below, the reality of course was quite the contrary. As for value, if her daily role was examined only within the context of monetary worth, reality still was quite contrary to "nothing." One historian estimates the replacement costs of only the childcare and housekeeping duties of a middle-class woman to be $250 per year over the cost of a woman's own maintenance. If Colby's cheese-making work were to be factored in, this sum would be much larger. Given the fact that a man could secure room and board for only $4 per week, her contributions added a considerable sum to the value of the household income.[13] So despite Colby's thoughts, as well as contemporary society's ideals to the contrary, she was accomplishing quite a bit.

As noted, Colby devoted a significant amount of time to household responsibilities. These duties, which varied, were numerous, time consuming, and for the most part, not enjoyable. They also were, without a doubt, laborious. Much of her cheese work was seasonal, which invariably affected other facets of her responsibilities. In addition, some of her household duties in themselves would have consumed entire days and some simply were never finished. Not surprisingly, since her journals were dedicated primarily to her feelings and thoughts, she shared very little detail about the tasks that consumed the majority of her time. Although, at times, she felt that her duties dominated even her journals. "Why do I ever write thus of the outward only, when there is a world within, which is my only *true life*. I hear its voice pleading for utterance."[14] Contrary to her protests, her references to the "outward" frequently were only brief entries, such as "worked all day" or "today's work is done."

The brevity of those descriptions should in no way confuse the reader regarding the actual labor necessary for the maintenance of a rural household. Nor should ideas about the Industrial Revolution lead to conclusions that new technology rendered women's prescribed labors significantly easier. For one thing, the ease of household duties was less positively affected than men's tasks by changing and new technology. Perhaps, more important, technology often actually added to a woman's work because of raised expectations. As premade, store-purchased cloth became more accessible at mid-century, people's expectations regarding the number of items of clothing they should own grew, which in turn increased sewing requirements as well as laundry. The advent of the cooking stove in the 1820s raised expectations for multi-dish meals, thus increasing planning, shopping, cooking time and effort, as well as cleanup. The details changed depending on region and time, but not the overall purpose of the tasks. Women's work remained just that—"woman's work"—regardless of technology, time, region, or specific expectations. Apropos to that perception, Colby's typical journal entries regarding 1850s' housework could just as easily date from the 1950s.

> Have washed and baked &c. to day in addition to my usual housework, consequently every bone and muscle aches with weariness.

It is bed time and I am tired and sleepy, have been up at four for two days and have worked very hard. Yesterday I did out a large washing and ironed the whole of it besides my usual house work.

Yesterday I washed . . . baked and ironed besides cooking and washing dishes, dairy fixtures &c . . . with the afternoon came the usual stupor of weariness so I read some, sewed and mended till supper time. Now I have washed the dishes &c. which &c. means numberless small chores.[15]

Entries such as these frequently served only as preludes to her primary purpose: to give voice to her frustrations with her daily life, which were twofold. "'Couldn't get time' is the death knell to many, very many, of my aspirations," summed up the first part of her frustration: housework required too much time and energy, which left insufficient reserves available to accomplish anything of value. The second complaint was housework's supposed natural status as solely within a women's sphere, or as Colby noted, she spent her days "doing all sorts of chores usually supposed to belong legitimately to 'woman's sphere.'" Colby followed her role as assigned, but because she held complete scorn for this notion of naturalness she often noted her tasks only with bitterness and sarcasm. "I must not pause long for the motto of the housewife must be 'duty before pleasure.'"[16]

Colby's writings provide very few actual details about her work, but the ideal of how this natural role as housekeeper should be approached is eloquently pictured in a nineteenth-century work by Catharine Beecher. Beecher's book, *A Treatise on Domestic Economy,* first issued in 1841 and reprinted annually until 1857, describes in detail the mechanics of "keeping" a house—a term that gained popularity during this era—and caring for a family. Ironically, like many female authors of the time whose very careers and lives were in opposition to the notion, Beecher's writings supported the idea that women belonged primarily in the home sphere. However, she also felt that the popular perception in which a woman's role as a wife and mother made her somehow inferior to a man needed to be eliminated. This book proposed to serve that goal. Key to this goal was her adage that a woman should "regard her duties as dignified, important, and difficult." Beecher advocated that if this attitude were coupled with the recognition of women's "far-reaching influence and usefulness," then the proper education and training of young women would move to the forefront of American society.[17]

As a young woman educated in the New England tradition, Colby would have been aware of Beecher's philosophy and very likely would have read the book herself. Obviously, many young women had. Part and parcel of Beecher's notions on proper training was the idea that the key to a well-run house was the development of "habits of system and order" for all aspects of housekeeping. This orderly system needed to have a foundation. Beecher noted that some women had achieved success with a schedule such as the following: "Monday . . . is devoted to preparing for the labors of the week. . . . Tuesday is devoted to washing, and Wednesday to ironing. On Thursday, the ironing is finished off, the clothes folded and put away, and all articles which need mending put in the mending basket. . . . Friday is devoted to sweeping and housecleaning. On Saturday . . . every department is put in order. . . . All the cooking for Sunday is also prepared."[18] Beecher covered subjects ranging from food preparation to health care, but she had designed her regimen with the urban, middle-class housewife in mind. This fact explains why much of her coverage of housekeeping, including this plan, which although it dictated a full week of labor, assumed the presence of hired help. Her prescriptions left little room for aspects of life that would have been the added responsibility of a rural mother and housekeeper such as Colby, like dairy work and full-time parenting.

Many tasks involved with running a nineteenth-century household were undoubtedly unpleasant, but one in particular—laundry—ranked among the worst. Regardless of any other work, every household had to devote considerable time to this one job, even if hired help was involved. Beecher suggested that several days were needed to complete the washing, and she devoted several chapters—almost thirty pages—to its various components, which included the actual washing, ironing, and preparation of needed materials. Although her treatment of the subject assumed that in many, if not most, cases this job was hired out, in Colby's household, every indication supports the fact that she performed this task herself. A brief excerpt of Beecher's recommendations serves to demonstrate the enormity of this job and why it was a multiday job. It is important to keep in mind that piped water did not appear in most households until after the Civil War, so water for every "tub" first had to be hauled from a spring or well then heated. Beecher counseled that a woman should begin the night before in order to save labor the next day. She should "assort" the clothes and put the whites in warm water to soak over night. Then the next day, the real work began. "Wash the fine clothes first, in suds, and throw them, when wrung, into another tub of suds. Then wash them in second suds, turning them wrong side out. Then put them into a boiling bag, and let them boil, in strong soapsuds . . . moving them about, with the wash-stick. . . . Take them out of the boiling water, into a tub, and rub the dirtiest spots. Then rinse them, throwing them, when wrung, into a tub of blueing water. Wring them hard the last time . . . and dip them in starch just before hanging out." This description covered only the "fine clothes." The book continued with procedures for washing other materials, proper starching and ironing techniques, as well as instruction on soap making.[19]

Beecher's treatment of the subject suggested how washing "should" be done, but besides her assumption of hired help and prescriptions on the treatment of the varied types of clothing that many rural families may not have owned, her descriptions seem to offer a fairly accurate picture of what it entailed. Susan Strasser's history of American housework, eloquently entitled *Never Done,* devotes a chapter to the "staggering" amount of time and labor involved in laundry. Ruth Cowan's examination of technology's effects on women's tasks, aptly titled *More Work for Mother,* notes that by mid-century laundry had become "a major component of woman's work . . . and arduous work at that."[20] Washing was obviously an extremely time-consuming and labor-intensive job and it was only one component of Colby's many household responsibilities.

Laundry was—and is—a largely thankless task that must be completed by somebody. It is an easy job to loathe. Colby's primary responsibilities as a mother also required significant time and labor, but these responsibilities were infinitely more complicated because they involved deep emotions. She obviously loved her children and was devoted to them; nevertheless, her frustration with what their presence implied regarding her ability to achieve any of her personal goals is apparent in her private writing. This dichotomy often contributed to her sense of self-loathing. Colby's approach to mothering in the late 1850s and early 1860s seemed to incorporate the prevailing cultural ideology that a mother's primary duty was to produce good citizens, but with an expanded definition of what that citizenship meant. Colby's hopes for her children went beyond the standard, gender-based prescriptions, and in Colby's diary entries about her day-to-day interactions with her children, the struggle to be an example for them, not merely "an unthinking drudge," was apparent and exceptionally poignant.

In addition, in a time when many people regarded the mantra of "spare the rod, spoil the child" as central to parenting, Colby's attitude regarding discipline was a progressive one. Nevertheless, like many aspects of her life, she was conflicted about what was best for her children's future. "I was surprised and grieved to night that my little Vine should tell me an untruth. She seemed much grieved when I talked with her about it, and I hope it may be her last error of the kind, though I have not proceeded with her in regular orthodox style of discipline. Have I failed in doing a mother's duty, that I did not whip her, and make her learn the text of 'all liars have their portion in a lake of fire and brimstone etc!' I could not conscientiously do so, and should have violated my own ideas of right and been guilty of a falsehood, had I done so." Colby continued to struggle with the subject of discipline as her children grew—especially because her opinion differed from her family's. Colby felt that "too soon for our happiness, does the child leave the flowery paths of youth. . . . Shall I spoil my children if I neglect to use it [the rod]? Time will tell; for my conscience upbraids me for ignorantly using it in times past, when I too thought necessary."[21]

Regardless of Colby's love, the children still represented a tremendous amount of work, and her conscience continued to add weight to that load. In the summer of 1858, Colby's three children were aged six (Vine), four (Branch), and two (Rose). Three entries from that summer demonstrate the frustration she felt as a result of an overload of work, which not only left little time or energy for intellectual pursuits, but also restricted her opportunities to be the example that she wished for her children. She expressed guilt and feelings of inadequacy. These emotions, no doubt, were fueled by her continuing perception that she was accomplishing nothing of worth, partly because her children required so much time.

> Rose this morning at four and made a vain effort to write, but could not, for baby thought something wrong was going on and so waked up and bothered me just as she is doing now. There is *no use* for me to try to be anything but a drudge for I am bound to the wheel as with an iron fetter, and yet I cannot give up the cherished dreams of years without many and *bitter pangs*. Here I am sitting on the ground under the locust tree but my heart is far away. Very pleasant is this spot, and had I but one kindred spirit by my side I'd try and be content. "Where is ma" and "where is ma" is echoed from mouth to mouth, and thus not one minute of quiet from morning till night is mine. My spirit gets *so* weary, my patience so often tried that I sometimes feel that I could die without a pang. And yet it is but a momentary feeling, born of despondency over which the soul triumphs by power of will. Would that I could maintain the ascendancy so dearly gained; but "the flesh is weak" and too often leads the spirit captive.[22]

A month later, she expressed weariness once again as the children tried her patience, and she had little energy left for thought or higher aspirations.

> Have given the children their usual bath and they are now chatting in bed, though Branch is already asleep. Rose was kissing her goodnight, while he was waiting for his turn, but he was so weary he said he "did not want to stand here all night waiting for kisses" and as soon as this was over he was

asleep. Rose keeps putting her little finger on the page where I am writing and says "what is that?" Hope she will go to sleep soon for I'm too weary to be patient with all her little wayward caprices. Wonder if other mothers ever feel too lazy to answer the thousand and one little queries that children only can invent?

She then turned her guilt inward as she chastised herself for her inability to stay current and her perceived lack of intelligence. "Have been glancing over several volumes of the 'Cultivator,' [*Ohio Cultivator*] since supper and reading the 'Tribune' [*New York Tribune*] before. Wish I could retain all the facts, both statistical, historical, and scientific, which I wish to, but my mind is too much like a sieve, it lets much that is valuable escape, while it retains the worthless, the light, trifling, funny things without any effort or wish of mine."[23]

The next evening, her self-deprecating feelings of inadequacy coupled with her guilt produced this over-compensating pledge regarding her children. "Sometimes I'm too weary to talk and it requires a great deal of effort to patiently answer all their questions. But I will here record a resolution and will strive to act accordingly to tell them instructive stories of men and things as often as possible while pet is going to sleep. I know this would be useful if my mental resources were what a mother[']s should be. But oh how sadly deficient! Still they have unbounded faith in mother's knowledge, for Vine very artlessly asks 'how comes it that you know so much?'" It is interesting to note that very same week that Colby remarked that a temperance meeting would have been made "more interesting if the women only speak the thoughts that are born within and often demand utterance." Ironically, her promise to tell her children "instructive stories of men," which included Robert Fulton, Ben Franklin, Samuel Morse, and George Washington, reveals that despite her feelings about the importance of women's potential contributions, she lacked alternative American historical examples and still felt compelled to reiterate the patriarchal story of American accomplishment.[24]

Society said that mothers had the responsibility to produce model American male citizens and duty-bound daughters. Colby's own ideals required that all her children be prepared for not only citizenry, but also a higher life, one in which each child lived a useful life not mired in drudgery or degradation. She obviously felt inadequate at times to do either. This view of motherhood's often overwhelming implications as well as the weight of her additional responsibilities may well have been the base for her comments regarding an old school friend's pregnancy. "Found two letters on the table . . . one from Nette Warren. She is blessed with another daughter! Such blessings come so fast to her home nest that I should think they would hardly be blessings at all." Colby's attitude regarding the frequency and number of children may have translated into some sort of family planning on her part, so as her "blessings" did not arrive so quickly. Colby made no obvious mention of sexual abstinence or birth control in her private writings; nonetheless, the timing of her children suggests some level of planning. She gave birth approximately every two years while in her twenties but bore no more children after this time, despite the fact that she theoretically had at least ten more childbearing years before beginning menopause. Between 1830 and 1870, information about contraception was circulated widely among women, particularly middle-class women who wanted to limit family size, so it is entirely possible that Colby made use of some type of family planning. Only speculation can be made, but clearly she viewed her family sufficiently "blessed."[25]

Her children's care contributed to her weariness, but they also represented a bright spot in her life at this time. Nonetheless, their unconditional love did not quell her desire to achieve something beyond her home life. Frequently, she lamented about the meaningless tasks that drained her energy and mental acuity. She viewed these chores with deep resentment. One of those duties that she continued to regard with almost as much dread as laundry was "visiting." As previously noted, Colby's attitude about her neighbors was not always positive. Time did not mellow this view.

> As a matter of duty I went a visiting today . . . remarked about the weather, asked her a baby's name, said it looked like its uncle &c, &c.; which &c means nothing of interest, nothing into which the heart, soul or intellect had any share, and this is called a visit. And worse than all Custom makes it imperative that we ask a repetition of the same tasteless affair. From all such visits "good Lord deliver me" is added to my "Ave Maria" to night. But the clock is striking ten and I must retire. Have written half a dozen introducing paragraphs to "Brookville Home" tonight. Wonder if it will ever be finished.

Brookville Home or the Still Silent Influence of a Woman was the title to her unfinished novel. The desire to complete this work was one of the primary reasons she resented the constant pulls at her time and energy. This book represented a concrete way in which her goals could be manifested. It embodied her desire to express not only her thoughts, but also her ambitions to be more than a "mindless drudge." "Could I thrill the heart of another by my written thoughts it would be a bliss that would reconcile me to this half way life, *if possible.*"[26] Books played an important role in her life, and she felt if she produced something that affected someone else in that same way, then her life would be "useful." She never viewed the effects of her day-to-day actions as having that kind of potential.

The process of writing a novel as well as the story itself represented both her hopes and frustrations in regard to her life. She believed its completion would place her within a sphere of higher culture that she envied and in which she wished to be more involved. Ironically, or perhaps even covetously, her book was the story of an educated woman who establishes a literary society to provide the young men in her community a place of culture to replace the temptations of, among other things, the saloon. Her heroine was able to accomplish this task because she was a childless widow who owned a home that served as the site of this lyceum. For several years, Colby occasionally referenced the fact that she had written pages for the manuscript, but unfortunately, the book was never completed. Her daily obligations made that wish impossible, and these stymied desires contributed to the constant frustration she felt.[27]

Meanwhile, she used her writing skills for a less noble effort, but one that nonetheless she hoped would free up some much-needed time for higher intellectual endeavors.

> Had a letter from West & Wilson last night. I am to have one of their sewing machines in a few weeks, and am to pay for it with the pen, provided it is a good machine, so that I can praise it conscientiously. I hope I shall not be disappointed in its merits, and that the exchange will be satisfactory all around. Have just finished the days work, at least so much of it as is done by day light, save preparing the wee darlings for slumber. What the record of the evening will be is still uncertain. Somehow I feel dissatisfied with myself to night—indeed I often do. I feel sometimes that my life is almost a cypher, When I long to leave a high holy impress upon those around me. To will is mine, but I fail totally in the execution, and I draw but little consolation from the agreeable couplet that tells us that—good God will note the hours.

Ironically, although the sewing machine did change the nature of sewing to a degree, it did not necessarily provide more free time. In fact, sewing machines often raised clothing expectations. In addition, they were temperamental machines at best. This agreement in which she wrote testimonial essays in exchange for a sewing machine may have been the only way that Colby could have afforded this new machine, which would have cost approximately $100—a considerable sum.[28]

Her diaries reveal that Colby spent many late nights, in essence, working, by writing essays in the hope they could be used in other "exchanges," most frequently as trade for newspaper and periodical subscriptions. Although it would seem that she was successful, judging by the number of references made to the different newspapers to which she contributed, she rarely displayed much confidence in this aspect of her writing.

> Again it is evening—and again I am alone with my pen, but with little courage to write. Have mixed in a page of writing with my work to day. Well two hours have passed, and I've just finished writing, folded and sealed an article for the Sentinel, [*Ashtabula Sentinel*] with a request for an "exchange." Wonder if the request will be granted, or will the article be a failure? Time will tell. I've also one ready to send to the Dollar [*Philadelphia Dollar Newspaper*] with a similar request, and next I must try my luck with the Olive Branch. Lewis is by me reading the Lamplighter [unknown publication], but it is nearly bed time. Wish I could sit up and not feel the vigil tomorrow.

Besides using her writing as trade for subscription or product use, she occasionally used it to earn cash as well. She entered a writing contest, in which the prize was to be $50. Of this essay, she noted that the "subject upon which I must write now or never is dull & just like work and I have to bring myself to do it as to any other task." She clearly resented the implications of writing for this purpose, as it turned something akin to higher culture into merely another task. In addition, typical of her constant self-doubts, she was extremely hesitant to actually send the essay. "But I must finish up that 'Essay' to night and get it off my hands. . . . There it is late, I do not know how, but I've finished that terrible essay, folded and put it in the envelope without daring to read it. I shall send it Monday and wait as patiently as possible till its fate is decided. Sometimes I have a faint hope of success, at others not a bit, but what is writ is writ. I've not spent much time about it but it has laid in my drawer unfinished till the very sight of it made me sick."[29]

She mustered the courage to mail the entry, but the decision weighed heavily on her. "I've been thinking of my folly in sending that Essay, for as the time draws on for the decision I feel more ashamed of it than ever." And again, although her efforts could be considered successful, she was not confident before or after. "A busy week is gone; I've written nearly every evening. Wonder if will pay—in dollars and cents, I mean, for that is the test by which people judge everything. I have just learned of the partial success of my Essay. Mr. Krum called tonight. He was one of the committee. He said that there were five competitors and that there were two Essays which they could not decide between, so they divided the premium between the two, so I shall get twenty-five dollars, which will help pay my debt."[30] Her attitude about money as an unfortunate but necessary evil surfaced once again in this entry. She associated nature with purity and morality, and urbanization and its accompanying focus on money, with many of society's evils. Her contempt for a world that she saw as growing increasingly materialistic is obvious; however, her actions show that she operated in a realistic fashion and was aware of the importance of money in her life.

Her sense of what was valuable only rarely translated into emotional attachment for an "inanimate thing" of monetary worth. Nevertheless, occasionally she was forced to concede the effect that money, or its lack, had on her life.

It is a most glorious day, and all the morning while doing my work I was longing to be out in the golden glory of the warm sunlight. So when I finished I called the children . . . and soon left the gloomy atmosphere of the house, determined to have one more revel with nature. We wandered around . . . and after we selected a sweet mossy knoll . . . we set the table! . . . [I] put my hand in my pocket for my pen—but it was gone. Instantly I was saddened, to me the pen was not merely a shining bit of gold . . . but a *friend* that has often soothed my melancholy, peopled my solitude and been to me the best of society. . . . I shall miss it in many a lonely hour . . . and I but illy spare the money to purchase another. Oh dear *it is hard to be poor.*

She reacted similarly a year prior while at the Ashtabula County Fair when she was unable to purchase books because of an "empty purse."[31] Money was only truly worthy if it was used to gain something higher.

Colby not only acted in a pragmatic manner in her existing outer world but also attempted to maintain hope that the ideals inherent in her inner life somehow could come to fruition and alter her reality to bring it closer to the life she had glimpsed in Illinois. Too often, however, in the months after leaving Annie in Illinois, the picture of the idealized life she had glimpsed actually served to fuel frustrations with her own life and heighten her sense of isolation. She feared that her efforts to obtain a higher life were bound to "fail totally in execution." As 1858 turned toward 1859, this theme of frustration was interwoven with a continued sense of emptiness. She longed for someone or something to fill this void. Colby's frequent correspondence with Annie provided a tenuous feeling of connection. "Am keeping silent company with Annie just now. Wonder where she is, and of what she is thinking and talking?" But her sense of emptiness remained strong. "I weary and turn disgusted in my search for human sympathy, and human love, which has power to make life so beautiful, so bright, so full of joy. Had a letter from Annie last night and have looked long and lovingly upon her soul lit features, and tonight she was the silent, invisible companionship of my walk. I love to feel the shadowing spirit presence of a loved one, even though distance stretched away between us."[32]

These intersecting themes of frustration, loneliness, and spiritual wanting left her feeling unconnected in any meaningful way with those people and events that made up her day-to-day life. The overriding feeling that pervaded Colby's life during this period was neatly summed up in her own words: "I am a strange incomprehensible being, and live in a hidden world. My outward and inner life are not the same, they have no points of resemblance. Like two vast continents, they are separated by an ocean of mystery." Her hopes were in opposition to her reality and although she entertained the idea that a change could be made, she made only intermittent efforts to do so. "I long to . . . live in the ideal world which my fancy creates, and which reason tells me should be the *real earth life* . . . but no."[33] In her view, reality allowed little else. Although many aspects of the wider world changed over the next several years, her personal situation remained much the same. As she struggled to find contentment, this divergence operated at times as an inspiration, but it also acted as a force to break down her will.

CHAPTER SEVEN

November 1858–November 1859

"I wish for a 'bright little isle' to be peopled with the good, the loving, the gifted"

IN NOVEMBER OF 1858, Colby experienced a brief ray of hope. Annie returned from Illinois to Ohio and she brought somewhat unexpected news. She was a new bride. "My heart is in a strange sort of a tumult tonight, full of strange emotions. Was surprised to receive a call from sister Annie and brother Ned today, now *one* in the eyes of the law, as they have long been in heart." Colby was "*so glad* to see her," and she hoped that Annie's presence would alleviate some of the worthlessness she felt pervaded her daily life. Annie and Ned remained in Ohio throughout most of 1859 and Colby was able to see her more often. Unfortunately, reality often interfered, and Colby's complaints reflect her continued frustration. "Last evening I talked with Annie till a late hour; the interview was pleasant. But I am ever sad after such. She has been with me for several days but has just gone. How often I wish for 'a bright little isle' to be peopled with the good, the loving, the gifted, where I would be content to fill a humble space, and breathe the pure atmosphere that such spirits ever diffuse."[1]

Colby's fantasy regarding this "bright little isle" recalled her idealistic views of life in Illinois, but it likely was grounded also in the knowledge that such communities existed. Utopian communities proliferated in the early and mid-nineteenth century. To Colby, these endeavors, such as the mid-1840s' transcendental community of Brook Farm, must have represented the embodiment of her ideal environment. The residents of Brook Farm strove to achieve an intellectually stimulating life within a tranquil rural setting. In essence, they hoped to access a higher culture without the toxic effects of urbanization. They also incorporated equal participation of the sexes and emphasized a spiritual, nonmaterialistic existence, rather than adherence to a particular religious dogma—all of which were endeavors that Colby admired. She realized that such an ideal environment was realistically out of her reach, but she still hoped to find a spiritual community that met more of her intellectual and emotional needs. To that end, she continued her search for what she called the "truth" by investigating other avenues of religious worship.

This search was given breadth by her rebuke of the idea that God's ultimate role was to mete out fiery justice to sinners. Colby did not feel she needed threats to act morally. In fact, she resented her childhood indoctrination and felt it contributed to her spiritual uncertainty as an adult. She noted, "I attribute much to the influence of a false education that taught me to fear God instead of loving him." In her eyes, a God who created the wonders of the natural world did not equate with the God envisioned by orthodox Christianity. "Poor soul, how I pity her, deaf and blind as she is to all the glory and beauty of the universe, always suspecting evil, and worshipping as her God a miserable creation of her own imagination who has but one attribute of what she fancies to be justice but seems wondrously allied to revenge."[2] This attitude allowed Colby to contemplate ideas that were considered unmitigated sin by orthodox Christians. Despite Colby's consistent complaints, she was not completely alone in this particular contemplation. Although Lewis had been raised as a Regular Baptist, he displayed a willingness to consider other options. His interest, however, may have been fueled by intellectual curiosity rather than an emotional need, contrary to Colby, who viewed this spiritual search as a possible means to fill a void. In addition, like other aspects of his sometimes apparent progressive mindset, ideas for change did not always manifest clearly as attempts at real change. Regardless of Lewis's motives, in a community in which societal norms centered on orthodox Christianity, his openness to at least hear about diverse religious ideas no doubt eased Colby's access to spiritual alternatives.

Universalism was one of those potential alternatives. The orthodox teachings of Colby's youth, as well as the evangelistic turn of her early twenties, provided a foundation that condemned the idea of universal salvation as supported by Universalism. Universal salvation, according to its critics, let the "unregenerated" escape punishment. In addition, these critics noted, without the threat of retribution, humanity was left "morally adrift" and thus doomed. Despite her earlier influences, Colby showed interest in the ideas of Universalism, as did Lewis. "Lewis went to hear Mr. Shipman at the town house and he came home with him and took tea with us. My curiosity was somewhat gratified in his elucidation of the peculiar doctrines of the Universalists. Years ago I thought them all that was evil, and that it was almost an unpardonable sin to go to hear them preach, but the hallowed impressions of my childhood are fast disappearing." As such, she found that her evolving belief system was in some ways in line with Universalism. "Yesterday I heard Mr. Shipman give a doctrinal discourse, containing a brief outline of the views of the Universalists, which was interesting as a fund of information respecting that much abused sect, and really contained many excellent sentiments; though I am not a universalist in all respects, yet I could but agree with many of the ideas advanced."[3] Lewis's thoughts are unknown, but despite her concurrence, Colby was not ready to commit wholeheartedly to another set of dogmatic boundaries.

Her search for truth in religion also led her to consider the merits of the spiritual sciences, such as spiritualism, mesmerism, and phrenology. As previously noted, the spiritual sciences were a significant cultural force in the mid-nineteenth century that proposed to use objective science to prove the earthly world's divine connection to the spiritual world, or God. After Charles Darwin's 1859 publication of *The Origin of Species,* people became less confident that science could offer insight into God, but until that time many learned people thought that the future of spiritual knowledge naturally was connected to science. Phrenology purported to demonstrate that people were "religious by nature" by an analysis, or "reading," of the shape of the skull. Mesmerism evolved from the premise that magnetism, or electricity, was a physical extension of God, so if a person was "magnetized," or put into trancelike state, then she or he formed a tangible link with God. In Spiritualism, science was not used merely to validate a particular religious view. Natural law was viewed as a physical manifestation of the spirit, so the observation of those laws at work in nature was in itself the religion.[4]

Although by the 1850s many spiritual science practitioners may have been little more than amateurs or charlatans, the ideas behind them were serious and never were meant to be merely parlor games. Many orthodox religious authorities thought the practices dangerous threats to not only a person's immortal soul, but also to religious institutions. Nonbelievers associated Spiritualism, in particular, with "free love" and the basest element of the women's rights movement, which exacerbated its sinfulness among many of the orthodox. Spiritual science no doubt appealed to Colby's love of knowledge. In addition, many people that Colby admired, such as Lucy Coleman, adhered to at least one of the facets of the spiritual sciences, which likely made these movements more appealing to Colby.[5]

This appeal led her to embrace the limited access to the spiritual sciences and consider their possible merit. Toward that investigation, she read a "strange and mystical" book she called *The Life Line of the Love One.* Its author, Warren

Chase, was a well-known spiritualist lecturer. She commented that although he was a "Spiritualist and Free lover," she thought it contained some "*very good* ideas." She also stated that she found it "Strange that it should! For they are said to be all evil." Her positive, although somewhat surprised, reaction to his ideas offers another example of her continued challenges to the cultural bias typical in this period. Despite the community's negative attitude toward unorthodox religious practitioners, Colby even had some limited opportunities to discuss the subject with believers. "Went to hear Mrs. Warner to day, but did not get converted to spiritualism." Like Universalism, she never did "get converted" to Spiritualism, but she continued to find the subject interesting. Her willingness to consider a different spirituality coupled with her disdain for orthodoxy produced an amused reaction when orthodox Protestant followers were forced to hear a Spiritualist speak because of the forum. "Heard Sophronia preach old Mr. Phelp's funeral sermon to day, and strange to say the use of the Baptist pulpit was granted for the occasion! I liked her discourse best of any I have heard from her. And to day she had a few hearers that have never before ventured to listen to a '*spiritualist*' or an infidel."[6]

Although she also continued to attend orthodox Christian services, she continued to disparage them. "Went to church to day. Heard Eld[er] Crandall for the first time. Was not particularly edified." Amusement and sarcastic dismissal often devolved into more bitter pronouncements and questions as her disdain for orthodoxy reached new depths. "Have been to church to day, both at the centre and at the methodist. Did not get profited at either place. Certainly many of Elder Crandall's statements *were false* without any mitigation. But they are part of his *sectarian capital*, and without such, he could not preach the gospel to the satisfaction of his orthodox hearers." She also openly questioned religious authority. "The new methodist preacher and wife staid with us last night. We had a long discussion upon the Scriptures and kindred themes, he starting with the assumption that the Bible is the word of God and reasoning round in a circle as the orthodox are apt to do. My remarks were so shocking to his wife that she left the room saying she could not listen to such conversation on Sunday night! She seemed to feel as though I must not only reverence the 'word of God' but his *minister* also, while I feel no more reverence for a priest than for a farmer, or humanity everywhere." This attitude showed the continued influence of her association with the Progressive Friends. They believed that ministers were not important to communing with God and, in fact, felt that people were better able to experience the "divine light" of God's direct connection with humanity without the interference of intermediaries.[7]

Her doubts regarding the "assumption that the Bible is the word of God" allowed her to apply a level of textual and contextual analysis not allowable at any level for orthodox Christians. In addition, she showed interest in the burgeoning field of geology, which, among other things, called into doubt previously accepted biblical ideas regarding the earth's formation and age. During the prior year, she read a book she called "Adam's fall refuted by earth's rocky records." Although in a self-denigrating manner she claimed that the author's proofs were "a little too scientific for my weak brain," her interest in these ideas clearly displays her questioning attitude regarding the veracity of biblically based religious dogma. Another work inspired her to analyze the various depictions of gods available in different literature, including the Christian Bible. "Yesterday I read the closing Book of Homer's Illiad. . . . And many of its marvelous and miraculous stories of 'the gods' and sons of the gods has a parallel in the strange stories in the old Testament; nor do I see that the *idea of god*, as developed by the old Testament writers, is much, if any in advance of the idea which the ancient heathen had of their warlike divinities. But there is a wide difference between the God of the Greeks, the Jewish God, both so mighty in the field of Battle, and the God of St. John."[8] The notion that "old Testament *writers*" had "*developed* an idea of god" (emphasis mine) was not something a "true" Christian would consider.

The clergy's abilities continued to provide a frequent target. "Last night I went to a preach at the Methodist house. Wish when the Lord gives a 'call to preach' he would also give the ability. Worked out of doors most of the time yesterday, and think I enjoyed more of the presence of God, heard more of his word while surrounded by his silent, voiceless ministers, than it would be possible to do while listening to the boisterous rantings of such an ignoramus."[9] As this entry shows, she dismissed the need for clergy to commune with God. Although she never embraced the spiritual sciences as her "religion," she expressed a consistent belief in the idea that nature represented the best earthly embodiment of God. Despite her contention that clergy for the most part were misguided, she admitted that, perhaps, some meant well. "Went to quarterly meeting at Wayne yesterday. It was a decidedly stupid affair, preaching dull as need be, and yet I suppose the clergy who were present really think they are 'the light of the world;' if so how great is the darkness. After the sermon there was a communion; but to me it seemed only a solemn farce! And I cannot believe that the great supreme looked upon it with approbation." She simply was unable to see how orthodox churches served her life or provided any of the spiritual sustenance that she so needed. "Sunday eve. Have been to church to day! Heard Eld[er] Yates preach, but I do not see as what is called the 'preached word' has much bearing upon everyday life of the hearers."[10]

Colby sought something that would sustain her through her everyday life, and unfortunately the things that most people used in this capacity—community and kinship support via church, family, and friends—remained inadequate to fulfill her needs. Not yet willing to completely give in to hopelessness, Colby attempted to mold these societal mainstays to fit her needs. Her forays into alternative and progressive religions represented this endeavor, and although she found areas of interest they failed to provide consistently uplifting results. As for her family Colby had often noted over the years her dissatisfaction that her family life did not live up to her ideals. In the following October 1859 entry, she expressed those feelings and provided a more fully articulated view of how this lack of support affected her path to potential happiness.

> And then the *sacred privacy* of a true home has not been mine. I can never cease to regret the fatal mistake that must shadow my life time, that was committed when I entered, not without many misgivings—the family, not to make and model our own future home, but to be trammeled, repressed and dwarfed by the opinions, prejudices, and cold mercenary spirit of others. I cast a backward glance to night over the weary toilsome years that are past, note the *few* hours of real home feeling that I've passed with my own loved ones when fate or fortune made a transitory solitude for me, and vainly sigh "*It might have been.*" Then fancy draws the picture of what an hour might have been had our home life been moulded after our own wishes.[11]

Colby clearly felt that if she and her family—"my own loved ones"—had made a distinct and private home, then she would be happier. This recurring sentiment seems to make allowances for Lewis's inconsistent level of support by blaming the environment rather than him. Her prevarication adds another dimension of doubt to attempts to discern Lewis's actual level of emotional and active support during this period.

As previously noted, like Colby, Lewis had been involved with various, reform-minded groups and activities, and this involvement continued throughout 1859. The couple attended occasional Universalism meetings and antislavery lectures, both together and separately. They again hosted progressive speakers, such as Lucy Coleman, at their home. The two also continued to periodically attend meetings of the Friends of Human Progress, although not as frequently as before.

They stayed active in their local temperance society and vocally condemned the use of both alcohol and tobacco. Occasionally, Lewis even displayed direct personal action that illustrated a progressive mindset. After an 1859 New Year's Day discussion between Annie and Colby about "woman's rights and duties, &c, then of her rights in reference to property—of wills &c," Annie introduced the topic to their respective spouses and "instant action was proposed. Accordingly four wills were written, signed and witnessed." These wills, one each written by Lewis, Celestia, Ned, and Annie Colby, left their property exclusively to the other spouse, which in a state that still allowed women only very limited legal rights was a progressive move.[12]

Despite Lewis's apparent accord on these progressive issues, however, evidence shows that also similar to prior years he failed to provide much actual physical or active support in her efforts to change the details of her life. It can be argued that considering the disdain her wider circle of family displayed for her progressive thoughts and publications that Lewis must have offered some level of emotional as well as verbal support. However, Colby perceived this support to be inadequate at times. Reasons for this variance can only be speculated. He was frequently away from home, so his absences may have compromised his ability to offer consistent backing. He also simply may have found it easier to bow to patriarchal norms in his own daily life. This attitude was far from uncommon, even in the most progressive households, and the couple lived within a household that displayed less than progressive daily ideals. Regardless of the underlying reasons, his actual everyday attitude—as perceived by Colby—was less than supportive. He offered little to no help with domestic work or the children and this inaction impacted her life in a more immediate and personal way than any show of progressive allegiance to a "cause."

Community, kin, and the church had failed her. In Colby's view, friendship offered her last real hope for human support. To this end, she continued her efforts to fill her life with enlightened individuals, and Annie remained key in that undertaking. Although Colby was nearly a decade older, she perceived Annie's role in her life as somewhat of a mentor. Annie served as not only a sympathetic ear with whom she could share her inner feelings and thoughts but also someone who inspired her intellectually. "I wanted to see Annie *so much* to night, but couldn't. It would do me good to sit alone with her . . . and talk as I never do with others." Colby had assumed Annie's return would mark the beginning of a period of sustained inspiration; in the months immediately after Annie's return, particularly in the weeks surrounding the turn of 1858 into 1859, Colby was inspired. The notation Colby made the day Annie returned ended with an indication of Annie's effect. "I've been lost in a dreamy reverie thinking things mutterable, all suggested by the brief interview of this afternoon. How different from the most of my visits, that leave no food for thought."[13]

These "things mutterable" turned out to be a more clearly articulated public position on women's possible roles. Colby's trip to Illinois the previous summer had inspired some private thoughts and conversations regarding society's view of women's potential. She even had broached the subject with a few select female friends after her return, but she had not taken the step to broadcast these evolving views in a wider public forum. Annie's return clearly inspired her to do so. She still did not publicly advocate "woman's rights" in name, but her evolved position on women's equal access to education, which differed considerably from her prior public opinions, mirrored that of women's rights activists. In addition, the following 1858 essay displays a sense of sadness in regard to her life's opportunities that had not appeared in print prior to this time. In this essay, she focused on a young woman, "Rosalie," with whom she had briefly come into contact.

> She was not a city belle—useless as the painted butterfly, idly sipping the sweet dew. . . . She was a worker in the social hive; silently and steadfastly working her way through one of the few colleges which will grant woman the simple justice of giving her intellect the same culture for which a thousand wide avenues are thrown open to man. Though young in years and slight in form, there was a strength of purpose in her soul. . . . She had a resource within herself, and scorned to lean upon the arm of a friend or brother and look tamely up to them for support. . . . I saw at a glance that hers was not a nature to bow tamely to the destiny of circumstances.

Colby's previous public words on female education had emphasized only its role in making better wives and mothers. She never had specifically broached the subject of women's access to higher education. Colby now presented a clear opinion: women had the right to education—for their own sakes. She no longer portrayed female education as merely an avenue to produce a happier or more satisfied mother and, therefore, a better housekeeper. Instead, education was represented as a right in itself for all people. This piece also displays her frustrations about the lack of female opportunities in general and her insecurities regarding her own abilities. In somewhat of a defensive tone, Colby linked Rosalie's educational success directly to her unique character. This character enabled her to go beyond the usual limits placed on women. "Her strong womanly independence earning her right to an education such as we are proud to bestow on our sons, while we bestow only the light accomplishments upon our daughters."[14]

This argument championed Rosalie; however, it also implied a greater amount of personal, or individual, fault for her own failure to obtain an education than reality supported. Colby's frustration on this subject was understandable, but her personal disparagement was not completely warranted. Even if her situation or "unique character" had been different when she was younger, she would have found it extremely difficult in the 1840s to obtain a college education on par with men. As noted previously, the higher education available to women was almost nonexistent. Even by the late 1850s, only a few colleges accepted women and they did not offer necessarily an equal education. The highly touted Oberlin offered women only a special "ladies['] course," except in rare circumstances— Lucy Stone being one example—and few other options were available. The 1862 Morrill Act, which funded higher education through land grants, helped turn the corner for women's educational opportunities. By 1867, a total of twenty-two coeducational universities and colleges existed, which by 1870 included eight state universities. These changes came too late for Colby, but they allowed her two daughters to become part of the "first generation" of college women.

Colby disparagingly described women who were "content to live a life of idle dependence." She harshly compared these women's futures with Rosalie's possibilities. "[They will] sink into mere drudges, and plod through the rest of their hopeless existence with no thought or hope beyond the bounds of their kitchen or parlors. Not for thee, strong, but gentle Rosalie, does such a future loom up, dark and cheerless as the storm clouds in its wrath; but a life of active usefulness, of intelligent pleasures, of intellectual enjoyment." Although Colby made no actual personal references, the tone of regret and the obvious admiration she held for Rosalie's life shows that Colby feared her existence was doomed to one of a "mere drudge." Her observation that Rosalie would not "bow tamely to the destiny of circumstances" offered succinct counterpoint to the terse journal entry that so often summed up Colby's view of her life: "Circumstances are destiny." This essay in many ways, and for the first time, placed Colby's inner thoughts about her own existence into a public forum. "There is a world within where we live a hidden life—a life widely different from the outward. . . . How often do we pine and languish for the sympathy of a kindred heart."[15]

In addition to placing her inner thoughts into the public domain, this essay provides the framework for the type of woman Colby admired and wished she could be. "I honor the maiden who fears not to tread the rougher path, to walk by her brother's side through the varied fields of science and literature, who is not content with the mere buds and flowers that adorn her path, but gathers also the ripe fruit, the golden grain of scientific research, and lays deep and broad the foundation for future usefulness." Usefulness was an important character trait in Colby's thoughts, and she felt that she fell far short of any accomplishment that could be labeled useful. Her continued frustration can be interpreted as an indication of her belief that change was still possible, but that hope continued to waiver. "Another day has passed in the same monotonous way in which all my days are passing. I've done nothing worth recording, save getting weary and perhaps impatient, or out of patience."[16]

Another factor contributed to Colby's impatience as 1859 unfolded. Colby had assumed that Annie's presence would provide additional ongoing support, but this was not always the case. "Ned and Annie came home with us and took supper. The short interview with Annie was refreshing, more from the thoughts and feelings, that spring up spontaneously in her presence . . . than from any words uttered by either of us, for we were alone together but a few minutes. Oh I wanted her to stay all night *so much*, for there was much within struggling for utterance."[17] Annie's new marriage compromised Annie's place as Colby's emotional and intellectual outlet. Colby's affection for Ned was never in doubt, but between her own responsibilities and Annie's new role as a wife, the two women's time together was far too infrequent. Colby never was satisfied by whatever brief time they could salvage from their days, and her attitude grew increasingly negative, despite Annie's presence. Her entries show she felt considerable frustration.

Although her public words—in print—spoke out boldly for change, in her private life she felt less and less adequate to be a force for change, as her July 1859 reflection illustrates: "Have been listening to the conversation of men who profess to be anti-slavery men, but sentiments which they have advanced would be very popular upon the rice plantations of the south. I am sick at heart to hear such sentiments uttered before my little ones and no dissenting voice is raised. How soon is an unjust prejudice against color raised in the minds of children. I longed to speak sometime, but remember that *woman* must keep silence and 'learn of her husband.'"[18] Ironically, this entry minimized the import of the many opinionated and forceful letters and essays that she wrote for publication. It also displays evidence of the strong hold the contemporary notion that women should not speak publicly had on Colby. Her ideas on the subject of slavery must have been known by those men to whom she was listening; nevertheless, she felt powerless to dissent vocally.

The contrast between her feelings of forced silence and her bold public words lend credence to her premise that her life was truly split between her inner life, which she dared to put forth in a public way only via a medium that allowed a sense of safe distance, and her outer life, where to speak out against a man was considered unthinkable for a "proper" woman. When she did dare to speak up vocally, she often privately chastised her efforts. In August 1859, she noted, "Last night I went to temperance meeting. Mr. R. Robinson was the speaker and his remarks were quite interesting, at least to me. After the meeting I had an introduction to the speaker, but somehow I shrink from it; for I find I feel my own insignificance *so painfully* and blush for the folly that I have dared to give my thoughts to the public. And yet they burn for utterance when the power of speech is denied."[19]

This hesitant attitude about "speaking" obviously was compounded by the influence of other members of her household. Colby's exact living situation is unclear. She and her immediate family shared a home with at least her mother-in-law and brother-in-law, but evidence indicates that the household also was frequently filled with people other than her immediate family. It is impossible to know exactly how many people lived in the house from month to month, but occasional references to various tasks, such as the number of people for whom Colby cooked, suggest that additional members of the extended family, workers, or perhaps even lodgers, also stayed with them at times. The following entry illustrates clearly not all of her household members were amenable to her more progressive attitudes, especially as to women's roles. "I've been listening while at the breakfast table, to a sort of discussion upon the relative merits of woman, and they seem to judge her by the same standard of excellence that they would a horse, viz: her *powers of endurance*, and her ability and disposition to do the *work of a man* in addition to her own. Oh how low, how unworthy, a standard of excellence is this. And yet by such a standard must I be estimated by at least a majority of those who make the social atmosphere of the spot I call home."[20]

If these entries reflect Colby's actual perception of her status within her social sphere, it is not surprising that a significant number of her private words concerning reform and change revolve around her generalized hopes for the future of the world and her children, rather than for herself. "I try hard to live as I ought—under the circumstances which are my destiny, but I am not, cannot be as cheerful as I wish to be. . . . I've looked at my little ones and tried to scan their futures. Could I make it *all* that I wish it, I could be content to 'labor and to wait' for the bright fulfillment."[21] Dreams for her children may have seemed attainable in opposition to dreams for her own life. This theory is given credence by the fact that although she frequently wrote of desires for change in her own daily life, these words often simultaneously reflect a depressed resolve that her existence was actually fixed.

She resented the role allotted to her by society, and she hoped for something more for her children, especially her daughters.

I hushed little Rose to sleep in my arms, and pressed her to my heart with fond, but anxious love, as I thought of her possible future. She is my sensitive child, and will feel *so keenly* if the dark lot of woman should be hers, "to make idols and find them clay," and "to pour unvalued wealth" upon a worthless shrine. She is my darling, my pet, and I have three of them, but for her happiness I fear the most. . . . Oh that I had wisdom to guide her in the way of truth, to mould her little mind aright. I do not wish to make a genteel lady of her, with not a thought for anything more lofty than the fashions, and not an opinion of her own unless it is connected with dress or the toilet, but my great desire is that my daughters may grow up strong, true, and earnest women, such women as are fitted for life's great duties, women who are prepared to bless, not only the home circle, but the world."

Colby clearly felt that too few paths led to fulfillment for a woman. The usual avenue—marriage—too easily could manifest as "the dark lot of woman," an unhappy life of drudgery, or a life of idle frivolous dependency. Colby was troubled deeply by this potential future. Her fears and hopes also extended to her son. Her desire that he become a man who was a worthy partner for a "strong, true, and earnest woman" is evident as she continued her entry. "And my boy, not for him do my aspirations culminate in 'the presidential chair,' but I would have him *great—a man,* who can rule his own spirit, and body, one to whom the dictates of reason shall triumph over every low and unworthy passion." Her belief in her ability to guide them to this path was somewhat tenuous. "Verily the mothers mission is a fearful and a holy one, and I am not equal to the task which rests upon me."[22]

Colby frequently linked reflections about her hope for humankind and her children to feelings and disappointments concerning her own abilities and accomplishments. This dissatisfaction regarding her accomplishments was not merely an undefined melancholy; she had distinct personal ambitions that were being unfulfilled. In the following entry, some of the specific desires not being met in her everyday life are revealed as she discussed her children's potential futures.

Little Vine is by me reading. . . . She has been talking about writing books, thinks she "shall write one sometime." Would that her childish thought might grow to be a reality for it would be a bliss to me if the genius which I so vainly covet, might be the dowry of my children. Have been dreaming of the future of my little ones all day as I often do. I long to see them fitted for a higher sphere than mine, for a wider circle of usefulness. Not that I should wish them to live a life of idleness, but that their happiness may be increased by a broader culture. That they may never feel as I do the pressure of that "iron shroud" of ignorance that crushes me on all sides. I would have the mind cultivated, the hand, the eye, the ear, the feet, even that they may be able to give expression to all the struggling emotions within, to embody the creations of thought, or copy the glories of nature upon canvas, to give a voice to the inborn music of their own souls, and move to the harmonies of sound.[23]

Colby's feelings about what sorts of things she felt were important for a different—higher—life are clearly displayed: books, music, art, conversation, and an appreciation of the natural world. Her enjoyment of these aspects of life is revealed throughout her journals. Happy times consistently involved one, or a combination, of them. She desired that her children feel the freedom and ability to express themselves in word, song, or dance without the oppressive disapproval of family or community to which she was exposed as a child and that she felt infected the atmosphere still. "Sometimes I fear lest they will have no aspirations after a higher calling than those around them, that they will be content to live as I have lived—a life of mere drudgery compared with the sphere I crave for them. But if I cannot give the talent and genius as a birthright, I trust they may at least inherit an *earnest aspiration*, which with a favorable culture may bear them upward unto a purer atmosphere."[24]

This hope for her children's future often led her to distrust her neighbors' possible influence on them. She once commented after a family moved in to a neighboring house, "hope they will not stay long, for I rather my children would play alone." Her disdain for outside influences affected her feelings about her two oldest children beginning school in May of 1859; it was not entirely a happy occasion for Colby.

To day Vine and Branch began their school days. I have looked forward to this event with strange emotions, and sometimes with a sort of nervous fear and dread. It seems like an era in their existence. I have always looked upon them as babies almost, as *mine*. Now they leave my care in a measure, and are more under outside influence, and what they may be I cannot know. I do not fear that the teacher will injure them, but how many wayside teachers, and wayside lessons, they may encounter and what their influence may be is a matter of doubt and uncertainty. But they must live in the world, surrounded by all its influences, and perhaps it is well that

they should be educated in the same school. But how pleasant it would be
to be able to do this work myself, to be the sole teacher of my little ones.[25]

Her pragmatism collided against her ideals. Realistically, she understood that
she could not isolate her children, but she had real concerns about the effect
of these outside influences. Once again the unpleasant reality of her workload
resulted in her sacrifice of something she valued; the outer world won out over
the inner life.

Colby not only desired a home life that buffered her family from these outside influences, but, as we have seen, she also felt her home environment offered
unsatisfactory influences. So perhaps not surprisingly given this conundrum,
Colby's thoughts regarding her daily life, at times, were contradictory as she
struggled to incorporate differing ideas about how to create a happy home. She
often wrote in public, as well as in private, about what qualities embodied a
"higher" life. She expressed admiration for women who spoke publicly on the
subject of women's rights and lived unconventional lives as women, such as
Abby Kelley Foster, Frances Gage, and Lucy Coleman. Despite this admiration,
she also gave every indication that she had little to no belief that changing the
structure of her life as a wife and mother was a viable option. Consequently,
she routinely envisioned unrealistic scenarios. On one hand, she used ideas
culled from popular fiction of the time and imagined an ideal home and family
life. She drew on the T. S. Arthur story, "Maiden, Wife & Mother," to support
her disenchantment with her existing home life. She felt his story provided
validation for her thoughts regarding the ideal living situation in which young
married couples formed their own homes in order to achieve "their highest
happiness" and the "mental and harmonious development of character that
united growth of the soul, without which there can be no perfect union."[26]
Unfortunately, this rewriting of the past was no more a real option than her
routinely imagined ideal of a "bright isle" where she could commune with like-
minded friends, but both indicated her discontent with her real outward world.
Although she never seemed to believe that a real alternative was available for
her life, thus her idealistic scenarios, she still desperately clung to the idea that
if she could simply achieve some sense of a higher "mental . . . development of
character" and incorporate it into her life, then she would be *more* content.

Unfortunately, the realities of the outer world offered little opportunity to
rise above the ordinary and strive for this higher character. Colby viewed the
concerns that occupied her neighbors' day-to-day lives, as well as her own daily
life, as monotonous. They provided no "food for thought." She shared this disdain in her correspondence with a woman whom she had never met, but hoped

she could share "kindred thoughts." Colby noted, "Money, butter, and cheese, cows, calves, horses, sheep and pigs are not only our 'staple productions' but also the staple theme for conversation at all chance gatherings. . . . When I return from such a gathering with 'my soul thirst and hunger' all unsatisfied, I am more than vexed, I am pained, deeply pained that the human mind should feed so contently on husks and chaff, and I feel a wild longing of soul for a higher and holier converse with my fellow beings." Colby's journals show that she felt particular disdain for the women in her community. She often made disparaging comments about her female neighbors and kin.

> Called upon "Aunt Anna" or rather in her flower garden, for I did not go in her house. She seems very happy when any one admires her favorites, and talks of but little else, but it is more interesting than this perpetual chatter about house work with which we are so often entertained. . . . Then we called next to see Mr. Gidding's cheese. The good woman began her dissertation upon milk, cheese and work in general, the instant we opened the door and did not stop a minute till we were out of hearing. Her cheeses were models, but it is pitiful to see the mind so narrowed down to the limits of the cheese room.[27]

Besides providing a typical example of her attitude, this entry also illustrates, perhaps unwittingly on Colby's part, the imbedded cultural paradoxes that formed her world. While acknowledging that *Mrs.* Giddings performed the work, she simultaneously referred to the product as "*Mr.* Gidding's cheese." This patriarchal structure ran contrary to Colby's ideals, but obviously was imbedded in her consciousness, perhaps contributing to her frustrations as well as her consistent disparagement of many facets of her daily life.

Colby's contempt also extended to friends with whom her family commonly socialized. Her journal notations on the subject were frequent, rarely complimentary, and provide additional demonstration of her feelings of detachment. Her attitude that her time would have been better spent writing was an obvious and recurring theme. "Have been alone . . . and was anticipating a good time with the pen, but fate steps between, for I am to have company and there will not be one word spoken but gossip—so adieu to my dreams." Her reaction to a gathering at her home was that "there is nothing said to arouse the intellect, or call a single faculty of mind to play." Company arrived to call at her home, and she complained, "Suppose I ought to go down and try to be sociable, but far pleasanter to me is the solitude of my own room."[28] It bears remembering that Colby's consistent complaints that she was alone too much were based on perceived emotional isolation because she was rarely actually physically alone. In fact, people frequently surrounded her. This irony added to her despair.

By 1859, Colby's despair began to manifest itself in more chronic fashion. Although she often had blamed other people's deficiencies for her feelings of isolation and unhappiness, she shifted the responsibility for her inability to connect to herself. The fault for her recurring depression lay in a defect in her nature.

> I'm utterly discouraged to day, almost hopeless. I've no energy to do, no courage to act, and in seasons of despondency like this my physical strength deserts me, and it is only by a desperate effort of the will that I nerve myself to perform my daily tasks. Life is no blessing to me, unless I can be a blessing to others. And much I fear this is impossible. I feel that I should be but little missed were the grave my home. I cannot make others happier, only in a very small degree. I can cook, wash dishes, and other household drudgery, and this seems to be the extent of my usefulness. Any one can do this as well as I, and many far better, while at the same time their social qualities may be such as to improve and bless all with whom they mingle. Oh why was I even born?

Her dismissive "any one can do this [cook, wash dishes, and other household drudgery] as well as I" provides another clear embodiment of the effects of the "pastoralization of housekeeping." Not only were the tasks viewed as of minimal "usefulness," but also easily could be done by others "far better." Although Annie's presence provided a temporary antidote for recurring feelings of helplessness in the face of "destiny," too often the reality of the outward world consumed her days and left little time for the pursuit of other interests. "The day has been a busy one, dull and monotonous outwardly, but characterized by an intense longing after the impossible, the unattainable. There are tears in my heart now."[29]

As day-to-day circumstances continued to challenge her ability to find the ever-elusive contentment, so did events in the wider world. Well over a year before South Carolina seceded from the Union and the Civil War began, Colby revealed a sense of foreboding as to how the question of slavery would be resolved.

> Well again it is the Sabbath evening. The little ones are not yet all in bed. I've been to hear [American Anti-Slavery Society lecturer] Parker Pillsbury to day. I was interested in his remarks, and yet my thoughts were sometimes painful, very painful—I do not know why, but sometimes I get discouraged, and despair of the ultimate triumph of the right, and the

future—not of myself in particular—but of mankind, and my children looks so dark, so hopeless that I shudder when I think of the *possibilities* that may be concealed behind its thick vail of uncertainty. But let what will come, I hope they may be found *equal to the times*, superior to circumstances and yet, I've no reason for this hope.[30]

Hopelessness became a dominant factor in Colby's life as she failed to find continuing sustenance. Annie's presence, although inadequate to quench Colby's voracious need—provided some sense of hope and support. Consequently, Colby was saddened deeply when Ned and Annie returned to Illinois to join Ned's parents in the fall of 1859.

Colby was troubled by the knowledge that one of her only avenues for emotional and intellectual support soon was to be missing again. "Spent last eve with Annie. The thought that this privilege is to be mine no more fills me with sadness. My spirit needs her influence to reconcile it to destiny, fate, and itself." Colby's bitterness regarding her life's direction shows in the following entry in which, in addition to the sadness at Annie's departure, she exhibited deeper feelings of fear and even jealousy.

Last night Annie staid with us, for the last time before going west. We sat up till long after the old clock in the corner tolled the knell of midnight, saddened by the thought that for the future, our lives must lead down separate channels, severed far and wide, never more to meet and mingle, until perchance we join the fathomless depths of Eternity. There is something inexpressibly sad, in the thought of this separation, and that *change*, more cruel than distance, will separate our spirits. I know that for her, a more elevated sphere will open, and a wider range of enjoyment prepare her for greater usefulness than I can ever hope for, and that consequently she will *soar* while I shall sink. Will this sever the bond of friendship that has been so sweet to me? . . . Long will it be, before my pathway will be brightened by intercourse with another spirit like hers. I shall miss her so often when my spirit is sad, and my courage low.[31]

It was unclear what Colby meant by a "more elevated sphere." Annie was a schoolteacher, so perhaps she continued to teach in Illinois, which certainly qualified as a "greater usefulness" in Colby's eyes. What is clear is Colby's perception that the monotony of her life posed a danger to the quality of their friendship. Annie would move on—and up—while she remained mired in mediocrity.

On the eve of the move, books provided Colby with comfort. "Let me turn to books for the solace earth cannot elsewhere give." Annie's parting gift to Colby was a copy of Lord Tennyson's dramatic poem, *Maud,* in which Annie had marked her favorite passages. This gift was representative of their relationship, in which books and discussions about books were an important element. After Annie and Ned left for Illinois, Colby noted sadly, "yesterday morning I had the last glimpse of Annie, as she went by, en route for Illinois."[32] They would not meet again for over a year. During that year, the nation stood at the brink of war, Colby's struggles grew increasingly difficult, and a sense of torpidity pervaded as she and the country waited for something to determine their course.

CHAPTER EIGHT

November 1859–February 1861

"I am accomplishing nothing"

IN THE FIFTEEN MONTHS between Annie's departure in November of 1859 and her return to Ohio in the spring of 1861, Colby's feelings of emotional isolation escalated while her efforts to counter this isolation stagnated. Annie's absence, no doubt, exacerbated these feelings, but other factors also contributed. Personally, her negative attitude about the inadequate nature of her home life and her place within her community intensified, but in addition, apparent unhappiness within her marriage also became a larger component in her dissatisfaction. On a wider scale, the nation moved closer to war, and Ohioans continued to display vastly different ideas about how, or even whether, to halt this approaching storm. Although Colby continued to contribute to this debate publicly, she turned increasingly inward in her private life.

In December of 1859, one month after Annie left, Colby turned thirty-two years old, and her comments marking the occasion eloquently sum up her thoughts about her own worth and the passage of time.

> My birth day! . . . I must confess the thought struck me painfully. Yes I *do* regret that I am thirty-two, *not* for the wrinkles and gray hairs that steal so silently upon us with advancing years, and which with me anticipated the flight of old father Time, and met me, even in my youth. But I feel *so sadly* that my years are passing away, and I am accomplishing nothing *worthy of Life.* . . . I begin to grow *miserly of time.* . . . My time is all frittered away in petty care, in little things, that weary the physique, and too often perplex the spirit but leave no worthy record behind. Were I to

trace the record of a day, it runs in this wise: arose at six, dressed, washed and combed the children, got breakfast, washed the dishes, swept and dusted the rooms, made the beds, got dinner, washed the dishes, swept and mended till supper time, got supper, washed the dishes, read a little, wrote less, mended or sewed more, and now it is bedtime. And all this has been spiced with a multitude of little chores, whose name is Legion; and yet with a few slight variations, such as baking, washing, ironing, making butter and cheese, it is the history of my life—my outer life. And this is *woman's destiny*! . . . For the outer life of the mass of womankind may be traced in a few brief paragraphs of "born on such a day, died on such another," *lived, toiled and passed away*. . . . But woman's life is made up of such a repetition of little things, her duties move around in a circle, and seem never to be accomplished; she seems always to be doing, never to have finished her tasks.[1]

This birthday soliloquy aptly demonstrates Colby's feelings of inadequacy; she was "accomplishing nothing worthy of Life." This perception of worthlessness was a byproduct of the conflict between Colby's ideal of a useful happy life and the reality of her daily life. In addition, unconsciously, or perhaps even consciously, it was an admission that in a society that increasingly placed greater value on work performed for cash, her duties—although prescribed in part by that same society—were deemed less worthy, therefore she was also less worthy.

This birthday-inspired articulation of her frustration was unique only in its length. In the months leading up to this benchmark, she noted her growing fear that her life was speeding by and her hopes were falling by the wayside. "The record of yesterday is the record of to day in every respect, the same restless fever is burning intensely within, the same useless aspirations are struggling in vain, as they must ever struggle. Oh Life! Oh Destiny!" A month later she noted, "Oh Time, why is it so fleeting! The day has passed all to swiftly for my plans as all my days are passing. I've worked very hard nearly all the time, while my heart was yearning for quiet and leisure to trace my thoughts, but the work is done and it is bed time, and with another dawn begins anew the weary round of toil and care. And *this is Life!*"[2]

The theme was recurring. Colby feared that she was destined to live only to work and that this work had no real value. The week of her birthday, in an attempt to fight against this fear for her future, she recorded a "resolution" in which she vowed, "After this winter I *will not work* as hard, have so little rest or leisure. I know that in my circumstances it will be far easier to make a resolution than it will be to keep it, but I am going to make the effort, never the less.

I am satisfied that I'm sinning against my own intellect as well as physical constitution by excessive toil and that the wrong doing will not be transitory but lasting." Despite this resolution, several months later, her attitude reflected that no respite was imminent. She remained decidedly negative. "I've been tracing a simple sketch . . . just then some unwelcome duty, some trifling chore, perhaps presses itself upon my attention. . . . My destiny is to act, to do life's humblest duties, in a narrow unknown sphere, to crush back the up springing aspirations that rise in my soul."[3]

The winter passed, and as Colby predicted, her resolution moved her no closer to a different reality. The responsibilities that made up daily life were her reality and they never seemed to abate. In fact, they often grew heavier, particularly when Lewis traveled. During his absences, in addition to the usual tasks necessary to maintain the dairy, the house, and her three young children, she took on increased management responsibilities. She made a notation in the summer of 1860 regarding yet another one of Lewis's absences from home that is telling for several reasons. Unlike entries from years past in which she simply lamented his absence because she missed him, she complained about her extra workload. "So many cares will be mine that work will demand all my energies and the mind must starve on. Why this antagonism between mind and matter and why the highest ever sacrificed to the lowest—the inner to the outer?"[4] It is clear that despite her integral role in the success or failure of the household, she attached little pride to those endeavors; instead, she bemoaned that the effort required to achieve the goals of the outward world diminished her spirit.

Motherhood remained the one aspect among her responsibilities in which she displayed ambivalent emotions. She both begrudged and cherished the time required to accomplish her "humble" duties as a mother. She loved her children unconditionally, but she was becoming more resolute about the nature of the sacrifice that society mandated should be made in their honor. "Then why should we grow weary in well doing, or faint because the end is not yet? These humble duties are not *all* of our life, even though they do engross by far the largest share of our time. They are necessary, and love and trust can make them beautiful. . . . A mother's mission is never accomplished till her sons, and daughters like precious stones fully polished are prepared to occupy a worthy place in the social structure. This is her work in a measure, though the means may be humble, her progress slow."[5] This entry acknowledges two intertwined facets that were woven consistently through Colby's thoughts on mothering: its significance and its requisite time requirements. Like many other aspects of her life, she struggled to find a balance between the two facets. This struggle's implications often overwhelmed her because, unlike housework or social obligations, she was deeply committed to the prospect of her children's fulfilled lives. Nevertheless, her ideas about what constituted a good mother had evolved over the years. As she and her children grew older, she showed increasing frustration with society's idea regarding how she should accomplish those duties.

Nearly ten years after her numerous essays touting the responsibility of the republican mother, her writing revealed this altered sense. In her view, the sacrifice of mind and body to constant work did not result in successful mothering. In fact, she proposed that this sacrifice hindered a woman's ability to act as a responsible wife and mother. "Think not that we would have women idle, or men either; but while willing to do our share of labor for 'the meat that perisheth,' we do protest most earnestly against fettering the intellect, and binding it an unresisting captive to the wheel of toil, imprisoning it for life with the narrow bounds of kitchen and dairy. And we have serious doubts, if a woman can perform her highest duties as a wife and mother, who thus crushes out her intellect, and voluntarily reduces herself to the level of a self-regulating machine." Colby's use of dehumanizing analogies in which she equated a woman's work to a "self-regulating machine" occurred regularly in her journals. As time passed, she also used them more frequently in her public writing. Colby was progressive on many levels; she had not only perceived that industrial growth had tainted the natural world that she cherished but also produced the much-vaunted problems of urban life. For a human to be reduced to the level of a mechanical "drudge" was the ultimate price for a life devoted only to work. This state could be mediated only if adequate time was allowed for higher pursuits. She believed strongly that this attitude must be conveyed to her children. In Colby's opinion, a mother who cultivated a thirst for knowledge in her children—not just by sending them to school or encouraging them to read but also by example—"will bless her children as the unthinking drudge never can." According to Colby, if a woman could accomplish that goal, then she "will win the sure reward of their love and confidence—a love mingled with filial pride, and the dearest word in all the language to their hearts, will be the name of mother, which she has made holy."[6]

Despite this outlook, her love and devotion to her children insufficiently mitigated her sensation of being trapped in the life that she had helped to create. She felt powerless to force a change in regard to her situation; circumstance had produced duty, and this responsibility could not be left behind. "Christmas day, but with me it is any thing but a merry one. There are many bitter thoughts surging within that I'm not even content, nor calm. I try to be all this, and cheerful, but I can only purchase calmness, by utter forgetfulness of *all* that made my early dreams of home so bright and I cannot forget, though I often wish I could. . . . Were not my life so linked with others, I could make a straight path for my feet, and I would make for myself a home, where there should be at least *freedom* and peace, where my every movement should not be watched with a frown."[7] Once again, because she foresaw no viable alternative within her reality, Colby resorted to idealistic fantasy, where she broke away from her family and made "*myself* a home" (emphasis mine). For years, Colby had complained about her dissatisfaction with her home life, but as she perceived the path to her future grow narrower, her bitterness grew. Subsequently, she complained about the quality of her home life even more frequently.

Beyond her extended family's general disapproval of Colby's desire for a wider sphere, she occasionally also hinted at specific underlying reasons for her deep discontentment regarding her living situation. Sometimes obliquely she noted, "Does it ever occur to us to reckon those [hours] made happy by the absence of some other people?" Other times, she was more direct. "Am alone just now, and to be alone is *so refreshing* to my spirits after the *presence* to which I am always confined during the day. Oh it is such a relief to shut the door between myself and him. . . . To bear the cross of daily life under some circumstances requires a degree of fortitude, heroism and patience not easily acquired." It is not clear to whom she was referring to as "him." Lewis was away from home and her father-in-law had already died, so a likely candidate is Cyrus, Lewis's brother. His apparent disability—he is listed as "crippled" in census reports—likely kept him somewhat confined, and his care may have been one of Colby's "duties." Considering Colby's resentment that she was "mingling day after day with persons whose very presence 'poisons the atmosphere for me,'" she likely begrudged any additional duty that prolonged contact.[8]

Her resentment toward her daily tasks would have been lessened somewhat if those duties had been balanced to any degree by intellectual or emotional stimulus. Unfortunately, she remained decidedly negative regarding the ability of her available pool of companions to provide any avenues to this stimulus. Consequently, although Colby deeply desired the support and companionship of friends, she remained unwilling to extend herself to those women whose lives connected with hers on a daily basis. She assumed these women lacked the capacity to fathom her need for a connection that extended beyond cheese. "And yet another weary day's work is over and my little room is warm and lighted for the evening. Would that I could welcome to its humble retreat two or three true friends, or even one to spend the fleeting hours with the sweets of the soul communion. But *such treasures are so rare!* . . . Tis better to dwell in solitude apart, self centered, and self reliant, than seek social enjoyment where it is not to be found. As well seek warmth from an iceberg, as social bliss from those who cannot understand our mental wants or spirit needs."[9] Although her life did not completely lack more meaningful interaction, in her opinion these opportunities, or "treasures [, were] so rare."

Contrary to Colby's attitude, it bears mentioning that her extended community was not completely bereft of attempts to engage in activities centered on higher culture. Historians find that nineteenth-century women routinely attempted to recreate the "civilized" facets of society, and Ashtabula County was no different. These attempts included the sharing of books and periodicals, participation in literary societies, formation of reading groups, and the support of temperance societies. It is important to note, however, that the rural nature of their lives dictated the extent of participation. In Colby's situation, many of these diversions occurred at most monthly, often in neighboring communities, and were highly dependent on season, weather, and time considerations. In addition, many of these events and societies offered no real counter to her feelings of gender isolation, as they often served to reinforce preconceived notions about roles. Consequently, they provided only a peripheral means of daily support and were insufficient in quantity or quality to quell Colby's thirst for more. "Went a visiting one day last week and had company one evening, but among it all there was *no conversation*—not a word uttered that would refresh the spirit, or strengthen the soul for the every day battle of life. Sometimes I feel like a stranger in a strange land, even among my kin. Wonder if I shall ever be a stranger to all around them, and most of all to those of my own household? My soul is longing for recognition, but longs in vain. But I *will* silence it oh, I will, *if* possible."[10]

Colby felt that a wide gulf existed between her interests and the interests of the women in her community and family. Ironically, although these women's everyday lives were actually much like Colby's, she worried over possible subject matter for conversation. She also spared no feelings in her private assessments of them, and she commonly degraded neighbors and acquaintances. A notation in which she characterized a neighbor was typical of her attitude. "Mrs. C. is a fair type of that class of woman who think that to *work* and *serve* is woman's highest destiny, and between such and myself there can be no sympathy." Despite this condescension, Colby was not immune to the notion that if she could only be more like her neighbors then, perhaps, she would be less unhappy. "Have visited . . . this afternoon, had a good visit *of the kind*. They enter, heart and soul into the practical duties of life, *love to work*, are happy, or seem to be in their way, and once while eating supper I looked upon them as models of their kind, and half envied them their dull, sluggish bliss, but only for an instant. No, I would rather suffer the keenest anguish I ever felt . . . than to be capable of no *higher* enjoyment than their highest."[11] In the end, however, her certainty that she could never be content with their level of "dull, sluggish bliss" rendered the possibility of any real connection unrealistic. The gap that Colby perceived to exist between her and those women, who more enthusiastically embraced the "domestic life cycle" prescribed by mainstream society, mirrored the gulf she felt lay between her imagined life and her actual daily existence. This distance left a void that had potentially life-altering consequences. Women, who made meaningful connections, especially with other women, lived more satisfactory lives. These connections need not be made only within a domestic sphere; they could be formed between people with shared passions, such as those bonds experienced by ultraist reformers. Unfortunately, Colby chose to eschew connections within her community, and her rural environment offered her few opportunities for ongoing daily connections with those who were like-minded. The results in her life substantiate ample scholarship that shows how vital supportive networks were—and are—for contentment.

In Colby's life, the early loss of her mother also continued to complicate any potential bonding. Colby's attempts over the years to cope with the lack of a mother, or acceptable mother-figure, manifested itself in different ways. In her writings, both personal and public, her mother was a highly sentimentalized ideal. This attitude complicated her relationships with other women who rarely lived up to her concept of what role a supportive female figure in her life should play. Her lack of a living mother had allowed, or forced, her to create a symbol of motherhood that would have—if a reality—filled the empty place in her life. *Her* mother would have supported her dreams, so that perhaps "the weariness of spirit would be but a name." Colby's vision of the ideal mother deemphasized her role as the so-called linchpin of the female-centered apprentice system that prepared women for their "duties." Despite Colby's neglect, this aspect of motherhood was important. Historical research shows that not only did this bond provide the necessary training to enable a young woman to function effectively in society's assigned sphere, but it also served a vital function in providing a "sense of inner security" as well as fostering acceptance within available female networks. This acceptance was vital because friendships between women in rural environments were shaped for the most part by the reciprocity endemic to those networks. Perhaps the training aspect of the mother-daughter relationship was tied too closely with her stepmother to allow for sentimentalizing. In addition, if Rose's depiction of Colby's stepmother was accurate—"unloving eyes . . . harsh words . . . insult and tyranny . . . submission"—then Evelina Rice certainly did not inspire a familial completeness that would have fostered "a sense of inner security."[12]

This insufficiency offers a foundation that explains why her efforts to find and maintain friendships with women who had shared experiences and hopes remained so vital to Colby throughout the years. Even a temporary mother figure aroused especially poignant emotions for her.

> Strange that there should be no record here of the past few days, when they have been fraught with so much pleasure and profit. Days to be remembered with peculiar emotions. Three times within the past week I've listened to the eloquence of Mrs. Gage [Frances Dana Gage], twice on the West Indies, and one on a "Mother's Influence." Then she staid with us one night and it was such a pleasure to listen to her instructive conversation, oh so different from that we generally hear from woman's lips. So long have I loved her that it was like meeting with a dearly *loved mother*, and I felt when she went from me the corresponding grief at parting. All day the tears would come, but . . . I would fain "bid the kingly moment live forever" that gave me the bliss of her presence. In such an atmosphere as she threw around me, life would be so rich, and full of interest, and weariness of spirit would be but a name. Her words have given me new strength, new hope. To one who has so long felt the pressure of the "iron shroud" of ignorance her example is almost an inspiration, and it shall infuse into me new courage.[13]

Frances Dana Gage provided another example of a woman whose life was worth envy in Colby's eyes. She was a native Ohioan, a writer, an abolitionist, and an early women's rights supporter. Gage was also a wife, and by 1842 a mother of eight children. She spent her early married life mostly devoted to home and family, but eventually she sought a way to move beyond this narrow sphere. She initially turned to writing as a means of widening her influence. Her earlier work as "Aunt Fanny" for the *Ohio Cultivator* fostered her image as a good mother. She served as a role model in the "republican mother" mode in which womanly influence operated as the only acceptable means for working for change. Eventually, she stepped beyond merely writing and beyond the republican mother mode and into more active lobbying for women's equal rights. She organized conventions in Ohio and lectured on women's rights. Gage's life, as well as her struggles with role expectations, would have resonated with Colby and served as an inspiration to Colby for what "could be."[14]

In Colby's view, Gage lived a useful life. As we have seen, the concept of "usefulness" was a recurring theme in Colby's writings. She consistently degraded her own life as nonuseful with her descriptions of herself as no more than a "mechanical drudge," thus negating her household contributions as well as any importance arising from her writing or efforts for social justice. She consistently reiterated her thoughts on the frivolity of too much time spent on so-called women's work. The "new hope . . . and new courage" inspired by Gage's visit provided the context for an essay written after her departure in which Colby chastised "the mass, contented in their ignorance, aspiring no higher than to excel each other in the beauty of their rag carpets and fancy patchwork, or at most keep the externals of home in perfect neatness and order." Using the dehumanizing industrial analogy again, she applauded those few women who were "perhaps, struggling feebly and alone, to fit themselves and their daughters for something more than mere household machines."[15] In addition, unlike a decade prior, Colby focused her public concern on the futures of American daughters, not sons.

Not long after Gage's visit and also within the context of women's potential futures, Colby addressed the irony of another woman's apparent dissatisfaction with her life. In Colby's mind, the life and work of an author was an important and ultimately worthy accomplishment for a woman, and it puzzled her to read a poem by Alice Cary, titled *In Vain*, that seemed to indicate Cary was dissatisfied with her life and her accomplishments. Cary was also a native Ohioan whose life had taken a course Colby may have deeply envied. She was unmarried and lived in New York with her sister, Phoebe Cary. The two sisters wrote prose and poetry and achieved prominence in mid-century literary circles before their deaths in 1871. Colby privately noted:

> Can it be true of Alice Cary, with her success as an author, or are the "unused powers" to which she refers, of a different nature. Does she pine for human love and the companionship of husband and children? It may be this, for it is different to think that it is *her* intellect that so pines. But I feel all the sorrow and the sadness, and my soul is ever sad "with a sense of its unused powers," till I query why such a soul was placed in my bosom, like a tuneful bird, prisoned in utter darkness, then I chide my self for my "secret discontent" and try to be happy; because those around me seem to be so with the same or less mental food upon *which I am starving*.

Colby could not imagine how a woman in Cary's position could be so dissatisfied with her life that her poetry could serve to illustrate the "dark words of my [Colby's] soul so well."[16]

Later that same month, Colby privately questioned why it seemed impossible to bridge the gap that separated her desires from others in order to make a connection.

[W]hy am I formed so different from those around me that there should be even here an "impassable gulf" between my soul and those of my kindred, must that gulf *ever* be impassable, will our spirits *never*, never meet? Alas no, the bounds *are* "eternal set—to retain us strangers yet." They look upon me and think, if they stop to think at all, that they have fathomed the depth of my nature, "of course they are acquainted with me, they've known me for years," and yet with all their keenness they have never seen beyond the surface of my outer life, and know nothing of the inner volume that makes up the only true life.[17]

This "impassable gulf" seemed especially painful as it pertained to her marriage.

All indications are that the Colbys' marriage began as one based on mutual love and respect. By the early 1860s, however, Colby showed signs that the marriage had become considerably less satisfying for her in both regards. The growing emotional distance between the couple likely exacerbated Colby's feelings of isolation. Scholarship focused on nineteenth-century relationships shows that romantic notions about marriage commonly incorporated the expectation that couples would travel a path of "self-revelation" and "disclosure." On the whole, couples did not anticipate that the emotional intensity of courtship would prevail over time, but they did expect a loving relationship in which a romantic bond held together a contented—even if somewhat predictable or boring—relationship.[18] Colby hoped this path would be theirs, but this level of intimacy, if ever attained, apparently was not maintained.

Several sources speak strongly for that interpretation. Colby wrote a letter, dated January 10, 1860, to someone identified only as "M.C.C.," in which she discussed marriage. Apparently, her friend was contemplating this move and solicited Colby's advice or Colby offered it unasked. In this letter, Colby wrote extensively about marriage in general as well as also addressing specific things a woman should consider before entering into a marriage. Colby opened by stating that marriage could be "either a cup of blessing, or a fountain of unmitigated woe," and as such should be treated as the "most solemn subject in life . . . [especially for] those whose lives are all within," like herself and the letter recipient. She offered suggestions for questions she should ask herself about how well she knew her husband-to-be because "many a maiden marries the object of her choice, and thinks she is marrying the object of her love, when in fact she loves an *Ideal.*" She also advised that they wait until they were at least twenty-five. "Many a maiden marries at the ages of 18 or 20, a man who is *then* her choice, but as time develops her mind and soul, she has new 'soul needs' of which . . . her husband never understands and cannot minister to and the same woman if free, would reject him at thirty as unworthy of her love; but if married *must* lay a heavy hand upon her hearts purest noblest impulses and crush them back into silence."[19]

This letter was purported to be one in which marriage, in the abstract, was examined; however, the parallels to Colby's own life lend credence to its commentary as an indictment of her own experiences. She had married for love at age twenty, and her expectations for fulfillment had evolved since that time. Her journals also often bear witness to her unmet "soul needs." Additional anecdotal evidence also offers contextual clues that indict marriage in general as well as hers specifically. A rare occasion in which she visited with old school friends gave rise to a pejorative comment about marriage. "A greater portion of this week has been spent in visiting—and good visits I've had, have spent two days with old school friends, renewing old acquaintances, and my time was all too short for this pleasant purpose. Visited Nette Warren and Sarah Case, the last of whom I had not seen since her marriage. I had a very pleasant visit with her; she has found mental improvement since her marriage, a thing so uncommon among women." Several years later, within an entry discussing her children's futures, she noted, "Still less can I bear to think of their . . . stooping to meet groveling spirits 'half-way,' making wretched compromises with earth and clay, and calling such compacts by the holy name of marriage." Remarks such as these contribute to interpretations that her marriage was unsatisfying.[20]

Poetry, however, was often Colby's choice for purging particularly difficult emotions, so perhaps most telling are two extant poems about courtship and marriage. In the first, "I Wouldn't, Would You?" she sarcastically impeached men's honesty during courting: "If I were a young lady just out of my teens, I'd never believe that a 'beau' talks as he means." The other piece, titled, "We Are Two," apparently offered a sad study of Colby's own marriage. This work is undated, but the fact that it was not written on foolscap, as was her earlier loose manuscript writing, but rather on smaller correspondence-sized paper indicates at least a late 1850s' or early 1860s' composition. A few stanzas provide an accurate reflection of the tenor of the entire composition.

> We are two, the ties are riven
> Ties that bound in days of yore
> God only knows how long I've striven
> To cherish a love that is no more
> . . . A score of weary wasting years
> I've tried Life's dusty path with thee
> Loved every flower with my tears

We Are Two
By Celestia R. Colby

We are two— the ties are riven—
Ties that bound in days of yore—
God only knows how long I've striven
To cherish a love that is no more.

Hungered and faint, my spirit came,
Seeking manna from thy own—
Weary was I, worn and lame
Instead of bread, thou gavest "a stone."

I gave the deep and earnest love,
Of girlhood's trusting hour,—
Alas! alas! that time should prove
Unvalued was the dower.

I left all other cherished things
To link my life with thine—
As toward the light, the tender springs—
Turned to thee, each thought of mine.

By the early 1860s, Colby's marriage was increasingly unsatisfying. The first four stanzas of her poem, "We Are Two," poignantly illustrate her discontent. Used by permission Colby Collection, Illinois State University Archives, Illinois State University, Normal, Illinois.

Tears born of mortal agony. . . .
I shrink from thy caresses
That link not soul with soul . . .
I've waited in sorrow and pain
For the coming of thy Spirit's feet,
I've waited alas in vain
We are not one, our spirits never meet.[21]

This notion that their "spirits never meet" contributed to her growing un-happiness and sense of personal isolation. According to historical research, this sort of "anguished and articulated lament for lost love" is found commonly among sources documenting "troubled marriages." Nineteenth-century mar-riage was often based on emotion, but ironically the ending of marriage could not be prefaced on the loss of that emotion. Divorce was sanctioned socially, and was legally available, only when someone failed to perform culturally pre-scribed duties. This irony helps to explain why, regardless of any progressive thoughts about women's roles that Colby harbored, she did not believe that unhappiness was a realistic reason for leaving a marriage. Instead, if a woman chose the wrong mate, then she "must lay a heavy hand upon her hearts purest noblest impulses and crush them back into silence." This dichotomy— if a cou-ple "fell" in love, but then society provided no alternative if one of them "fell" out of love—could be the foundation for a sadly unfulfilled relationship.[22]

One of Colby's published stories echoed this sentiment. In this two-part work, she described "Mrs. Weldon's" "early dreams" in which "love, purity, and intelligence shall be the household trinity." Unfortunately, Mrs. Weldon's hus-band felt that being a "good provider" meant that he was a "model husband," and he "never dreams that he is piercing it [her heart] with wounds incurable, and closing its portals against himself forever."[23] Again the parallels to her own beliefs lend credence to the notion that this story was a fictionalized depiction of her personal dissatisfaction within her marriage. She had long complained about the void in her life where a loving mother, like-minded friends, spiritual sustenance, and intellectual stimulation should be, but now it seemed that her partnership with her husband had also failed to live up to her hopes; thus her perception of isolation had further fuel.

Colby's desire for something more in her life is poignant. As the belief grew that the support necessary to bring this idealized world into reality would con-tinue to elude her, she continued to struggle with her perception that she was alone with her dreams.

> Once more it is Saturday evening, my little ones are in bed, though still "telling stories," but for them my solitude would be unbroken; even now I am "*too much alone*." My spirit is hopeless and sad, and desponding to night. I shall never learn the lesson of *self reliance* that alone can give me strength to live. I *am* something *more* than a machine, or an animal; I have *soul needs* that are just as imperative wants, necessities of any being, as is the *air* I breathe. But alas Earth has no food to nourish them, none that is attainable to me, save the solitary, silent appreciation of the pure and beautiful of which even *my* destiny cannot deprive me. But I do so long for the *social pleasures* that can double, yea more than double this, for a presence ever near me to whom I can utter every thought and win a return.[24]

She attempted to accept the lack of support and gain strength from it, but she consistently felt as if she were failing. She longed for a sense of "sympathetic" reinforcement, but increasingly doubted the possibility of its presence in her life and condemned herself for her weakness in desiring it.

In the wake of these feelings of isolation, Colby turned as she had in the past to writing, but she began also to rely more frequently on the written word for the emotional support that she failed to find elsewhere. She always had been an avid reader, but her comments began to show early signs that she hoped to garner more from reading than entertainment or distraction. In November of 1859, after Annie's departure, Colby felt alone, so she turned to Percy Bysshe Shelley's prophetic poem, *Queen Mab*. This work would have appealed to Colby's radical sensibilities with its condemnation of institutional religion and dogma as the true source of social evils. She described Shelley's words "as full of truth as they are of poetry. And yet poor Shell[e]y was called an infidel. He may have [been] for ought that I know, but there are many gems of truth in this poem that bear evidence of a deep and earnest integrity of soul, and they cannot but arouse thought in even the most unthinking."[25]

In contrast, a popular novel called *The Confessions of a Pretty Woman* provided little inspiration. "It may be *well written*, indeed I think it is, but the characters with but one or two trifling exceptions are vain and frivolous, so that the work elicits no higher interest than a mere idle curiosity as to 'how it will come out'; It does not arouse a single aspiration after a greater degree of excellence."[26] This expectation that a book should "arouse . . . aspiration after a greater degree of excellence" echoed her desires for her life, but more and more often she looked to the written word rather than humanity for this feeling. The beginnings of a shift in emotional emphasis in which books were expected to substitute for human support had begun. Although reading had provided "pleasant company" in the past, Colby began to expect it to serve in a greater capacity, or as she described: the only means to "furnish food for my solitary life." This shift gradually escalated over the next several years. Her reliance waned when she felt energized by other more proactive means of support, but it always rose again as her perceptions of isolation grew. As the next few years unfolded, Colby was aware of the inadequacy of this substitute, and her journal entries display mounting despondency during these periods.

Women's use of substitute forms of emotional support was not uncommon. Throughout the nineteenth century, educated women, in particular, turned to books as a way to mitigate solace and stimulate imagination. Nonetheless, Colby's feelings of emotional isolation sometimes pushed that reliance to extraordinary depths. The Great Depression and the Second World War journals of Martha Friesen illustrate that coveting a replacement for missing companionship was not limited to the nineteenth century, as, like Colby, isolation affected Friesen's perceptions. Friesen was a rural farm wife, and her almost daily entries provide a glimpse of her daily experiences. Over the years, her children grew up and left home, and her husband's dependence on alcohol increased, which led to a growing rift between the couple. Her life, which was largely characterized by both emotional and physical isolation, led Friesen to form—in her perception—real emotional connection with the world that was broadcast over the radio. Her radio "friends" served as a quasi-substitute for the connections and support that she did not have in her real life. Colby did not experience the same level of actual physical isolation as Friesen, but her perceptions of emotional isolation could be as debilitating. These perceptions sometimes led Colby to reach for, and eventually come to rely on, the word on the page with an urgent need. A year into Annie's absence, Colby was feeling especially low. "Last night I read till nearly two o'clock, then my oil gave out and I tried to sleep, but the disenthralled brain still went on in its strange, weird way, weaving its web of fancies around the characters following them through light and shadow, till morning dawned and recalled me from the world of fancy to that of reality; only sometimes I wonder *which is* the world of fiction or fact, which is the '*real* life' that which thrills us upon the poets page or the dream of the novelist, or that which is apparent to our eye in the outward life of those around us. Which is it? Which is it?"[27] Once again, Colby retreated to notions of an idealistic and fictional scenario when the reality of her unchanging outward life offered little support.

As the weight of her outer life smothered her past hopes for her future, her journal entries became less frequent and emotionally darker as she sank into a period of despondency.

For an hour my fingers have thrilled with unutterable longings for the pen, and so many things were crying for expression all at once that the tears would come, for at such times the broom & dishcloth are not the most interesting society, and yet the old tyrant—necessity—compelled the intercourse. Ah well, perhaps "the Hereafter" may have a recompense for all this, perhaps—well—perhaps it is well that my life is so repressed, that my soul has no voice, no visible life. I've been wondering, if it is *really me* that is moving about in the daily round of care, or a phantom of myself, endured merely with physical life, and a weary sense of a void, a death in life. I've been fancying that I am dead, that my soul died years ago and somehow there is half a luxury in the thought.[28]

Her despair was reaching a point in which her hope had become a notion that her life was not really "real."

Occasionally during this period of despondency, however, Colby found the energy to continue in her effort to find something to fill the void that she perceived dominated her life. Toward that goal, she continued to periodically seek spiritual fulfillment in unorthodox places. Although not "converted to spiritualism," she did not discount it completely as a possible avenue of enlightenment. She participated one evening in an extremely rare occurrence by Colby's reckoning—a pleasurable social experience—that involved a combination of the prevailing spiritual sciences: mesmerism, phrenology, and a self-proclaimed Spiritualist preacher. "Last evening was spent at a sort of 'circle' at Mr. Higbee's. It was rather pleasant—a company that can furnish good music and *real conversation*—not gossip—is a rare pleasure. Then the 'manifestations' if manifestations they were—were quite interesting. Mrs. W. [likely the aforementioned Spiritualist preacher, Mrs. Warner] gave my phreneological development while in a state of 'impression' and if she guessed at it she made some *good hits.*"[29] Nonetheless, this feeling of connection was extremely rare; for the most part, Colby felt only distance between herself and those around her.

This feeling of distance continued to extend to the community with whom she was forced to have contact. In the first six months of 1860 she noted various events in a negative fashion. After a week spent attending three separate winter events, she described the final party as "a dull insipid affair." Later that spring, she attended a "surprise party" and commented that there were "but a few present with whom I could wish any social intercourse." Another set of visitors inspired the observation that "it is hard work to entertain people when all the time you are wishing them forty miles away." She felt disdain for many members of her community, but continued to desire connection. This seemingly no-win situation plagued her as she went through the motions of adhering to community norms, particularly religious norms. One diary entry provides an apt summary of the opposing forces that she felt as she tried to balance the need for community with her own need for spiritual and intellectual satisfaction. It also illustrates the repercussions that her questions and opinions had in her life.

> Have been to church to day, and though among the orthodox, church going is considered one of the cardinal virtues, yet I do not feel that it was "good to be there." I hesitated between spending the day with the pen, or going to church and finally went without exactly willing to do it, and came home feeling that my time had been spent for naught. . . . One trifling incident rather amused me. While the speaker was going through the sterreotyped form of praying for "backsliders," old Mr. Cornell who sat where he was perfectly hidden from my view, feeling that I must be hit, leaned over at right angle to look at me full in the face, with a look as much as to say *"that means you."* But somehow I didn't feel hit.

At times, her need for community led her to wish that she "could be as firmly established in the truth . . . of the bible," so that she was not always on the outside searching for truth. [30] Despite this desire, she simply could not reconcile her personal beliefs with those espoused by the orthodox church. This lack of reconciliation resulted in her ongoing struggle to negotiate an accepted religious space in her community. This negotiation involved rather ineffective attempts at an outward show of acquiescence to orthodoxy while at the same time she privately expressed extreme doubts and publicly questioned this orthodoxy through her actions.

This ongoing struggle with religious truth is important because in many ways it paralleled her frustrating attempts to come to terms with other aspects of her life. Societal norms structured the performance of women's roles. Colby's vision continued to be at odds with these expectations regarding her capacity as a wife, mother, housekeeper, and social moral reformer. The coming Civil War fueled greater national debate on slavery as well as other progressive issues, particularly women's roles. The war altered the way that some people viewed these norms. Initially, this shift gave Colby hope, but eventually the war only exacerbated her frustration in her inability to successfully negotiate a space, or identity, for herself as what she considered a whole functioning member of society. As her level of personal isolation and feelings of hopelessness grew, Colby's personal and public demands changed in focus. She kept her discontent about many aspects of her personal life to herself, voicing it only to her journals. Over time, her private words show an increasing sense of despair as she turned emotionally inward, but for a brief time she publicly voiced her thoughts on events crucial to the nation and, in particular, she attempted to seize the moment in order to advance the idea of a fulfilled womanhood.

CHAPTER NINE

February 1861–November 1861

"Dark and fearful must be the struggle"

In April of 1861, the first official shots of the Civil War were fired at Fort Sumter. The conflict behind these shots, however, had been brewing for years. The tension centered over what, if anything, should be done about slavery and then splintered into almost every social, political, and economic disagreement of the time. Divisions extended beyond the line dividing North and South and affected even supposedly coherent groups: churches tore apart, reform organizations divided, political parties split, and communities and even families squabbled. In the final years leading up to the war, people responded in various ways to this undercurrent of tension. The local Ashtabula County newspaper documented some facets of that county's response, particularly aspects that were political in nature. The *Ashtabula Sentinel*'s position on slavery remained clear: legislation was the key to ending it. This opinion resulted in the paper's emphasis on politics and the marginalization of other avenues, even to the point of ignoring some of them almost all together, such as the 1857–58 AASS speaking tours that included Abby Kelley Foster, Stephen Foster, Lucy Coleman, and Andrew T. Foss.[1] The newspaper's focus, for the most part, echoed the popular sentiment. Despite the presence of some progressive proponents, the choice of traditional legislative solutions over radical social change resonated with the majority of the area's residents throughout most of the 1850s.

Nevertheless, as time went by, avoidance of more radical approaches to ending slavery and the reliance on the federal government's ability to foster a solution proved a difficult strategy to uphold. As the 1850s drew to a close, hostilities grew as sectional distrust escalated and rifts based on strategy grew deeper.

Politically, these rifts deepened as the Republicans gained greater control over Northern legislation. Their growing congressional dominance contributed to conflict within abolitionist camps when some radical reformers softened their political opposition and looked to the Republicans for possible action. Even radical leader William Lloyd Garrison loosened his previously stalwart stance against politics in hopes the Republicans actually could make real changes. Despite the *Ashtabula Sentinel's* political and legislative focus—the paper also pinned its hopes on the Republicans—by the close of the 1850s, even its editors felt compelled to applaud some levels of affirmative action. In 1859, an escaped slave was captured in Oberlin, Ohio, and a crowd of antislavery proponents freed him. During the melee, a former Cherry Valley attorney was arrested. Subsequently, *Ashtabula Sentinel* editor Congressman Joshua R. Giddings led two thousand people to Cleveland to protest this arrest and the Fugitive Slave Law.[2] Clearly, even those people who were part of the system were on edge.

Then in October 1859, an incident raised the level of tension and mistrust to the point that it proved to be one of the most significant national precursors to the war. Because this action involved many men with local ties, it had special significance to northeastern Ohioans, including Colby. She had been sadly anticipating Annie's departure and her own thirty-second birthday when John Brown Sr. once again grabbed the nation's attention with his actions. Brown, three of his sons, and a small group of followers, which included numerous local Ashtabula County men, seized a federal arsenal at Harpers Ferry, Virginia, with the intent of arming slaves and inciting a rebellion. Their attempt was a complete failure. Within a day, the resulting chaos was over, but not before more than twenty-five men had been killed or wounded, including two of Brown's sons. Brown was captured, and his place was secured as one of the most controversial figures of his time as well as within the context of historical analysis.

In the South, this incendiary act furthered fear and resentment regarding what Southerners feared was the real intent of Northern antislavery sentiments. In the North, many people, especially politicians who hoped that a compromise still could be reached on the subject of slavery, condemned Brown. Among antislavery reformers, the reactions were mixed. Several prominent people among the abolitionist community showed support for Brown's actions, even before the raid, by supplying money and advice. Many radical abolitionists, however, were torn; Brown's actions represented a moral dilemma to those who had sworn to uphold a policy of "nonresistance." As an adherent to the idea of nonresistance, Abby Kelley Foster was among those loath to applaud his violence; however, in reality she was somewhat ambivalent in her reaction in that she "agreed with John Brown in a certain sense and in another sense disagreed."[3]

Colby, however, was quite clear in her opinions. Privately, she predicted, quite presciently, that this event would add considerable fuel to an already seething situation. A full year before the war began she wrote:

> The day set apart for the execution of "old John Brown" but his death will sanctify the gallows and make it glorious as the cross! I suppose that when the good old man is gone that the heart of the slaveholder will cease to quake, but "conscience makes cowards of us all" and not long will their sleep be quiet for if they think that by the taking of Brown, they put an end to the love of liberty, and hatred of oppression that is inborn in the soul, they have made a *fearful mistake*. I look upon this affair in Harper's Ferry as the beginning of sorrow to the slaveholder, and sometimes fear of the ultimate triumph of *the right*. Dark and fearful must be the struggle, ere the victory is attained.

Although privately she expressed fear that things would not turn out satisfactorily, publicly, she was more militant. Brown's scheduled execution served as the focal point for her discussion of the broader themes of politics and morality in an essay written on December 16, 1859—the eve of the coconspirators' execution. Unlike antislavery proponents who looked to the Republicans for possible answers, her faith in the government's ability to bring about a solution to the moral problem of slavery had by this time almost disappeared. "[Four] men . . . are to be *legally murdered* . . . [by those] wearing the uniform and receiving the pay of the United States." Unlike many abolitionists who were avid "non-resistants," Colby saw no moral dilemma in her support for Brown's actions. In her view, if morality and legality cannot be reconciled because the leaders say that morality cannot overshadow the law, then "let every true hearted man and woman spurn the weak sophistry that reasons from so low a standard, and be ever ready to 'fling to the wind the parchment wall that binds us from the least of human kind.'"[4] In the spirit of vintage William Lloyd Garrison, the "parchment wall" served as her metaphor for the mere paper documents—ultimately the Constitution—that kept right from triumphing. Clearly, her opinions about the state of the Union and the government's ability to resolve the looming crisis had not softened.

Colby's neighbors may also have been sympathetic to John Brown. He had family as well as friends in Ashtabula County. In addition, various members of the community reportedly were aware in varying degrees of Brown's broader intents, if not the exact method. During his earlier controversial stand against slavery in Kansas, even the usually rather socially conservative *Ashtabula Sentinel* deemed him to be "the Ethan Allen of Kansas." Nonetheless, any sympathy that the community harbored for a local and infamous radical did not translate into communitywide support for radical abolitionists and their corollary progressive opinions. In particular, citizens continued to balk at the idea that organized religion held any responsibility for slavery's perpetuation. Colby's position—in which she condemned orthodox Christianity and found authority for slavery in the Christian Bible, therefore tainting its value—remained unpopular. The *Ashtabula Sentinel* occasionally even took space away from its regular coverage of the political battles against slavery to condemn these sorts of arguments. An 1860 editorial summed up the official feelings of the *Ashtabula Sentinel* in regard to the idea that there existed some sort of biblical authority for slavery. "Permit no man to depreciate the sacred book by raising such a suspicion. Authority for slavery is only found in writings originating in the source of evil."[5]

By the autumn of 1860, Northern debate between immediate abolitionists and more moderately minded advocates grew even more volatile, as evidenced by the inflamed opinions of some Ashtabula County citizens. A speaking tour sponsored by the Western Anti-Slavery Society, which included Parker Pillsbury and Josephine Griffing, sparked significant local interest. After Colby's attendance at one of the lectures, she noted, "My spirit was refreshed." Not all observers had the same reaction. Parker Pillsbury was one of the most notable and impassioned abolitionists of his time. Like Stephen Foster, his formative years were spent in New Hampshire, and like Colby, he had been raised in a stern Calvinistic home and later embraced evangelism. Pillsbury even served briefly as an evangelical Congregationalist minister. By the 1840s, however, he had adopted a position that condemned all Northern churches as proslavery. He was extremely proactive in his attempts to pass along this message and as a result was more vehemently vilified than many other reformers. Communities often refused him access to meeting venues, such as in October of 1851, when the citizens of Andover, Ohio, denied him the use of their meetinghouse for a speech.[6]

Almost a decade later in September of 1860, Pillsbury did speak to local Ashtabula County residents, but many of them still found his message to be quite indefensible. His lectures inspired both readers and contributing *Ashtabula Sentinel* editor Congressmen Joshua R. Giddings to challenge Pillsbury's criticisms of established religion and government. One reader, identified only as A.D.O., sent a series of responses to clarify what he saw as "not merely his [Parker Pillsbury's] gross blunders, but his willful and malicious perversities, and libels." Giddings's and Pillsbury's newspaper debate over the subject was more civilized in tone, but the underlying differences remained. Giddings acknowledged that perhaps Pillsbury was well meaning and presented an "eloquent and powerful" argument, but he characterized Pillsbury's stance in which people's consciences, and not government action, held the answer to end slavery as similar to "waiting for the Devil to convert the world to righteousness."[7]

Despite the prevailing views in her community, which were considerably more conservative than hers, Colby continued to address publicly the slavery issue, as well as other progressive issues, in her own way. In regard to slavery, she frequently focused on the shortcomings of the political system. Just weeks after John Brown's execution, she delivered a harsh critique of Republican members of Congress after their acquiescence to the choice of William Pennington as Speaker of the House in 1860. Pennington's record on slavery did nothing to inspire Colby's confidence. Although he favored exclusion of slavery from the territories, he also had supported the Fugitive Slave Act. He was no friend to the abolitionists. Colby blasted the Republicans, especially Ohio Republican John Sherman. Sherman lost the vote for the Speaker's seat, but then, as reported by the *Ashtabula Sentinel,* gave an "eloquent" congratulatory speech celebrating the success of the Republican Party. Colby declared this so-called victory "a success that contained every element of defeat except the name." She condemned his brand of "anti-slavery sentiments . . . [that seem] to be very popular among slaveholders and their apologists." Her opinions ran contrary to the majority in the North who were inclined—because of misplaced belief or blind optimism—to accept as true Sherman's confident boasts that the election of a Republican president would solve the looming crisis and ensure that the "union was safe."[8] Sherman was unfortunately incorrect in his judgment. The November 1860 election of Republican Abraham Lincoln to the presidency did not stop the looming crisis; instead, it provided the catalyst that brought it to a head.

The year of 1861 began with a series of political events that helped to set the course for the next four years. After Lincoln's election, a South Carolina convention of delegates voted unanimously for an Ordinance of Secession, which declared the state's ratification of the United States Constitution repealed and the union with other states dissolved. This act was followed quickly by the secession of five other Southern states that culminated in the February 1861 formation of the Confederate States of America. From this point until Lincoln's April 1861 inauguration, the Congress made last-ditch efforts to find a compromise while President Buchanan did little but wait for his term to end. Patriotic fever flared in both regions, but it manifested itself mainly as strong rhetoric as the nation also waited for the new president to take office. Although patriotic tension between North and South remained mainly rhetorical, Northern abolitionists were subjected not only to verbal attacks but also to occasional physical attacks. Many Northerners were especially angry over the loss of trade with the South and blamed abolitionists for raising the pitch of the debate to this point. Many people felt that the radicals owned a large part of the blame for the volatile state of the union, which meant that it was potentially dangerous to be an ultra or a disunionist in this highly combustible time.[9] No evidence indicates that Colby ever backed away from her long-held position of disunion, but while this waiting game played itself out, she briefly turned her public attention from the politics of antislavery to another volatile subject: women's rights.

Until this time, Colby had written only obliquely on the subject, addressing it only as it intertwined with other reform issues. Her reasons for choosing this time to take her views on women's rights public are not clear, but perhaps have their root in both her personal evolution in thought regarding women and her personal situation during this period. Clearly, her public opinions on women's issues had evolved during the last decade. Her essays regarding justifications for female education display that progression and—as the next chapter illustrates—her thoughts on temperance reform also show evolution. Her direct public declaration as an advocate of "woman's rights," however, actually coincided with the virtual disappearance of an active and vocal call for women's equality; the nation's attention—including most women's rights reformers—turned to the war. This timing adds to the sense that her personal situation was paramount in her decision. The foundation for this decision rested on her increasing frustration with the limited nature of her role and her clear desire for more for her daughters. In the autumn of 1860, however, about the same time as Parker Pillsbury passed through Ashtabula County, another event brought her feelings to the surface. Colby's youngest daughter Rose suffered some sort of illness or accident that left her an "invalid" and forced her—and Colby—to be confined for months. During this time period, Colby's frustration and despair regarding her own situation as well as her daughter's intensified.[10]

During the months between mid-September of 1860 and mid-January of 1861, Colby acted as a full-time nurse to her daughter in addition to her other duties. As Rose "wasted to a shadow," Colby worried that "when, if ever she gains the power of locomotion is very uncertain." During this period, Colby found time to write in her journal only six times, and each of these entries served mainly to describe books and note her need for additional "mental refreshment." Isolation and stress led her to lament that she had "been wondering is it really me . . . or a phantom of myself." When she recommended writing more regularly, her despair as well as her need for a different kind of life had escalated. This "hunger of heart," as she termed it, was the context from which a brief prewar foray into women's rights emerged. She boldly had expressed her opinions on controversial topics before; however, unlike some of her other passions, the expansion of women's legal, economic, and social rights had potentially significant personal consequences for her life. A personal stake in reform can make the act of public declaration more daunting, which may have contributed to her hesitancy before this time. As late as June 1860, she expressed trepidation after she read an essay at a temperance meeting because "some persons were present of whom I am so foolish as to stand in mortal fear." Clearly, despite her strong beliefs and occasional bravado, she was not immune to the pressures exerted by community members. Nevertheless, her limitations of the last few months seemed to have reduced the power of those fears and quelled the last doubts she held about going public.[11]

Early in 1861, Colby displayed her attitude about women's proper sphere in a somewhat oblique fashion in an essay in which she discussed societal prescriptions for little girls. According to Colby, "Nature . . . gave her [a little girl] the same needs of air, exercise and active sport. . . . [But] the little girl, almost as soon as she leaves the cradle, must be subjected to a manufacturing process, to be made over into a miniature lady. . . . The poor little thing must be cramped, fettered and curbed till her free wild spirit is crushed out . . . and be a sort of living doll." She protested the ignorance of mothers who attempted to make "little ladies" of their daughters while they encouraged their sons to run "wild and free." In Colby's estimation, both boys and girls benefited from "constant motion" that "bath[ed] the lungs with pure fresh air" and provided the "vigor and vitality" that helped protect them from disease. She declared that you simply needed to look at a young woman, who as a result of an active lifestyle, radiated "perfect health . . . and a peaceful consciousness" to realize that "she is acting well her part in her own proper 'sphere.'" Beyond providing a forum for Colby's thoughts, essays such as this one also may have served as a valuable counterpoint to the array of toys, games, and literature geared toward girls that stressed the indoctrination of "proper" gender roles.[12]

Another early 1861 essay written on the heels of Colby's winter confinement, titled, "Equal Rights—circulating Petitions, &c.," demonstrates her new public attitude quite forcefully and directly. In it, she described the various responses received while circulating a petition "asking a modification of the existing laws relating to women." She noted:

It is a little amusing to listen to the various excuses, remonstrances, &c, by different classes of individuals when you present them a petition . . . and ask their signature. One man when asked to sign, says "no" very abruptly, and very decidedly, as if to refuse were a matter of pleasure, as well as duty. Ask him why, and the reply is, "they have *more* than equal rights now. . . . There must be one head of the family, &c, &c, . . . No use of reasoning with him, for reason only irritates, never convinces him on this point. . . . One rather laughable instance of refusal was by the wife of a man given to intemperance. She commenced reading the petition, and when she reached the sentence "that you place the wife upon an equality with her husband"—she handed it back with a look of disgust saying with such a tone of irony, "on an *equality* with her husband, I want no more of it." . . . Another will not sign, because she "has no rights," another because "women can't have any rights, nor men either," another thinks, "it would make discord in families;" men earn the money, do the "providing" and ought to have sole management, &c.; and so on.

Colby's style of writing tended to vary with the intended venue, as well as the subject. In her contemporary antislavery writing, she exhibited an angry and frustrated tone. Her attitude in her work focused on women and education often alternated between resignation and condescension. In contrast, she used a humorous, almost sarcastic, tone in her women's rights essays to demonstrate her apparent dissatisfaction with her appointed role. This essay, as well as others on the subject, at times achieved a tongue-in-cheek quality as she described her frustrations. Despite the quasi-humorous tone and the fact that she couched her feelings in a somewhat nonconfrontational style, she was not ambiguous in her demands or in her belief that society's hesitancy to grant further rights to women was based on "prejudice and ignorance."[13]

The above essay clearly demonstrates that Colby had chosen to take a public stand on the subject of women's rights. She purported to be commenting on her experience gaining signatures for a petition, but whether these encounters actually occurred is more difficult to ascertain. In the months before writing this work she was severely restricted in her movements by Rose's situation as well as the winter weather. In addition, Colby made no mention of this petition activity in her journal. It is, of course, possible that the outing occurred months prior and that no entry was made that day and was subsequently not recorded in later entries. It is also possible that she used poetic license to make a point. Either way, her attitude regarding society's need to awaken and address gender inequalities is clear. In addition, whether the essay was a product of her mind's eye or reality, it provides a good example of what she considered to be a useful action.

Colby's decision to lobby more forcefully for women's rights did not place her on the leading edge of this issue, but she still was within a small minority within the larger context of antebellum reform. A small band of agitators had begun to speak out on women's rights decades before Colby ventured into the public eye. Initially, these women spoke primarily within the context of anti-slavery work, but by the 1830s some of them had begun to speak to the subject of women's rights more directly. By the early 1850s, a small segment of Ohioans demonstrated at least some level of support for the idea of female equality. Even as much of the northeastern reform community focused on antislavery, Ohio hosted many women's rights conventions. The first took place in 1850 in Salem, Ohio, and others followed. Two state conventions were held in 1851, one in Akron, Ohio (the site of Sojourner Truth's "Ain't I a Woman" speech), and one in Mt. Gilead. State conventions followed in both 1852 and 1853. Cincinnati hosted a national convention in 1855. The primary focus of state as well as national conventions was the development of strategies to expand the social, legal, and economic rights for women, who, especially after marriage, retained little if any power over themselves, their earnings, their property, or their children. A vigorous campaign to expand women's rights in Ohio succeeded in forcing some legal changes in 1857, such as the limited control of women's own earnings and expanded property rights for widows, but suffrage was defeated.[14]

The fact that conventions and organized efforts were undertaken during these early stages in the fight for women's expanded rights should not be equated with the notion that there existed, at this time, a unified coalition that controlled the movement. The story of the struggle for women's rights is a continuing and multifaceted subject, but for the purpose of examining Colby's place in the movement a few basic ideas are important. In the years prior to the Civil War, the endeavor to expand women's rights was an extremely malleable concept. No one central agency, publication, or even dominant voice provided direction. Women, particularly married women, lacked even the basic legal rights or their own authority over almost every aspect of their lives, whether public or private. This almost complete subjugation provided numerous targets for protest. These targets ranged from the symbolic—although literally physically restraining as well—trappings of "proper" dress to the very real economic and legal limitations that too often blocked women from pursuing any avenue beyond marriage. No matter the manner of protest, it was met overwhelmingly with ridicule or anger, if not being dismissed outright. The prevailing cultural norms in regard to a woman's role simply left little room for expansion of women's rights. She was queen of the home sphere—to what more could she aspire?

So regardless of Colby's newfound public passion, her community as a whole was not inclined to encourage expansion of women's roles into traditionally male territory, especially in a time when attention was supposed to be focused on the crisis at hand. An *Ashtabula Sentinel* death notice that praised the life of a prominent Ashtabula County woman offers evidence of the "type" of woman likely looked upon most favorably by Colby's community. The added emphasis, which appeared in the original publication, further confirms this conclusion. The deceased was praised as a "woman of the . . . New England type character . . . [who] was well informed . . . without being *political* or *theological*." Colby consistently challenged both of those restrictions in her public writings, and by February of 1861, regarding women's equality, she "[felt] more than ever the need of action upon this subject." She hoped to awaken the hearts and minds of her peers and "stir up a deeper hatred for domestic and home oppression, which we see in different degrees, almost every where, and which is so common that both oppressor and oppressed are sometimes half unconscious of it. And this stage marks the worst state of the wrong—the semi-consciousness of their own degradation that marks the contented slave." To counter that status and challenge her community further, she read a "long essay on 'woman's rights' covering 15 pages" at her local temperance meeting.[15]

Another factor likely contributed to Colby's bravado of early 1861: Annie had returned to Ohio. Although Colby had written many forceful reform pieces during Annie's absence, her presence always spawned initial feelings of hope and raised expectations. Given the long periods of perceived uselessness and isolation Colby experienced during the previous eighteen months, she hoped Annie's presence would provide some much needed comfort and support. Unfortunately, this hope was tinged with worry as well, because Annie fell ill. "Annie has been with me, but has just retired. Her presence soothes and strengthens me, and yet it makes my heart ache to look at her, and see the trace of suffering upon her brow. Shall we ever renew the old time vigils, that were *so sweet to me.* Oh I *cannot spare her.* While I know that she lives, no matter how distant from me, yet has the power to bless me, as few, very few present friends can do. And sometimes I think that nothing can weaken or destroy this power; that it will survive all change and be immortal as the soul that gives it birth."[16] Colby loved Annie and hated to see her suffer, but she also was troubled by the fact that Annie was unable to offer substantive companionship. After the months spent nursing Rose, Annie's illness was especially painful for Colby to watch.

Colby spent as much time as possible with Annie over the next few months. Annie remained ill, however, and her sickness diminished the brief sense of hope her arrival had inspired. Subsequently, Colby felt more and more anguish about her living situation and the isolation she felt even while surrounded by family. "All I would ask of life is a true and happy home, where none but the loving and the loved should ever enter, where coarseness and vulgarity, could not shock its inmates, and harsh words and unkindness could never wound a single heart. . . . I shall never call such sanctuary mine, and yet I long so earnestly to shrink away from censorious eyes to hide myself from the faultfinding gaze of those who are my self elected mentors." Contrary to the bravado and pragmatism that characterized her public words during this period, her private journals reveal feelings of hopelessness. "Oh why must all this outward turning of life go on, this eating, drinking, sleeping, working, and talking . . . when the heart *is dead*."[17]

Meanwhile, as Colby wrestled with her personal demons, the nation continued headlong into war. In March of 1861, President Lincoln took office. Despite his inaugural hopes that the "mystic chords of memory . . . will yet swell the chorus of the Union, when again touched . . . by the better angels of our nature," on April 14, 1861, the first gunfire at Fort Sumter marked the beginning of the Civil War. Lincoln's subsequent blockade of Southern ports prompted the secession of four more Southern states. The border states were then up for grabs, and after several months of grappling—and the eventual split of Virginia into West Virginia and Virginia—every state south of Missouri, Kentucky, and the newly formed West Virginia adhered officially to the Confederacy. Of course, patriotic tendencies did not merely follow border lines, which is one of the reasons why this bloody war was so emotionally gut-wrenching as it literally pitted family against family.

This patriotic fever initially served to swell the military ranks of each side with volunteers. These soldiers—along with those people remaining at home, North and South—predicted quick victories, with neither side really understanding what was to come. In July of 1861, the Battle of Bull Run near Manassas Junction, Virginia, about twenty-five miles west of Washington D.C., provided a deadly dose of reality. Before the battle, so many Washington residents were sure of a quick and easy victory that they brought picnic lunches to view "the show." What they experienced, however, was not a show, but a horror. As the battle escalated, Northern soldiers panicked. As they attempted a retreat, the road to Washington was entangled with soldiers and civilians alike. The North was routed in this first real show of force. Both sides realized that victory might not be quick or easy; the reality of war was not parades, ribbons, or picnic lunches, but death, injury, and possible imprisonment of loved ones.

Colby used the specter of this battle to publicly declare her opinion that emancipation could serve as the only legitimate purpose of the war. In an essay written as a reaction to Bull Run, she vehemently argued that the war goals should be focused on complete emancipation, not to save the Union. She noted that the "seeming blindness of our rulers in so resolutely ignoring the real cause of the war, is at times truly astonishing." She wondered why the North was "expending our blood and treasure, bringing desolation and woe to thousands of firesides, merely to fasten again upon ourselves the galling fetters of the slave power." After a very vivid description of the horrors of Bull Run, she asked whether it was "fitting that they should suffer all this, merely to establish, if it were possible, the Union as it was?"[18] Despite the public's realization of the war's potentially bloody outcome, her views did not mirror those of the majority of Northerners who rallied around the flag in a seemingly cohesive consensus for the first time in several years.

In addition to calling for emancipation, Colby also used the war's societal shake-up as a platform to raise the level of her women's rights demands. She perceived that the war might actually awaken the nation to the inequities of society and perhaps provide a time for a real change for women's status. Her public words pushed more vehemently for that change as she exhibited strong ideas about women's need to take the initiative. Toward that end, she wrote an essay in the week after the Battle of Bull Run that focused on the topic of women's status, which appeared in two parts as front-page material in *The Mayflower*. This periodical was created specifically as an outlet for women and their concerns, and it regularly printed pro-women's rights material.[19] After *The Anti-Slavery Bugle* ceased publication in May of 1861, *The Mayflower* provided a frequent forum for Colby's writings. This lengthy work contained a thorough exposition of her views in regard to women's rights, and if anyone in her immediate community had been unaware of her stance before this time, then they surely were aware of it now, as she read this entire essay at a meeting of the Cherry Valley Literary Society.

She confronted point-by-point common indictments made against expanding women's rights and the "strong-minded" women who claimed those rights. Her tone in this essay, like others on the subject, occasionally was somewhat mocking, but she was quite clear in her demands. She began by addressing the ideals put forth by those people who desired that a woman be confined to a narrow and separate sphere. "They tell us in tones meant to be very sweet, I suppose, of our superior refinement, purity, loveliness, and what not—call us 'angel of the hearth,' 'presiding divinity of the household,' and disgust us with other unmeaningful flatteries—only adding by way of mental reservation, that we are a little lacking in judgment, inferior in intellect, and quite incapable of the lofty attainments and proud achievements of men." She added that it had been true that women, as well as men, had been satisfied too long with the status quo, and if a woman believed that she had no other recourse than to "ask her husband at home" and then "meekly swallow the few crumbs of knowledge he was able or willing to bestow," it was not surprising that she felt limited. She called for the willing not to "swallow this sugar-coated pill that is offered up to woman under the name of 'social courtesies'" because in actuality it was one part "empty compliments . . . while the remainder is made up of contempt, injustice, and social and domestic tyranny."[20]

In an essay published just a month prior to the above, Colby harshly criticized the foundation for this sort of attitude in which women needed to be coddled because they were the weaker sex. "She [woman] is stronger—not in the mere physical sense, and yet in the physical endurance, few men could bear the wear and tear, the constant tax upon the physical system, that is borne uncomplainingly by those who are called weak and delicate women." She continued by describing the "trials common to woman's every day life . . . that in their reaction upon her physical system are more exhausting, more crushing than the severest manual labor . . . borne year after year, in secrecy and silence." She lamented the "crushed" spirits of woman who "must waste her energy and dwarf her intellect." In this essay, Colby merely laid out complaints and applauded women's "silent heroism."[21] The very next month, however, she demonstrated a stark change in tactic as she boldly demanded solutions.

Her demands were straightforward. She declared that the "most zealous advocates of woman's rights ask for nothing more than simple justice." They will accept nothing less and will "never cease their efforts till full and exact justice is meted out to all the sisterhood, black or white." Colby explained the many ways in which society fell short of this goal. Women's opportunities were denied in many arenas, and they consistently were treated unfairly by the economic, social, and legal systems of the country. She touched on examples of this subjugation, noting that women were afforded no real control of their own finances; they had no access to equal education; they received no payment or acknowledgment for labor within the home sphere; they were denied equal wages for work outside the home; laws limited their property rights and widows' property inheritance rights; guardianship rights for their own children were not guaranteed; and, finally, they were denied the innate right of United States citizenship—the vote. After outlining the list of grievances, she complained about what she perceived to be a common reaction from men regarding women's rights, which allowed that men perhaps could go along with a mother's right to her children, "but that we go too far when we ask for the right of suffrage, and the right to time, person and earnings." Sadly, in regard to the cause of fulfilled womanhood, it is interesting to note that over one hundred years later, activist and women's "libber" Robin Morgan outlined remarkably similar grievances in her book, *Going Too Far*.[22]

Colby continued her critique of the societal norms that supposedly justified women's continued subjugation. As she explained, the justifications were based on three—in her mind, faulty—main premises: a perceived need to keep peace within the home sphere, an assumed inability for women to "understand politics," and the need to protect women's purity. She outlined her opponents' underlying thoughts for each of these stances and then argued against them. She described the "peacekeeping" argument for women's inferior position, as well as denial of the right to vote, within the framework of current events. "They very gravely tell us there *must* be one head of the family, and solemnly hint at domestic discord if all this is conceded, which means so far as I understand it, that if woman has the right to think, act, and vote according to the dictates of her own conscience, that her husband will rebel, perhaps *secede*, as this is a day of 'secessions' . . . and they seem to imply that woman must submit to a certain amount of despotic rule in order to keep peace and harmony in the family." Her response to this argument was succinct and to the point, and incidentally echoed her feeling about the war effort, "Give us justice, and there will be no breach of the peace."

Colby countered the argument that women's ignorance constituted a valid reason to confine them to a narrow sphere by admitting that perhaps, as it stood, many women were uninformed. However, since this condition stemmed primarily from the prevailing notion that it was considered disgraceful for a woman to "read politics," this deficiency easily could be remedied. In addition, she was disdainful of the level of awareness of the population in general. "Yet with all this popular opinion in favor of feminine political ignorance, the mass of women are scarcely more ignorant of the political history of our country than are the men. There is too much ignorance among us both." Her stance was that ignorance was no barrier between men and the vote so why should it be for women? She used the same vein of argument to provide a counterpoint to the position that the political atmosphere surrounding the vote was too vulgar and corrupt for a woman. In a strategy often employed by women's rights advocates during this period, she also simultaneously used the opposition's justifications as a foundation for her own conclusion; she employed the stereotype of women's purity as a reason *to* grant the vote.

Ah, a *vulgar crowd,* is it, that surrounds the ballot box, who are swaying the destinies of the nation, who are sending representatives and senators to enact laws by which woman is to be governed, judges before whom she is to be judged, and executives who may pervert the righteous cause. Dare she send her son, her husband, her brother into such a vulgar crowd? Will not they too become corrupt and lose their purity, and compel her to share their degradation? Truly, if the atmosphere that surrounds the ballot box *be* so foul and unhealthy, and we fear it is, there is a need of woman's influence to purify it and keep it pure.[23]

She then shifted her rhetorical strategy from defense—against man's justifications for oppression—to offense, by citing arguments to support her premise that women were entitled and able to assume a position of equality. She first employed an analogy from the American Revolution. She noted that although "taxation without representation" was perhaps a mercenary reason, each year women contributed thousands of dollars to the public treasury with no say to how it was spent. "Where is the justice in this? And if this is wrong, this outrage drove our forefathers and foremothers to the sword and bayonet for redress." And for those people who perhaps thought that women were incapable of the challenge of this responsibility, she cited examples of women throughout time who had held responsibilities far beyond the vote. She named Catherine of Russia, Maria Theresa of Austria, Isabella of Castile, Madame de Staël, Joan of Arc, and Queen Elizabeth, whose name, Colby reminded her readers, encapsulated one of the most distinguished eras of English history, the "Elizabethan Age."[24]

She lamented that in the United States every step women took toward progress had been made "up the 'hill of difficulty'" and that man, instead of encouraging woman, had "met her with frowns and thrown every possible impediment in her way." Ignorance had been his main weapon. This ignorance was maintained by barring women from any avenue to education except for female academies where girls were taught only things "appropriate" to their sphere, such as fancy needlework and quilting. She applauded those few brave pioneers who broke through the barriers and "opened the way to a wider sphere of usefulness." She also noted that these women were abused by so-called gentlemen who attempted to drive these fearless women back to their sphere. Despite these impediments, a few of these women persevered as doctors, artists, poets, and writers.

And while we look with pride and admiration, and with deeper, sweeter feelings of love and gratitude for the many, many names in every department of life, who show us what woman may be, what she should be, and will be, when the masses become fully conscious of their unused powers, no one can feel more deeply than do the advocates of woman's rights, the degradation and ignorance which have bound us as with chains of adamant, "lo, these many years"—chains not of our own forging, and we wear them not willingly, but will struggle for ourselves and our sisterhood for a higher life, and to fill as well as we can our ideals of woman's mission.[25]

Her wish for womankind was that the so-called sphere would expand be-yond the kitchen, so that a woman could aspire to something "nobler than to excel her neighbor in the beauty of her rag carpets." Her public words echoed her private desires for her own life, but rather than being cloaked in a blanket of despair, these public demands indicated hope for a different future. Perhaps she was speaking unconsciously, or even consciously, to herself when she also addressed those women who claimed contentment with their current limited status. These women needed to be enlightened as well so they would realize that an elevation of their sphere would bring them greater satisfaction, as it would their husbands, who would gain "loving companion[s] of equal intel-ligence," and that their homes would no longer be places typified by conscious or "unconscious, tyranny on one side, and ignorant submission and obedience on the other."[26]

In this essay, as well as others on the same subject, Colby used language com-mon to women's rights activists in the mid-nineteenth century. She employed metaphors of slavery, warfare, and nature that helped to place the subject with-in a framework of public current events, thus legitimizing it as a subject of debate. This rhetoric also rejected the use of metaphors that would have been consistent with the idea of "woman's sphere," such as ones that employed do-mestic duties. This language use, in essence, rejected the ideals of domesticity and republican motherhood and placed women in a different context. Analysis of the language used by women's rights activists during the 1850s found that this strategy—the use of identifiably male metaphors and the rejection of so-called female metaphors—was an effective one on at least two different levels. It not only helped to place women in a different and public context, but it also served as an effective means to elicit responses. Whether the responses were negative or positive, the response itself helped to legitimize the debate.[27]

As the Civil War escalated, the direct vocal call for women's rights stalled as many reformers turned their full attention to the crisis; nevertheless, the day-to-day reality of ordinary women's lives continued to add nuance to the debate, even as it simmered on the back burner. It was not uncommon for con-temporaries of the Civil War era to note that in many ways the constraints on women's so-called traditional roles were loosened. Women took on expanded roles in the absence of their spouses and aided the war effort in a variety of ways. However, the reality of the home front and the war front was that, for the most part, expected roles still were gendered. Just as before the war, men manned the public front and women were expected to keep the private home fires burning. For the vast majority of women, their war work was conducted within the context of a "woman's sphere" and viewed as unpaid volunteer service in contrast to men who, whether they had been drafted or volunteered, expected payment for their services and received it. Despite their status as unpaid volunteers, women's war work, like their housework, contributed real value. An 1867 history of women's war contributions estimated its monetary worth to the army alone at fifty million dollars.[28] However, again like their housework, it was conceptualized by society as a natural extension of women's sphere, therefore not work.

The war put this ongoing dichotomy into an altogether broader and more complex context. Women long had been expected to contribute themselves unselfishly to the greater good of family and community because it was natural—their innate moral instinct. However, as the war progressed, they were increasingly expected to contribute their time, labor, and skills—still unselfishly and without compensation—to a national agenda that at times was unclear to many women. As the battle marched on, women reacted in different ways to this call. Attitudes about race, class, and gender reflected women's assumptions about the "nature of social order and authority." Cultural and intellectual forces, such as the church and popular literature, as well as their families, neighbors, economic situation, and access to political power, all helped to shape women's perceptions about accepted behavior as well as means to pursue change. These influences meant that most women continued to answer their so-called moral imperative for selfless duty, although many of these women did attempt to keep the focus local rather than national. However, some, like Colby, struggled to take another route.[29] During the prior five years, Colby had been increasingly influenced by the radical message that devalued established institutions and placed emphasis on an individual's responsibility to value his or her own moral compass. This context influenced how she responded to the societal chaos of the war. Because she had little faith in the fixative power of the existing institutions of church and state, she resisted joining the patriotic clamor for "saving the union." Instead, she idealistically hoped that the chaos could lead to real social redemption. Over the next year, frustration and increasing feelings of gender isolation operated to try to stymie her efforts in this regard, and although she eventually gave in to despair, her initial efforts were valiant.

CHAPTER TEN

September 1861–December 1862

"He is the true patriot . . . whose patriotism is only another term for the love of truth, justice and humanity"

IN SEPTEMBER OF 1861, as the entire nation grappled with the escalating war, a personal tragedy changed the context and the nature of Colby's struggle and contributed dramatically to her perception of emotional isolation. The fear that had been a constant for months was realized: Annie Colby died. According to the local newspaper, she had succumbed to "Pulmary Consuption [*sic*]." Colby's journal displays her painful sense of loss.

> How much of life goes from us with the death of a single person! For two weeks sister Annie has been *gone,* and I've made no record in this neglected journal. I do not realize it yet, cannot bring myself to feel that it is *all over.* And when I stood by the open grave, and saw the dear form buried from my sight—I could not feel that the unrelenting grave had really closed between us, that her presence and sympathy was no more to bless me here. All summer I've seen her passing away, like a fading flower, often longing to say much to her, that still remains unsaid, and now she is gone how complete seems at times the solitude of the place. . . . The blank which her death has made in my life can never be filled. So linked has she been with my inner life for the past six years, that a part of my very being seems gone with her. . . . There are so few to whom my spirit clings, that they are doubly dear, so few who have in the least understood me, and oh it is so sad to live on without this sympathy.

Annie's death left a palpable hole in Colby's life. She referred to Annie only infrequently after this time, but those brief mentions were wrought with emotion. "Oh for an hours chat with Annie. But never more, never more!"[1] Like the unfilled place left in the wake of her mother's death, no one person or thing adequately filled the space left by Annie's death, and the torment of war only increased her sense of grief.

The monotony of her life also magnified her grief. "The waves of housework, patching, darning, etc, crush me with their resistless sway. . . . *Must I come to it at last and be no more than the mere household drudge*, the thought of which fills me with terror? *Can it be* that this *is* woman's *only* mission—the end and aim of her creation?" Spiritual avenues also were tiresome and inadequate as a means to soothe her inner self. "Have been to a meeting in the woods today—a great crowd of people drawn together to listen [to] the rantings of a poor miserable ignoramus who calls himself a '*minister of God.*' But my soul rejects the ministrations of such teachers and can find more of truth in the silent ministry of leaf and flower, in that God has made. And to me the scene was painful—so vast a crowd listening to such nonsense, and calling it—the 'word of God.' And yet the multitudes, with but a few exceptions, seemed to swallow it—without a doubt." Consequently, unlike many people who turn to their religious convictions during times of personal or national tragedy, she rejected orthodoxy even more strenuously than before. Instead, in the months after Annie's death, she turned to the only means of support that in the past had been consistently reliable—words. Colby found some comfort in reading other people's works, including *Bleak House, Robinson Crusoe, Mill on the Floss, Old Curiosity Shop, Aurora Leigh, Adam Graeme of Mossgray,* and *Jane Eyre.* However, despite the consolation of these books, she desired something more. "So monotonous is my outer life that there is nothing worthy of the pen to record, and the inner life can have no record made visible. Sometimes I almost stifle it, and am almost indifferent to its want and needs, then *it conquers me* and its demands will be heard." This attitude led her to continue to turn her words outward as a way to cope with her grief and give voice to those "demands."[2]

During the war—particularly through the first two years—female writers most commonly used their access to public forums to celebrate women's patriotism as wives and mothers. Early in the war, Colby also contributed—briefly and in a somewhat ambivalent way—to the construct of the patient, long-suffering, female patriotic model. She wrote two separate pieces that approached this theme in differing fashion for *The Mayflower.* The first, a satirical poem called "While Darning Socks," spoke of "woman's mission" and admonished women who worried about war news when they could be darning. The second, an essay titled, "Silent Heroism," called for people to acknowledge women's contribution, even though "no pomp and circumstance of glorious war" accompanied their "loneliness of watching, the anguish of waiting." Although neither piece clearly challenged the role women were expected to play, neither did they offer a show of clear contentment or support for that role. By the spring of 1862, her doubts regarding these role expectations and her ability to resist them were clear. "What is duty, is often a query that I cannot always solve, and sometimes it seems that I have no choice left but . . . to act by train of circumstances over which we have no control."[3] Despite this assertion to the contrary and throughout the first two years of the war, she clearly endeavored to assert some control. Although she struggled with the "jagged rocks of circumstance" that she felt confined her in the role of the patient patriotic woman, her early war foray into upholding the image of the acquiescent waiting woman did not last long. Her conscience soon pushed her to make her views known. She longed to embrace the role of strong-minded woman that her conscience desired instead of society's prescription regarding her duty. Nevertheless, as in the past, ambiguity between her private thoughts, her public words, and her ability to act continued to plague her.

Through the first stages of the war, Colby's immediate community displayed only marginal tolerance, at best, for the opinions of the most radical abolitionists and disunionists. The most common prewar attitude had been support for the Republican Party's political efforts, and the immediate response once the battle commenced was a patriotic call to save the Union. Nevertheless, as fighting escalated and it became clear no quick victory was imminent, some of Colby's fellow citizens considered the validity of more extreme stances. In the months after the July 1861 Battle of Bull Run, a Cherry Valley group organized for the express purpose of drafting a document to present to Congress urging the government to use emancipation as "the most powerful battery against the rebels." Colby served as the elected secretary of the group. The opinions of the men in this group, who represented some of the most prominent as well as the founding families in the area—for example, the Krums, the Giddings, and the Creerys—illustrate the strong emotions that the war elicited. These opinions about the need for emancipation, which in many ways mirrored Colby's earlier views, aptly demonstrate the link that contemporaries made between slavery and the war. This link was not necessarily grounded in the same sense of social consciousness as Colby's, but rather the acknowledgment of slavery's role in the cause of the war, so therefore its importance in ending it was understood.[4]

Their comments, as reported by Colby to the *Ashtabula Sentinel,* ranged from civilized rhetoric to volatile condemnation. One man was "opposed to the petition—would not degrade his manhood to ask a favor of so mean a body of men as the Congress of the United States—would sign a petition to have the

President and all his cabinet hung, Washington City burned, etc.; and every person who had ever crossed the threshold of the 'White house' hung; and that the slaves should be armed and instructed to kill every man, woman, and child who had ever owned them." This radical attitude was apparently rather singular, although it is interesting that Colby gave it considerable coverage. Most of the participants showed less heated emotion and more patriotism. Mr. Krum offered a typical and less vitriolic assessment. He stated that the Constitution was "the wisest and best the world ever saw with the sole defect of slavery alone to tarnish its glory," and that the Confederates had "by their acts" relinquished their "former Constitutional right," so emancipation under war powers was no violation of the Constitution. Regardless of the difference in tone, the group agreed sufficiently to set up committees—all male—to coordinate the circulation of the petition.[5]

Considering Colby's prior public and uncompromising words on slavery and her contemporary public views on women's roles, it is ironic that although she was called to record this meeting her views were not reported. It is unknown whether she was the only woman in attendance because there was no roll listed or female opinions recorded; however, the circulating petition committee was exclusively male. If she was the sole female in attendance, then her presence indicates a rather unusual acceptance of a woman within an otherwise exclusively male domain, even though she still took a secondary role. However, if both men and women attended this meeting, but only males "officially" spoke or acted, then it indicates she played only a traditional female role. Both conclusions, nevertheless, display acquiescence on her part that must have been difficult given her strong views on the subject at hand. Recent historical scholarship illustrates that the activities that helped construct rural New England's public culture very often were mixed, although this mixing did not translate into freedom from the gender conventions that dominated society. As one historian describes it, women were expected to remain listeners not speakers; consequently, women commonly took compliant roles when participating within these mixed-gendered groups. Colby's role in this meeting certainly validates that conclusion.[6]

Later that same month, perhaps inspired by this feeling of forced acquiescence, Colby did not hesitate to voice her opinions. In a November 1861 essay, she discussed the concept of patriotism and clearly articulated her criticisms. As discussed previously, no matter what opinions Northerners held regarding emancipation or the constitutional status of the South, patriotic fervor during the early stages of the war for the North—the Union—was at a high point in most communities. Similar to Vietnam-era rhetoric one hundred years later, that is, "love it or leave it," anti-Union language was not likely to be well received. Colby's stance, which was published in her local paper, demonstrated her willingness to take responsibility for an unpopular position.

> We hear much said at the present day about treason and traitors, and the prevailing idea of those who thus stigmatize their friends and neighbors, seems to be simply that treason is any oppositions that a person may have against the government under which he lives, of which he was born a citizen or a subject, and in whose foundation he had no voice, thus making patriotism a thing of birth of circumstance, and even of latitude and longitude.
>
> In this latitude, a veneration, almost an adoration for the "Stars and Stripes" passes for patriotism, and the person who looks upon this emblem of our country as less sacred, less holy than the rights of the lowest and the weakest of mankind, who dares to regard it even as the emblem of oppression, the protector of the oppressed, who dares to be true to the voice of God in his own soul, and boldly proclaim that "*Man is more than constitutions,*" is at once stigmatized as a traitor; socially and politically he is a marked man, bearing the brand of treason as a reward for his *fidelity* to *humanity.* Let those who almost deify the flag of our country, who regard patriotism as being only a love for the land of our birth, regardless of its crimes and wrong-doings, remember that the word has a higher and holier significance than that; that he is the true patriot whose love of country is governed by his love of right, whose patriotism is only another term for the love of truth, justice and humanity.[7]

Colby was stalwart in her belief that to save the Union complete with its current stance against human equality was not an option for those people who truly revered the idea of natural right. In her opinion, laws higher than civil mandates existed.

> If the country of our birth and the laws and constitution under which we were born, legalize and sanction crime and oppression, then it is the duty, the stern and solemn duty of a true patriot, to resist and overthrow the wrong, even at the risk of the destruction of old time constitutions and laws. They are *not sacred things* if they crush the divinity out of the lowest, even, of our race. . . . The time has come when our reverence should be transferred from the musty parchments and constitutions of a past age. . . . And whatsoever laws and constitutions crush and trample upon the

rights of lowest of the human race, they must pass away and give place to the better and purer organizations that shall be developed by a loftier type of civilization and a nobler outgrowth of humanity.

Research focused on women writers of the Civil War era finds that during the early war years, as one historian notes, an "oasis of consensus in the North" existed. On the whole, women writers were "united in their support for the war."[8] Colby's words certainly defy that consensual conclusion. Despite possible repercussions for being thought of as disloyal, she strongly questioned the notion that a person should blindly follow the flag regardless of the government's actions.

Colby firmly placed herself in the minority with essays like the above. With the exception of a few radical antislavery activists, most women writers did not "ruminate publicly" on the causes or meaning of the war. What women were supposed to offer the war was their willingness to sacrifice. As one historian explains, women's sacrifices were to be of the "apolitical" and "altruistic" kind. Northern women were portrayed contemporaneously, as well in the postwar patriotic histories, as the "ideal embodiment of self-sacrifice, virtue, and disinterested benevolence that symbolized the values threatened by the Confederacy"—in short, true womanhood wearing the stars and stripes. In reality, what all this high-toned rhetoric described, albeit in romantic terms, was—for the most part and for most women—nothing beyond the usual "woman's duties" of sewing, cooking, and nursing.[9] For Colby, the very idea that her ideal wartime role should be more of the same—household labor, except for wartime use—went against her inner desire to be useful in a meaningful way.

Colby's attitude about the war, women's roles, and what changes should come of the uprising was best seen through her writings—both public and private. Publicly, she protested, and unlike many women writers whose narratives in the first two years of the war centered on the heroic patriotism of the women who stayed at home and waited, Colby only briefly explored that genre. Instead, she initially displayed a political slant that placed her within a minority of antislavery activist writers who used the war as a context for public discussions for overall social reform, rather than patriotic cheers.[10] Rather than solely focus her public concerns on emancipation or the actual war effort, Colby centered on the need for women's roles to expand. Unfortunately, Colby's efforts to change society's thoughts regarding women's appropriate spheres of action seemed to have made little impact in Cherry Valley, which, no doubt, contributed to the growing despondency in her private words. These limiting expectations for women frustrated Colby's sense of idealism because they opposed her hope that the specter of war would open social eyes to wider inequities, but she also experienced frustration of a more mundane nature. While the war effort affected most people's daily lives in some capacity, Colby's day-to-day existence to a great degree varied little from its status before the war. An epic battle consumed the nation, and its physical intrusion in her life often was so minimal that her days marched forward in the same relentless routine as the past, except with an added air of despair. "Oh for one week of perfect rest—rest of mind as well as body. I need it so much." Her exhaustion was clearly affecting her emotional state as well as her physical being. "Have just laid side my work, and mentally written 'Finis' to my days work though there is much more that might be done. . . . I ought to be satisfied. . . . [And] wonder if I shall stagnate at last, and be content in my ignorance?"[11]

Her ability to "act" was limited and did little to stave off stagnation. Beyond her contributions to Cherry Valley Soldiers' Aid Society, she served as the editor of a Civil War newsletter, which the female members of the Total Abstinence and Literary Society instigated as a forum for their thoughts. Although extant copies show Colby as the primary source for this endeavor, it still provided only a marginal avenue for more useful work. Considering the extent that the war reached into many people's lives, her daily routines stayed remarkably unchanged. Her extended family network remained basically intact, despite the fact that in March of 1863 Lincoln signed a conscription order for men from age twenty to forty-five. Her family apparently escaped military service with the sole exception of her younger brother, Jay Joel Rice. He enlisted in 1861 as a part of the Twenty-fourth Ohio Volunteer Infantry Company A and served until he was discharged in June of 1865. No evidence indicates that any other members of the immediate family served in the military despite their ages. Lewis Colby was in his middle thirties during the war, as were Colby's other brothers. The conscription order made allowances for certain exceptions and also allowed for paid substitutes for soldiers, which perhaps accounts for their lack of military service. The lethargy of daily circumstance that seemed to define her life, even during this time of immense national turmoil, led her to lament, "I do not, *cannot* live in harmony with my highest convictions—cannot embody my own ideals of life."[12] Ironically, despite this recurring certainty that her own destiny was fixed, in the first two years of the war she publicly continued to lobby for broader social evolution. Specifically, she focused on the inherent components of cultural bias that governed women's roles and her vision of how those components should be changed.

In her effort to point out areas of concern regarding women's options, she frequently addressed specific economic issues. Although she found society's preoccupation with money to be detrimental to the growth of "higher culture," she also was well aware of money's very real, as well as symbolic, importance. These economic-centered pieces placed her squarely within a so-called male-restricted domain, the public arena of the market economy. These forays into the male world of business and finance provide another example of her use of rhetoric designed to strike a nerve by confronting issues outside of "woman's sphere." Colby had spoken to economic concerns indirectly in many earlier published articles in which she discussed the business of farming. In those pieces, she demonstrated the extent of her understanding and participation in the market economy as it related to farm products. She wrote about ways to maximize profits in the sale of cheese, butter, cows, and wheat as well as farming techniques designed to enhance productivity. By the 1860s, she used this understanding of the market economy to directly attack the prevailing economic framework in which wages for working women were less than those of men.[13]

From its earliest incarnations, the women's rights movement has been criticized for a lack of concern for working-class women. Admittedly, this criticism has validity, but it is not strictly accurate. During the nineteenth century, factions of the movement looked beyond prevailing, middle-class concerns, such as property and inheritance rights, to everyday working women's concerns, which centered primarily on employment options and wage issues. An early reform paper, *The Woman's Advocate,* was devoted to the rights of the "female industrial class," and other reform papers, such as *The Lily* and *The Una,* also covered women's economic issues, albeit mostly from a theoretical perspective. Colby demonstrated an interest not only with the theories behind economic issues but also with the practical results of wage inequities, which were based "not [on] capacity, but . . . sex."[14]

Colby confronted the issue of wage inequity in an essay written in response to an article that appeared in the *Farmer's Advocate.* The article's author—a man—had put forth the popular and familiar premise that women were already "superior to man"; consequently, those women who complained about their place in society and who were not "satisfied with their positions" should be more appreciative of "the blessings bestowed upon them." Colby's direct rebuttal to this man's letter argued her counterpoint with specific examples as well as some wit and sarcasm. She indicated that it would be "a little strange" to be so unappreciative if in fact women were "supremely blest with her current condition, if it is the beautiful and perfect one that men tell us it is!" The first "blessing" Colby confronted was the fact that female teachers were paid less than male teachers. Colby's earlier teaching experience served as a base from which she could draw memories to fuel these protests about wage disparities that were especially egregious in the teaching profession. Among those people who taught common school classes in Ohio by 1865, a higher percentage of them were women, and these women made significantly smaller salaries. For example, by 1865, at the common public school level, men averaged $36.25 per month compared to only $21.25 per month for women.[15]

As a self-described "district school teacher," or common school teacher, Colby had experienced this wage differential firsthand, and nearly fifteen years later its unfairness clearly still touched a nerve.

> Strange that the intelligent, educated and accomplished woman who has spent her youth and her means to fit herself for the responsibilities of a teacher, and is acknowledged to be peculiarly fitted by nature for the mission, should not be content to perform more labor in the recitation room for half, or less than half the sum which is so freely bestowed upon the male teacher, whose acquirements are no greater than her own, and whose needs are no more imperative than hers. A "Professor" would feel his dignity insulted by the mere paltry sum which a woman is compelled to receive for her services as a teacher.

Colby once again used rhetoric designed to legitimize the issue by placing it within a "male" framework. Similar to her prior use of the metaphor of "taxation without representation," Colby addressed wage inequity within the framework of justice as well as capacity. She frequently brought the question of fair pay into her discussions about women's rights. "I know this test of pay to be a low one by which to test the justice of woman's position; but it has the merits at least of being a masculine test, as well as an American one, and as it appeals to the pocket, may be more readily understood than if addressed to the heart, or a sense of justice."[16]

Despite her acknowledgment that appeals to simple justice were inadequate motivators for social change, her sense of injustice is evident as she used the notion of "woman's sphere" to argue against the practicality of the idea itself. She challenged the very base of the ideal of gender separation—the concept that woman's sphere was "natural." She cited as evidence to the contrary the present dissatisfaction among the "most intelligent and enlightened" women as "proof positive" of the untruth of the ideal. As she pointed out, "Is it necessary to make a legal enactment to keep the trout in the sparkling stream, or the bird . . . in the free air?" She noted in one essay that "many women are not blessed with homes." She questioned that if a woman's sphere was deemed to be limited to home, then what about those women? "Have these homeless women no sphere of action—no duties?" Beyond pointing out the impractical-

Colby's public stance on women's rights emerged in the early 1860s. This draft of her essay, "Some Things We Want," displays her use of subtle sarcasm that only barely masks her frustration with the continued lack of progress toward equality. Used by permission Colby Collection, Illinois State University Archives, Illinois State University, Normal, Illinois.

ity of the whole idea of a "woman's sphere," she again returned to the prag-matic problems stemming from the prevailing thoughts about the real—that is, monetary—value of women's work. These thoughts were the foundation for women's inferior wages, which, in Colby's view, were particularly unfair to those women without homes. She described the futility of the struggle for a woman who may "wash or sew for the wealthy if she can secure their patronage; and for many hours of weary toil, may receive enough compensation to keep themselves in plain food, the plainest of clothing but not enough to make even a dream of a future home seem possible."[17] A simple and straightforward solution existed to solve these problems—equality for all women. She never wavered from her belief that only radical changes in women's social, legal, and economic status would suffice.

In the spirit of that belief, Colby's public advocacy for temperance also intensified during this period. Although it can be argued that Colby's efforts for temperance never directly addressed women's rights, they do provide valuable insight regarding her evolving attitudes about the notion of womanhood. Colby's initial involvement in the temperance movement had been the least controversial of her early social reform interests, but as the 1860s opened, her message began to change. Her earlier public words on temperance, like her early expressions toward slavery and female education, had been focused on the traditional themes of home and family. These early arguments used alcohol's threat to the family to justify women's active involvement; the prescription that a woman's perceived "duty [was] to use her influence" to stop its entrance into her home was based on ideals of the proper female sphere. Colby's early temperance work also fitted in well with the mainstream, antebellum, temperance organizations' messages, which focused on stopping the sale of alcohol, illustrating its horrible effects in order to discourage drinking, and providing charity and pity for the family who suffered. The purpose of these organizations was not to offer advice or recourse for women who may have sought alternatives to an intemperate situation. Instead, the depiction of the wife as the "noble" sufferer was the common theme that ran through much of the popular literature aimed at garnering support for temperance efforts.

During the 1850s, the temperance movement became more political and women's place in the movement more controversial as it often entangled with women's rights issues. Women's rights advocates offered new thoughts on possible recourses for women beyond noble suffering. Options, which ranged from it being "a moral duty" for a wife to leave an intemperate husband to suggestions that intemperance should rightly be considered proper legal grounds for divorce, were met with outrage by some and uneasiness by many. The subject of divorce was the most contentious of these options. Despite its increasing occurrence, divorce was a topic that inspired deep divides of thought and was still considered quite controversial. In 1852, avowed women's rights activist Elizabeth Cady Stanton publicly disclaimed any proposal that viewed "divorce as a remedy for the evil [intemperance]." Nevertheless, even during the 1850s, Stanton's opinions regarding divorce were more layered than this simple conciliatory statement, and as the decade unfolded, Stanton's strong advocacy for the expansion of women's legal access to divorce contributed to the growing debate. Colby's early 1860s' work reflected the more liberal spectrum of this contentious cultural discussion. Her disdain for the "rum-sellers" and "drunkards" remained a constant, but her belief in women's responsibility and men's ability to be rehabilitated altered, as did her position on "women bearing up nobly." Her focus shifted to pleas for social justice specifically for women, rather than redeeming intemperate men.[18]

In an essay written for *The Mayflower,* she used a "true" story to illustrate the horrible effects of alcohol on the family. Contrary to earlier works, this piece, "Reverie for a Drunkard's Wife," displayed no pity for the "degraded drunkard." Colby described in vivid detail the "downward path" the couple took from happy newlyweds to total despair. Colby depicted—in highly emotional fashion—the wife's efforts to use her love and the love of her children to stop her husband from drinking, but "they were powerless before the love of strong drink; and now the drunkenness has destroyed the last lingering emotion of love that warmed my heart for him." Colby continued by detailing the death of the children and the wife's future, which unlike earlier temperance writings, was not depicted by Colby as one of "noble suffering." Instead, the wife cried, "My living soul fettered to a mass of corruption! Surely it is literally so; and more merciful fate was that of the poor heathen widow burned to ashes on the pyre of a husband she may have loved, than such a lingering living death as is this life of mine. Endurance is all that is left me now. Hope is dead, and aspiration is buried in the grave of hope." Colby's words in this essay were clearly inflammatory and meant to arouse an emotional response. Although she also wrote straightforward essays that explained the purposes of practical methods to fight alcohol abuse, such as temperance societies and the "Pledge," her rhetorical evolution can be seen most clearly in her graphic portrayals of "drunkards" and their families.[19]

Colby often placed the abuser within her own community. This technique allowed her to berate those neighbors who claimed they were against alcohol use, but refused to condemn local merchants because "the rum-seller at home is a gentlemen, and it would be very impolite and improper to insinuate that there is a crime in the traffic." Her position on that theory was a simple one. "We are apt to realize the evil more fully when we see its effects, and perhaps our efforts in the cause of temperance might not be so fruitless, if they were more concentrated, and aimed at a tangible object—visible evil." Exposing this neighborhood "evil" also potentially allowed for a greater sense of intimacy that perhaps could operate to mitigate the cultural prescription that said a true woman's role was to quietly provide purifying influence—no matter the sordid details or sacrifices.[20] No evidence from her private writings indicates that anyone close to her suffered from alcohol-related problems, but in a community of over six hundred people there no doubt existed at least a couple of abusers. Regardless of whether her portrayals were modeled after actual community or family members, her emotional approach clearly was a calculated rhetorical device used to elicit response.

In this quest for response she did not shy away from graphic illustrations as she portrayed this "tangible . . . visible evil." Toward that goal, she provided another explicit image of a Cherry Valley neighbor and how his alcohol abuse affected the lives of even innocent bystanders. She described this neighbor as a good father and husband when sober, but unfortunately he was a vicious drunk as well. Colby described in detail the scene as witnessed by a passerby, who discovered the man "with one hand clenched in the hair of his helpless wife, and with the other one he was pounding her head, face, and shoulders, while the blood was streaming from several cuts and bruises upon her face, and the frightened children were screaming loudly for help."[21] In this essay, she offered no advice for a wife who may be caught in the grip of this type of scenario; she merely used her story to display the horrors of intemperance in the private sphere. By 1862, Colby moved beyond merely illustrating the effects of alcohol as she publicized the stance that women should no longer suffer in silence.

Although Colby did not employ the word "divorce," she strongly advocated leaving an intemperate husband in the following essay, which aside from appearing in a newspaper, she also read before the Cherry Valley Total Abstinence and Literary Society in 1862.

Blame her not for this. If man, the stronger sex, as he is called, will go to destruction for the fleeting pleasure or appetite, if he is wedded to alcohol, he has no right to drag down with him in his fearful descent an innocent woman, and his own helpless babes. And the woman who is thus wedded to a hopeless inebriate, if she is true to herself, and true to humanity as represented in her own offspring, will cease to be a wife till reformation shall make her husband worthy of her respect and love. . . . Woman owes society a higher duty than a fruitless effort to save one who "is joined to his idols"—the loathsome beverage of the distiller—and as the wife of the drunkard she can never fulfill this obligation.

This essay displays Colby's belief in the value and potential of a woman's usefulness as more than a silent prop for her husband. A woman was more than her
husband's chattel, so if he deprived her of an opportunity for a useful life, then
she had not only the right, but also the obligation to unchain herself. Within
this same idealistic framework, she confronted the part that popular literature
played in perpetuating this "noble" status. She pointed out that novels consistently offered stories in which a wife followed her husband on his downward
path. Colby described how these fictional accounts often show this journey as
"the beauty of woman's constancy and devotion, how tenderly and truly they
cling to that mass of corruption which was once their husbands." In reality she
explained, this path has no moral charm, only a "dull, terrible reality, without
a single redeeming feature." Colby maintained that a woman's greater accountability should be to her children and society as a whole. This debt superseded
a woman's debt to an intemperate husband and validated her right to "cease
to be a wife." This attitude placed Colby firmly outside orthodox views on the
subject; as one historian describes the debate, Colby aligned herself with the
former in the battle between "infidels and Christians."[22]

Colby's publications, public actions, and even the occasional public reading
demonstrated her strong commitment to social, legal, and economic equality
for women. The backdrop for this bravado was the reality of the Civil War: the
home front, which in her case entailed a daily routine she perceived scarcely
altered from its prior status, and the war front, which seemed to show no signs
of peace. As time went by, the lack of movement or progress on both fronts
contributed to her growing sense of isolation and a decreasing sense that she
could make a difference in anyone's life, especially her own. As her expectations
increasingly stagnated, her personal despair grew. This personal despair appeared in her private writings while she still publicly appealed for reform. "The
little ones have just kissed me 'good night' and I'm alone, with my own *shadowy
thoughts* how I long sometimes to make them tangible to the eye of others.
Wonder if I ever shall? Sometimes I put the old dream aside for a time and it
ceases to haunt me with its power; again I smile at my folly in daring to dream
that *I could create a book* that should throb with life—with the wild, restless,
but hidden life of my own soul. And yet to realize that dream, to embody my
ideals would be *a luxury.*" Her actual daily life, unfortunately, did not mirror
her inner beliefs. She continued to experience dissatisfaction with her living
arrangement and her expected role within the household; more importantly,
Colby's live-in family saw her writing as a waste of time. As one of the few pastimes that provided her any sense of accomplishment, this disparagement was

particularly suffocating. "Am all alone in the house, but not a bit lonely. There is no one to look on with censorious eyes if I do take the pen for a few minutes, which is a real relief, a relief so great that I shall venture to use it, and shall feel not a pang of conscience for so doing."[23]

Sadly, a dream not shared or supported often fades away in the face of obstacles, and after 1862, little evidence suggests any further effort by Colby to complete her book. She no longer mentioned it in her journals, and the extant manuscript consists only of some incomplete chapters and a rough outline. Her feelings of isolation spread even to her other mainstay, reading. After Annie's death, even that pastime changed character. "My reading is so solitary now. How much I miss Annie in this. A book does not seem *half* enjoyed, until it is shared by one who enjoyed it too." Books always had claimed an important space in Colby's life, but her growing sense of isolation affected their function as well. More frequently, she expected books to fill a more sustaining role. Elizabeth Barrett Browning's poem, *Aurora Leigh,* which she felt spoke to her ideals, was a particular favorite. Of Browning's attempts to "elevate and redeem woman" Colby noted, "I reverence the author for her noble daring in the *aim and purpose* for which she wrote." Colby cherished Browning's poem and even declared, "Its presence cheers me as does the presence of a friend." Contrary to this sentimental declaration, the very next day Colby conveyed how unrealistic that notion actually was. "Again the chores are done, the evening lights are burning, and my spirit is longing so vainly for communion with some one who understands the needs of my soul. There is no one near me, no one to give me back my thoughts. Books are near me, but sometimes we need human love, human sympathy. Conversation is just as needful for the minds growth as is thought and reflection and it must rise above the level of daily toil or it only wearies."[24] Again it must be noted that Colby was not living a physically isolated life. Family surrounded her almost at all times. When she claimed, "There is no one near me, no one to give back my thoughts," she was lamenting the quality of company, not the quantity.

As time went by, her public written protests represented the extent of her efforts to turn outward and engage with others. Increasingly, in her private life she turned inward to the written word for support, but as she noted herself, this support was unable to sustain her needs. Despite this acknowledged inadequacy, as the war continued to rage and her role continued to stagnate, her love of reading continued to turn from a means of distraction, entertainment, and education into a replacement for the human contact that had operated as a support system in her daily life. As 1862 grew to a close and the war ravaged on, Colby's private writings as well as her public writings grew fewer and fewer.

In June of 1862, Colby noted, "Oh for one week of *perfect rest*—rest of mind as well as body." She continued this entry with a lament on her growing inability to cope.

> I do not know whether I'm sick or lazy, or only nervous, but I'm weak, *so weak*, and there is such a pressure of care, that the thought tires me, and all the restless motions of the little ones almost craze me. Life is so terribly *real*, so *intensely* earnest—and then it is but the physical that lives at best. Life is such a mystery, such a puzzle, and sometimes there seems all "the weight of this unintelligible world" pressing on my weary brain, all the mysteries that I would, but cannot comprehend, all the doubts that I cannot solve, but the solution of which seems so *necessary*, so imperative.[25]

Following this melancholy June 1862 entry, five months passed, and the entire cheese-making season went by with only two brief notations, one in July and one in September. Not even the marriage of her sister Cirlissa Rice to Hiram Fleming in October 1862 merited a mention. Then in late November, she resumed her journal writing only to lament, "Month after month passes—the same dull round of duties claim my time, fetter my hands, and the same unsatisfied yearnings struggle within—and *this is life*, or we *call* it life. Why, oh why do we live on—only to eat, drink and die. There is, there *must be higher* life here, and yet we, or few, make any effort to rise into its sphere of enjoyment, and the few who do, are fettered by ties that hold them down."[26] Colby's perception that she was "fettered by ties" grew, as did her weary acceptance that her place as a woman, even in this time of crisis, was essentially to be a caretaker. She felt that this role, which was basically to wait, was isolating and provided no support for her dream of a "higher life." As this awareness grew, her dependence on nonhuman forms of support grew as well.

If Colby's public words offered the only source to gauge her perceptions of not only her private life, but also women's roles in general during this time, then she appeared ready to confront with bravado the challenges of society's limiting prescriptions. However, her private words paint a very different picture of her state of mind. Those words indicate that despite the bravado, this defiant public mood did not translate into her private life. Her words also indicate that she was aware of this split in her life. "How strange and unaccountable is the hidden life! Will the outer and inner life ever be harmonized? Or are we created to be only the sport of destiny!"[27] Her public words represented the hopes innate to her inner life, but her private reflections demonstrated that her actual life, her outer world, continued to fall short of her hopeful expectations.

This dichotomy had been present for quite some time, but the continuing war exacerbated it as her awareness of the uselessness of her prescribed role grew. Annie's death in 1861, as well as the death of another close female friend, Jennie, also in the late summer of 1861, further intensified these feelings.[28] Despite the fact that her publications indicated a belief in an opportunity to widen women's place, she personally felt she was losing the battle to chart her own course. Her private thoughts revealed helplessness and an increasing perception of diminishing support for her efforts to move beyond the traditional women's sphere. She lamented, "there *must be higher* life," but although Colby's public words demonstrated that she advocated different roles for women in general, this evolution in roles was not a reality in her life. While she lived in a community that was progressive on many fronts, the expansion of women's roles was not a societal norm. Despite the Civil War's disruption, this view would not alter to any great degree for many decades. In fact, the years during and after the war would see the fight for women's rights lose momentum and focus. Colby's own experience would parallel this arc. Colby's publications during the first half of the war had demonstrated her attempt to capitalize on this apparent acceptance of women's widening roles, but by early 1863, her publications were predominantly children's stories, and her private journals display increasing despondency. As the war continued and it became obvious to her that her role was in reality "to wait," her sense of purpose waned and her feelings of uselessness and isolation grew. Initially, she had been tired of waiting, but as 1862 wound down, she merely seemed tired.

PART III

Expectations Stagnate

Acceptance or Defeat?

CHAPTER ELEVEN

September 1862–April 1865

"And we women . . . can only wait, and wait"

As 1862 was drawing to a close, Colby had sadly lamented, "there *must be higher* life," and expressed bitterness that "any effort to rise into its sphere of enjoyment" was restricted by "ties." During the previous five years, this sort of defeatist tenor had been common in many of Colby's private words, but despite this attitude she had periodically attempted to rise above her circumstances. She had displayed varying levels of frustration about her limitations, but she also had demonstrated her desire and belief in the possibility of change. Although she acted on these beliefs only sporadically, her actions were passionate when unleashed. In short, she felt despair, but still endeavored to maintain hope. She even closed her sad and bitter November 1862 entry with the statement, "I cannot, will not believe that life must be so, it is we who make it so by being '*content with merely living.*'" Despite her recurring hopelessness regarding the heartache of war and the mind-numbing "same dull round of duties," she desperately had clung to the notion that she maintained some control over her ability to change her life. Nonetheless, her tenuous hold on that notion began to unravel as the winter of 1862 turned toward the spring of 1863.[1]

In March of 1863, Colby resumed journal writing after several months without an entry, and these reflections display a palpable level of despair. Over the next several years, although she made entries less faithfully than in the past, her unhappiness clearly resonates. In years past, when depression had seemed poised to overtake her life, Colby had opted to act in some fashion to counter it. Contrary to these past patterns, this growing sense of emotional isolation and despair seemed unaffected by other distractions. As previously discussed, Colby periodically turned inward and resisted active engagement with the outward world, but heretofore her sporadic efforts to change both her circumstances and her expectations provided a sense of connection to a broader sphere and invariably acted to mediate her withdrawal to some degree. Most recently, the advent of the war had ignited her belief that real social change could be on the horizon. This belief served to temper her despair somewhat as she engaged in work she hoped would be useful. However, by 1863, she gave no hint that she felt useful, only tired, as her hope for support in these endeavors clearly had dimmed. "The winter has passed without a record! And yet many and deep are the records of toil, weariness and pain that its passage has traced upon the physical system. . . . It has left its impress traced deep upon me, and spring finds me weak."[2] For the first time in nearly a decade she showed no signs that she would eventually rebound with an outpouring of public protest. Rather she demonstrated an increasing tendency to turn inward and surrender to apathy. Without mitigating support she appeared destined to sink into even deeper depression.

Colby's feelings about the lack of human support were not new, but in the past she quite frequently had responded to this perception by increasing her public and passionate output for social justice. She had helped to not only counter feelings of increasing emotional isolation by reading books but also garner sustenance from her writing. She wrote many of her most eloquent reform-minded essays, especially those on women's rights, in periods when she perceived that human support was at its lowest. In particular, she had attempted to mitigate with writing the loneliness linked to Annie's absences, her prolonged sickness, and her death. Colby's frustrations and despondency, which were byproducts of her private dissatisfaction, actually served as fuel for her increasingly radicalized public opinions; as her personal future narrowed, her demands for equality in society grew. In essence, Colby used her writing to connect and gain the emotional support missing in her life from those people in the wider world who she perceived as like-minded.

As 1862 drew to a close, however, Colby reached outward less often and inward more often as her attempts to garner support from the wider world stalled. From late in 1862 through the end of the war in mid-1865, she did write some works for publication, but the number of those essays that focused on reform—or any issue that may have been considered controversial—dropped to zero. She stopped using her public access to try to connect with like-minded souls or contribute to social causes; instead, she wrote pieces that were primarily sentimental in nature. During 1863, she continued to contribute essays periodically to *The Mayflower,* but none made the militant demands of years prior. Many of them were nostalgic or maudlin pieces that romanticized people she had lost, in particular Plummer and Annie. She contributed primarily to the *Little Pilgrim,* and these pieces consisted predominantly of puzzles, words games, and stories about children for children. In years past, her child-focused contributions often interwove themes that highlighted the importance of play-time activities that did not teach, or expect, girls to be little ladies. Contrary to that end, these children's pieces, like her other work during this period, were often sentimental and nostalgic in nature. By 1864, even these contributions had diminished to almost none. Only one essay and one poem clearly originated from 1864, and the poem, written in a letter format, illustrates the depths of her melancholy.

> To ——,
> No art, or skill to one belong
> To grace this page of thine. . . .
> No woman soul should suffer ill.
> I know not why, I only know
> That perfect bliss we never find . . .
> That the mission of sorrow is never vain
> That blessings follow footsteps of pain.

She wrote possibly two other essays in that year as well, but beyond that—nothing.[3] Her private journal writing also diminished and became sporadic at best. Considered as a whole, her public and private words provide a picture of a woman who considered her life's options narrowed to the point that she only could go through the motions of her outward day-to-day life without hope. Today, this emotional state possibly would be diagnosed and treated as clinical depression, but regardless of possible, modern-day definitions her reality offered little refuge from its effects. She provided no self-analysis or explanation as to the reasons for this prolonged—and unopposed—slide into apathy, but likely contributors were her age, her living situation, a betrayal, and the continuation of the war.

The Civil War tormented her. Although the other factors were perhaps more intimate in nature, the war had been at least as invasive because she had entertained personal illusions regarding its ability to instigate real social change and her ability to contribute to that effort. The loss of those illusions of change and control left a deep void. Her thoughts and beliefs regarding the war's meaning had gone through several stages. Before the war even began she had believed slavery's elimination required true resolve. Her November 1861 essay on the duties of a true patriot declared, "It is the duty, the stern and solemn duty of a true patriot, to resist and overthrow the wrong." As early as 1854 she had written, "Slavery must and will be abolished; if not in peace it must end in war and bloodshed, and our own cherished ones may be crushed in the overthrow." As this effort at "overthrow" persisted without resolution, privately, at least, her firm resolve began to show signs of wear. As 1862 dragged on, so did the war, and the North was not faring well. In the last days of August 1862, the North was routed once again in a second major battle at Bull Run. In September 1862, as the horrors of the prolonged conflict became increasingly real, she noted in her journal, "And now after the long chronic heartache of this war, I am in a state of mental torpor, and can hardly realize it exists. . . . And so the summer has passed, waiting for news of battles lost and won—war the only theme of thought or conversation almost. Oh it is so terrible! And we women are so helpless—can only wait, and wait, and try to trust that this terrible carnage, shall yet come good to humanity. If we could do something—could shape and mould events, instead of waiting for their slow, uncertain development, it would seem easier than to wait in our forced inaction."[4] The North and the South remained basically deadlocked as 1862 ended, and the moral imperative of ending slavery, which Colby had hoped was just cause for the carnage, seemed no closer to reality than a year prior. Clearly, the waiting had begun to wear her down.

In the new year, the tide slowly began to turn in favor of the North, but regardless of this 1863 turn, many bloody days of war lay ahead. Lincoln issued the Emancipation Proclamation in January of 1863 and though, in reality, it freed slaves only in areas where the government had no real force of compliance, its symbolic meaning was felt nationwide. Despite the Proclamation's symbolic reverberation, many radical abolitionists were quick to point out its obvious weaknesses. The presumed justification for the war remained at the center of the abolitionists' disagreement with Lincoln. Lincoln remained committed to saving the Union as his primary goal, while ultras still demanded that the war be fought more directly for freedom. As a consequence, many radical abolitionists viewed Lincoln's emancipation gesture as little more than political positioning. Colby recorded no entries through the first months of 1863 and did not address the Proclamation publicly, so her opinion is unknown. A copy of the Proclamation in her scrapbook acknowledges her interest; however, she made no notation that offers more information. Nevertheless, a March 1863 entry confirms she still believed universal freedom remained the only possible justifiable reason for the bloodshed. "It sometimes seems were this terrible war but ended in the triumph of universal liberty, that I should forget weakness and pain in the general rejoicing. But the dark and terrible possibilities of the future, the sickening uncertainty weighs down the spirit and unnerves the body."[5]

Colby was not the only woman who registered concern that the nation as a whole seemed unclear as to the primary purpose behind the war. Historical scholarship finds that by mid-war, women writers overwhelmingly displayed frustration with what one historian terms the "seemingly fragmented understanding of the war's purposes." Even when their individual understanding regarding legitimate justifications for the war differed, women, on the whole, expected the war to have a "moral meaning" to a much greater degree than did men. Colby's sense that the war's meaning had become diluted clearly contributed to her June 1863 entry, in which she questioned her previous determination that these matters of "Right and Wrong" be decided in bloodshed if necessary.

> The shadows are beginning to fall, and I've been out among the roses, listening to the vespers of the birds, trying to *forget all thoughts of war*, and to "Dream still of peace, and only peace," Oh if only this horrid war were over, if the nations would learn war no more, what a good world this would be, & how much of joy we struggling mortals might find mingled with our toil. But where will the end of all this carnage be? Are we as a nation doomed to complete destruction? I feel so weak physically that I have hardly the heart for the contest that seems gathering over even our own once prosperous North, I can hardly realize that I am living in historic times, in a heroic age. I who used to long to feel the stirring impulses of such an age, when Right & Wrong should struggle for the mastery, now know that the deathless strife is still raging, and can only "*wait*," with no strength to "labor."[6]

No answers served to mitigate her struggle to find greater meaning in the war or in her life. In addition to the war's explicit emotional effects, it also exacerbated her frustrations regarding her "place" as a woman. How was she to find meaning in a life whose prescribed purpose was "only to '*wait*'"?

Despite this despair over the war's actual significance as well its possible implications for her own life, she kept abreast on the progress of the struggle, primarily via newspapers. A scrapbook documents her interest in the war effort and demonstrates that her focus remained on the social and political battles waged both during and after the war, including extensive clippings regarding Lincoln's assassination, Jefferson Davis's capture and trial, and Andrew Johnson's impeachment.[7] She also continued to participate in one of the few organizations available to a married rural wife and mother, the Soldiers' Aid Society. She took part in not only "woman's work," such as collecting clothes and making bandages, but she also served as the society's secretary. Nonetheless, for a woman who held such strong views on freedom and equality, this inability to actually "act" intensified her existing feelings of gender isolation and uselessness.

Of course, as stories of female soldiers, spies, and nurses testify, other women did step across boundaries and do more, but Colby's private words illustrate that by 1863 she felt additional action was beyond her reach. An important, and another uncontrollable, factor likely contributed to this inhibited view of her future possibilities: her age. During the Victorian era, doctors commonly warned women that if they wanted to ensure a relatively healthy, post-childbearing life, that is, "old age," then they needed to make serious lifestyle changes by the time they were forty. These lifestyle changes amounted to a withdrawal from the outside world so as to save their limited energy for their families. Women were advised that they needed quiet, so they should avoid mental activities, engage in no new activities, and renew their commitment to domesticity. In December of 1863, Colby turned thirty-six years old. In previous years, she clearly had demonstrated that the passing of time was a troubling phenomenon, and she regretted that she had so little to show for its passage. In an era when a woman's "old age"—thus her uselessness—was thought to begin at forty, and menopause was considered the beginning of the end, this approaching milestone must have loomed large on the immediate horizon. Colby's own words demonstrate that despite her progressive stances on many issues, she fell in line with this popular assumption. In an 1861 essay, she chastised women who spent too much time on making useless and frivolous bed quilts. "A woman who has anything to do, a mission in life, will find very little time for patch-work quilts, unless it is at the expense of her intellect." She condemned "half crazy mothers who feel that woman's mission in life is to make bedquilts. No wonder the world is full of weakly women." After this harsh treatment, however, she added a codicil that the pastime was acceptable "when a woman is past forty, and can find no more useful or profitable employment for her heart and hands."[8] This looming stage of her life magnified her assumption that soon her greatest fear was to be realized: a life whose entire purpose was defined by mindless drudgery. Apathy more often was becoming her response to this assumption.

The passing of time also contributed to other changes within her family that likely exacerbated her inner turmoil. As she grew older, so, of course, did her children. In the summer of 1862, Vine, Branch, and Rose had turned ten, eight, and six years old, respectively, and although they remained the bright spot in her life, they were becoming increasingly independent. In the autumn of 1862, Vine took her first step toward that independence when she went away to school. Colby reacted with pride and a bit of melancholy to this event. "Vine has been gone several days, and if we can stand it without her, will be gone three months. But we shall miss her so much. Dear girl is constantly in my thoughts. But she commences her first term of school away from home today." Colby clearly wanted her daughter to obtain the best education she could, but she also felt her absence deeply. Colby often noted Vine's household help, so her absence added not only to Colby's emotional angst but also to her workload. It is unclear where Vine attended school. By the early 1860s, Ohio was home to numerous educational facilities, including at least twenty female seminaries. It is also unknown how long Vine continued her schooling away from home, as events of 1863 possibly interfered and kept her at home.[9]

During 1863, the Colby household endured changes wrought by fate and the passing of time. In early 1863, Branch experienced some sort of accident that confined him at home for a time. Luckily, this injury apparently did not lead to a life long disability, but its temporary effects were debilitating. Colby noted in April of 1863 that Branch was "yet unable to walk." The extra responsibilities linked to Branch's temporary state of disability were compounded by her mother-in-law's status. Lewis's mother, Naomi Colby, also was ill during this period. The presence of possibly three people with limited mobility—Branch, Naomi, and Colby's "crippled" brother-in-law—added to the normal workload associated with cheese season and most likely meant that Vine was needed at home. Naomi passed away in October of 1863. Colby made no note of her illness or death in her journal, but the newspaper reported that Naomi's death followed a "protracted illness of great suffering, which she bore with Christian patience and heroic fortitude." The paper failed to report how well the caretaker, most likely Colby, had endured the "protracted illness" of a woman who viewed Colby's personal aspirations with disdain. During this same period, Colby's stepmother, Evelina Rice, was also ill. She died in November of 1863, and like her mother-in-law, Colby made no mention in her journal of her death.[10]

In fact, the magnitude of both Colby's workload and her growing apathy may be inferred from the lack of entries made from July of 1863 until February of 1864. Sadly, this pall of apathy was lifted not by a sense of purpose or inspiration, but by a betrayal. In an early February 1864 entry, Colby confronted this apparent betrayal that colored much of her following year. Unfortunately, this unburdening admission adds questions about her emotional struggle without much information to provide answers.

What a blank there has been in this outer record of my life! Ah what would the record be if *truthfully* written out. But it is traced in *letters of fire* that are burning deep into my heart—*eating my life away*. And yet with this hopeless cancer eating into my soul, I must live on, nerve myself to meet the gaze of others, and force myself to wear an outward calmness, while I am *dying by inches*. Oh why is it that the body must live on when hope is forever dead. Oh my tears blind me. What shall I do? All day I sat benumbed by agony, unable to work from very weakness, longing to die, yet clinging to life for the sake of children three, as only a mother can cling who feels how much those children need her. Oh God be pitiful, and help if help can come from there! Oh there is not one human heart to whom I can turn for sympathy, not one. Alone, all, all alone, with a soul solitude peopled by dark and bitter memories, all made dark and bitter by those professing the purest love, the strongest friendship. Oh how *false are friends*. . . . But to lose confidence in those we love; to be taught the dark lessons of distrust by those loudest in their professions of friendship, is indeed terrible, and yet *such is my destiny*. . . . But a month ago there was a *sudden death in my heart*, just a month yesterday and I've lived an age of woe all condensed in that little month. I have written that it was a sudden death and so it was, yet there had been a long life and death struggle, when oft death seemed sure, and that the death pang was one but sharp, and *sudden*, and awful came the stroke, and then I knew that there had been life still lingering even when I thought it gone. Just as truly did I *weep for the dead that day*, as if cold and icy, was the brow that I pressed—mortal agony.[11]

As lengthy as this excerpt is, it is only a piece of the outcry for that day. The self-reflective nature of Colby's journal entries often presents challenges in interpretation when attempting to reconstruct her feelings about her place in her world. If she had simply outlined actions or events and then documented her emotional responses, this reconstruction would be simple. More often, as we have witnessed, she wrote extensively about her feelings without supplying the entire context from which the emotions rose, and therein lays the challenge. These elusive glances can be extremely frustrating. More than once, Colby provided an outpouring of emotion without supplying any details about the event to which this emotion was connected. Nevertheless, for the most part, when other sources are layered into the interpretation, the combination allows extrapolation with a great degree of confidence. This quotation, however, offers a particularly frustrating example of when that extrapolation becomes more problematic. Several entries made in the early months of 1864 expressed her agonized feelings in regard to some type of betrayal. Unfortunately, for seven months prior to this entry she had not written in her journal. As we have seen, some events in that period can be reconstructed without her private words, but none lend themselves as possible answers. Her previous observation was written on July 15, 1863, so contextual journal inferences are difficult, if not impossible, to attempt. She commented on her emotions in regard to this event again and again, but she never revealed any further details about what actually prompted the feelings. This inability to "know" what happened is one of the particularly frustrating aspects of using private writings; personal expressions not meant to tell a story do not take the readers' needs into account.

What we do know does not necessarily answer the question with any great confidence. She had alluded previously to her dissatisfaction with her marriage, and in this entry she spoke of a prolonged struggle. This struggle could be interpreted as her attempts over the years to mend this rift. In addition, she closed her extended lament with comments about her "pure and clean" conscience and worries whether her children will "be strong in the hour of temptation, will they be true and pure." Those comments may point to an infidelity on the part of her husband, a friend, or perhaps both. She was obviously extremely distressed. A few days after the above entry she noted, "I sometimes close the door of my little room with the feeling that I would like to shut out the outer world—and never meet their gaze again."[12] It is really impossible to state with any certainty what actually happened. She never revealed any further details, but it continued to overshadow her emotional well-being.

After the initial shock of this betrayal wore off, her apathy grew deeper, and melancholy permeated many of her entries over the next several years. In the depths of her inner self, Colby still desired that her sphere be one defined by a "broader culture," where the ideals that she held to be important—reading, writing, conversation that served a greater purpose than idle gossip, and communion with those who felt like-minded—were also valued by those around her. However, in regard to her outward world, sadly, she increasingly doubted the possibility that any level of this ideal would ever be within her reach. "Have had company today, but am not lonely now. I do not believe I was formed to depend upon the presence of a great many for my social contentment. And yet I like society, and enjoy it immensely when I do enjoy it. . . . How full of satisfaction life might be, if around the evening fire, heart met heart, and thought met and interpreted thought; if poetry and books of real worth were read in a social way and all the real interests of life were discussed." She continued to struggle with her sense of emotional isolation, while she simultaneously shunned the company of those people available. This dichotomy dominated her inner dialogue as it had in the past. She still had a deep longing for something more, but she increasingly blamed her own weaknesses regarding her inability to find peace. "We, some of us at least, get so hungry for our proper mental and spiritual food, get so famished, that the wild cry of the soul for its proper sentiment becomes *almost unendurable*. . . . We cannot always be strong and self-centered, self-reliant. Though there are times that this is possible, but when there are those around us to whom we naturally look for sympathy of thought, for love and a pure and holy intercourse of soul, who bring us only 'husks' instead, then we are weak, and cry out in spirit for strength to *endure*." In this entry her sense of betrayal manifested as self-loathing in which she berated herself for reliance on someone who had proved unworthy. Whether this person was Lewis is unclear, as Colby's entries only very rarely mention him. He physically was gone at least some of the spring and summer, as he "went South for cows" in March of 1864, but whether this dearth of notice was due solely to Lewis's physical absence or further evidence of escalating emotional absence is unverifiable.[13]

As 1864 continued, Colby felt a void, but despite her dissatisfaction she functioned in her outward life as society expected. She made fairly regular journal entries from the spring of 1864 until late that same summer. Although these notations reflect undertones of sadness, the urgency of her distress had eased back to apathy. Rather than extended soulful outpourings, she more often merely noted the mundane facts of her life, such as letters sent and received, company, daily activities, and attendance at the occasional Literary or Temperance Society meetings. She participated to varying degrees in the activities that made up the cultural fabric of her community. She still loathed and dreaded the task of visiting. "Have been visiting today—the third day in succession!! A most remarkable circumstance for me. And the day has seemed six weeks long. I do not know why, and the hours seemed to drag—as though they never would pass off. Oh I am less alone in the solitude of my own room, or out beneath the blue sky than elsewhere, and feel less pressure of the iron mask that perhaps all wear." Colby perceived that her outer life was predicated on a facade—an "iron mask"—so her grudging involvement in Ashtabula County's society did little to stave off her emotional isolation. As she noted, "I am less alone in the solitude of my own room." This attitude contributed to her increased dependence on the written word for solace. "Some pleasant hours, made sweet by the companionship of books have been mine and some new ones added to the home list of favorite volumes, 'Aurora Leigh,' 'Walden' & 'Tennyson's Poems' are among them, and much is the pleasure their society has given me."[14] Of course, Colby's notation about the "sweet" companionship provided by reading was not in itself odd. Books had long been vital components in her life; she had been an avid reader for years. Her diaries are full of notations regarding stories and authors; nonetheless, by 1863 the character of those observations changed, and a brief look back illustrates the nature of this difference.

During the latter years of the 1850s, her reading list was quite varied. Her fictional selections included classics, such as *Arabian Nights,* Daniel Defoe's *Robinson Crusoe,* and Shakespeare's *Coriolanus,* as well as popular domestic novels—the "romance" novels of the nineteenth century—by fashionable writers of the time, such as Catherine Marie Sedgwick, E. D. E. N. Southworth, and T. S. Arthur. She also enjoyed the autobiographies of important contemporaries and historical figures, and works that examined religious, historical, and scientific topics. In addition, she perused many newspapers and periodicals, including the *New York Tribune* and the *Atlantic Monthly.* Her journals provide consistent commentary regarding these many selections. An 1857 reading of *The Virginians* by William Thackeray left her unimpressed. "Can't say as it is yet very interesting, though I suppose it must be good from the reputation of its distinguished author." She gave Homer's *Iliad* higher praise. "It has strange interest for me, yet I think I cannot appreciate its merits. Ignorance has ever been a fatal barrier to my happiness, especially when reading a work of this kind. There are too many allusions that I do not understand that it mars the enjoyment of reading." She enjoyed *Rip Van Winkle* by Washington Irving, as well as *The Bride of an Evening* by E. D. E. N. Southworth, which she found "rather exciting [although] I wish I were less interested in works of fiction." She could not put down *Jane Eyre.* "Spent the evening with her last night, breakfasted with this morning, and sadly she interfered with work today. . . . There is a strange fascination in it. The authoress has a rare power of delineating character, of analyzing feeling and emotion. I like it very much, and yet I do not like the ending of the plot." Charlotte Brontë was a favorite and she had positive reactions to *Villete* and *The Professor.* In the autumn of 1859, she ventured into Charles Dickens' work, which received mixed reviews. "I finished reading 'Pickwick' last week . . . I suppose I shall lay myself liable to a charge of a lack of taste not to like it, but I must confess that I did not enjoy it as well as I expected." A week later, her next foray into Dickens was better received. "Commenced the day by lying in bed till half past seven reading 'Christmas books' by Dickens. I like it so much better than 'Pickwick.' Thus far the characters, though poor and lowly, some of them, are rich in soul. And how poor is all the other riches."[15]

These examples represent only a handful of the totality of comments Colby made throughout the 1850s, but what they have in common with the majority is the nature of her critiques. They have the tone of a fan and an amateur scholar. Although she sometimes complained about her lack of intellectual capacity, her comments, for the most part, were not confessional or consistently full of emotional angst. As Colby's more needful and personal connection to the words on paper began to emerge in the early 1860s, this tone clearly changed.

Also as a consequence of this need, her reading list narrowed. As her desire grew that books should provide a higher level of emotional support, she began to rely more exclusively on poetry. Her favorites in this regard included the Romantic era poems of William Wordsworth, Samuel Taylor Coleridge, and Percy Bysshe Shelley and the more contemporary Victorian styles of Elizabeth Barrett Browning, Alfred Tennyson, John Greenleaf Whittier, and Henry Wadsworth Longfellow.

Colby's experience with the written word corroborates historical scholarship that shows female reading was not merely "passive consumption of textually determined meanings"; women transferred their own meanings onto the written word. As Colby's needs changed, her choices evolved, as did the personal significance she assigned to her reading. She found that the "beauty" of Longfellow's poem *The Ladder of St. Augustine* "consists in the fitness it has to minister to my soul needs." She began to look for "truth" applicable to her own life within these works. She had a sympathetic bond with the "soul famished" character of Maggie in *The Mill on the Floss.* "There is more of truth, than of fiction, in the history of these heart struggles and to many persons life is but one long record of these heart struggles, that never find a fulfillment here. Will they ever?" Of Longfellow's poem, *The Courtship of Miles Standish,* she saw "many beautiful things in it, passages where Truth lends her beauty to Poetry and sanctified it forever." She often had found a sense of truth in poetry; although, in the past, that truth sometimes had inspired her. After late 1862, however, it more often served to underscore her unfulfilled aspirations and sense of isolation, rather than simply providing benign companionship or inspiration. As time passed, Colby displayed an increasing self-awareness of her growing dependence on books as intimate companions, as well as a realization of their inadequacy as a real substitute for human contact.[16]

No matter how inspiring the written word, she knew it still inadequately supplied the emotional support she felt she needed. This self-realization was often poignantly articulated. In March of 1862, Colby had written publicly about the power of Browning's words in *Aurora Leigh*: "We do not love to be disenchanted, even when we know we are idealizing; we love to think our reveries real . . . we fear the loss of our ideal. . . . Such were the fears with which I opened 'Aurora Leigh.' . . . I had learned to love, as well as admire the author . . . and love her too because she had given the world such a sublime example of what woman may become." A year later, in March of 1863, she privately noted the comforting influence of *Aurora Leigh,* but in her next entry, made only two weeks later, she spoke to the true feelings of loneliness in her life. "To night I'm wishing that within *calling distance,* were spirits with whom it were joy to meet, who would refresh the weary soul, by drawing me out of myself. Oh I remember one whose silent presence was a blessing, into whose *eyes* it were joy to look. *Oh Annie* how much we need thee here! And Jennie, where art thou, and hast thou found rest for thy spirit in some quiet spot, and learned indeed to 'starve the soul' and thereby found content? How sweet indeed were an hours communion with them, what strength would they give both to mind and body."[17] She clearly was disenchanted with the idea that words could provide a substitute for real companionship.

Human companionship remained her truest desire, but because she felt little hope in that regard she attempted to believe that the words on the page could offer real support. "Wish I had something *new* to read, for I'm *mentally hungry*, if not spiritually so. Then I've been wishing that the one true friend for whom I ever long so vainly, were near me, for a social chat would be so refreshing. But *no such friend have I*, so I commune with my own heart (a sad comfort at best) and hold silent intercourse with books and strive to be content. Have been reading Tennyson's 'Idylls of the Kings' [*sic*] this last week. I love to read his poems and never weary of them, and these I had never read before." She frequently noted sharing her day with Tennyson's works, as well as her favorite, *Aurora Leigh.* Clearly, poetry served a deep need that fiction could not, because unlike years past, by 1864 she only infrequently commented about reading other material. Nonetheless, despite her attempts to make poetry stand as a substitute for human companionship, she still felt that, in reality, she was "alone as all my life must be spent." She felt cheated that the poet's words failed to sustain her, but she failed herself as well—she had stopped writing. In the past, these two interlocking facets had acted as a salve for her dissatisfaction, but as previously noted, by 1864 her writing had ground to a halt. Colby herself noted in her journal several times, with disgust, that she had "wrote none," or had "written none."[18]

Her day-to-day life continued as it had in years past, but the outlets she had used to balance against the unhappiness and dissatisfaction no longer acted as adequate substitutes. For a time, her passion for social justice had helped to make up for the lack of "higher culture" in her immediate life. Her campaigns for abolition, temperance, and women's rights had provided her a foray into a wider public arena and a link to a higher life. When her will to battle seemed to fail, other authors provided that link to a degree, but not even the best poetry could cure her "soul solitude." Her life continued to drag on in a sort of "half-life," her "inner self unknown," and by the end of the summer of 1864, Colby grew weary of even journal writing. She felt she had nothing new to record. One of her last entries in 1864 noted sadly, "My outer life gives little variety . . . and the inner life has no voice."[19]

Colby's inner life truly appeared to have been quieted, and as such she was left only with her outward world, the unrelenting role of housewife. Over the years, Colby's private words often linked her outer life's responsibilities with her mental and physical weariness and increasing sense of hopelessness. As the 1860s unfolded, Colby detailed her specific duties even less than before, but commented more frequently as to the sameness and relentlessness of those tasks as well as the effect she felt they had on her well being. Catharine Beecher glorified women's subordinate role as one that was voluntary and necessary for the success of a republican nation. Ironically, Beecher also documented her findings that in general women more often were sick than well, and that chronic illnesses were common among them. Historical research that examines the existence and treatment of this nineteenth-century condition, termed by contemporaries as the "hysterical" female, concludes that role conflict may have been the major underlying factor in these illnesses. The often significant inconsistencies between the ideals of female socialization and the realities of the life of an actual wife and mother may have precipitated some women's regression into "hysteria." This hysteria could have served as an unconscious method to register their dissatisfaction with life. The effects of this role conflict also could be registered in the less severe symptoms that nineteenth-century doctors found in many women, such as nervousness, depression, crying, chronic fatigue, and disabling pain.[20]

Over the years, Colby frequently noted physical and emotional symptoms that were similar to those described, and although none of these incapacitated her, she did show signs that they affected her daily life. The most severe signs of this "hysteria" coincided with the time period in which Colby stopped actively fighting societal expectations. The unanswerable question remains: did she stop fighting because her depression grew too stultifying or did her depression grow because she stopped fighting? The infrequent entries made in 1864 and the extremely infrequent ones from 1865 illustrate her obvious depression, but do not clearly display a sequence of cause and effect—perhaps because they are too intertwined to realistically separate. Clearly, the idea that she would never fulfill the aspirations in her life affected her physical and emotional health. More than once she mentioned that she even contemplated death.

From the July 1864 entry in which Colby noted the unrelenting sameness in her life until February of 1865, only two entries were made. In the February 1865 entry, she demonstrated an even darker and more hopeless attitude. "Months have passed without a record. . . . But alas so changed am I from the old time self that I used to know, that I almost fail to recognize my inner self. . . . And we all mask our real, sad selves from the unpitying gaze of the cold world. We put by our dead selves, bury our own dead hopes, and toil on, the *semblance* of *the being* that once lived, loved and hoped, as well as toiled. And yet how strange and unreal it all seems; so ghostly and how shadowy we feel, poor miserable bodies, with the souls of life gone from out of us, ever while we live. And yet we must wait."[21] She clearly felt as if her life were merely a sham. She no longer really lived, but only existed until death claimed her. She made only infrequent entries after this one and none of them gave any indication that her assertion of "dead hopes" was inaccurate. She was not writing for publication, and the few entries made were less about personal exploration and more informational in nature. She had—at this point—given up any dream of claiming a different life.

Regardless of her lack of hope, the spring of 1865 brought change for Colby and the entire nation. After years of bloody battles and a final, nine-month siege at St. Petersburg, Virginia, Sherman's infamous "march to the sea" secured victory for the Union forces. On April 9, 1865, four years to the day after the shots at Fort Sumter, General Robert E. Lee surrendered to General Ulysses S. Grant, and the Civil War was over. The formidable task of reforming and rebuilding a unified nation began on a tragic note with the assassination of President Lincoln the very next week. Sadly, the nation experienced unprecedented human loss over the war years: 620,000 lives lost and another 400,000 injuries. Apart from the human loss, other major changes also significantly altered the country's future. The South's economy and parts of its landscape were decimated by the war. The North's economy had experienced significant shifts, particularly in the form of increased industrialization. American society as a whole was altered permanently.

In northeastern Ohio, rapid shifts in the dairy industry were on the horizon. The forces of modernization had been operating to affect the way of life for many Americans, particularly in the North, for quite some time. Well into mid-century, dairy families had been able to incorporate modern technologies and participate in the national markets while they remained, in many ways, preindustrial. Dairy families had operated on a seasonal schedule, controlled their own work process, and owned their own land and tools, but major changes were in the works by the end of the Civil War. The wartime blockades of Southern markets forced the expansion of overseas markets that subsequently raised prices significantly. This rise in prices encouraged the fledgling enterprise of cheese "factories" to produce more cheese. Between 1860 and 1875, centralized cheese production became a profitable alternative for a few entrepreneurs, and home-based operations became increasingly obsolete. In addition, modernization forces, particularly improvements in transportation and communication, and also economic diversification and expanding educational opportunities, slowly created new visions of future opportunity. Change was everywhere. The war had ended and economic progress became the national agenda. "Progress" in the dairy business necessarily resulted in the decline in home-based cheese production. By 1885, 90 percent of all cheese was factory made. This decline altered the fabric of life in "cheesedom." As many of its citizens sought the economic brass ring, Cherry Valley's stable community drifted away. In particular, many second- and third-generation Ohio dairy farmers were ready by war's end to take advantage of these perceived opportunities.[22] The Colbys were among those dairy farmers who left the business and moved on. Consequently, despite Colby's apathy, her life was about to change drastically. Change, however, is not always progress, so whether this different life revived her "dead hopes" is more difficult to determine.

CHAPTER TWELVE

February 1865–July 1900

"If I only could leave behind all the darkness . . . and forget the past"

IN FEBRUARY OF 1865, Colby returned home after visiting and was somewhat surprised to find that their home was "no longer ours." She never articulated specific reasons for the decision to sell or the subsequent move. Possibly, the family dairy already was experiencing the effects of the decline of the home dairy industry. Lewis also may have anticipated an opportunity to take advantage of the booming economy in a less laborious field. Regardless of her apparent lack of control over the decision to sell the house, Colby did not register any deep despair over the impending move. Despite the fact that Cherry Valley was the site where "every tie of my life has been formed," she never had been satisfied with the community as a whole. She noted only that she would miss the fields, woods, and flowers: "for *I love them all* with a love as strong as death." Those aspects of nature had been like "friends" who always offered their "silent sympathy." She made no claims of that type about her family or neighbors. She also anticipated that relocation could provide new opportunity and renew her sense of hope. "Oh if I only could leave behind all the darkness and gloom that has thrown its dark pall over me here and emerge into the clear sunlight of happiness, and forget the past." The official end of the war just two months after the sale also may have acted to fuel that hope.[1]

On April 11, 1865, Colby started writing a letter to a friend that illustrates this slightly more hopeful mood. This note—it is unknown whether she finished and mailed it—coincided with the week after the Confederate Army surrendered, but before President Lincoln's assassination. In it, Colby expressed her wish to see "Friend Nellie" once the "roads get good." The women evidently had been passing along shared copies of the *Atlantic Monthly* because Colby apologized for a delayed delivery in March. The two friends also were sharing a copy of a manuscript—whose authorship is unclear—with at least one other woman. Colby was planning to include a copy of this manuscript along with suggestions about where it should be sent for possible publication. She also provided her thoughts about a new poem of John Greenleaf Whittier's, "The Eternal Goodness," as well as the forum in which she read it: an unknown publication she referred to only as the "Baptist." Her comments demonstrate that Colby retained her irreverent attitude regarding orthodoxy. She noted the paper provided "nearly *three columns* of comment upon it which was so *liberal* in its tone considering it was written by the Editor of a Baptist paper that the commentary *surprised* me as much as the poem pleased." Colby did complain that she had nothing new to read, but her tone lacked the deep melancholy of her journal entries leading up to this point.[2]

The few entries she made between April 1865 and the family's move later that summer, however, demonstrate that her melancholy had not dissipated completely. She may have felt the move carried hope with it, but as they began the process of leaving, she remained balanced on the edge of despondency. By May of 1865, the family was living in a rented home in Cherry Valley, and Colby began to say her goodbyes. The bonds that Colby felt most distressed about breaking, however, were not human ones. Her attachment to the living natural world around her has been noted, but in the final weeks of May 1865, she had to say an even more difficult farewell. Her comments regarding her visit to Plummer's gravesite demonstrate that her hope was precarious at best. She noted, "went to the graveyard and sat down upon the grass by that little mound over which roses and lilies have run wild for twelve weary years. . . . Pleasant was the companionship of the hour [a copy of the *Atlantic Monthly*] and of the scene [Plummer's grave], and yet as the human heart ever must, I longed oh so intensely for *one true soul* to whom I could give frank utterance to every thought and feeling, and win the same in return. I felt *alone* in the world, and this utter solitude is full of bitterness."[3] Colby's longing for worthy companionship echoed earlier laments about her dissatisfying home life, and she clearly was unhappy still, but at least one of the most restrictive impediments on her path to contentment—her relationship with in-laws—was no longer a factor.

As previously noted, Lewis's parents, David and Naomi Colby, had both passed away. Naomi's death in 1863, perhaps, severed some significant ties of obligation to the area. However, although the remainder of Colby's extended family displayed varying degrees of mobility over the next several decades, much of the Rice family stayed in Cherry Valley. Colby's father, Joel Rice, remarried again after Evelina Rice's death. He also outlived this third wife, Dorcas Barker Rice, who died in 1873. Joel remained in Cherry Valley until his death in 1881, living most of his last decades with his son, Jay Joel Rice. Jay had returned from Civil War service in June of 1865 and had married. He and his wife, Jennie, had one son, also named Joel Rice. Jay and Jennie Rice also remained in Cherry Valley until their deaths in 1905 and 1915, respectively. Colby's oldest, and only full brother, John Bradley Rice, lost his first wife and son in 1865. He remarried in 1868, and he, his wife Christina August, and their five children also stayed in Cherry Valley. Later correspondence places Colby's sisters, Cirlissa and Flavia, in the Cherry Valley area as well. Colby's other sister, Cordelia, remained in Illinois, living in a small community called Blackberry in Kane County, but she too eventually returned to Cherry Valley, most likely after the death of her husband in the early 1880s. Another Rice sibling ended up in Illinois; Napoleon Rice and his family settled in Aurora, also in Kane County.[4]

The Colby clan showed a bit more mobility after the war. Colby's daughter, Vine, wrote a letter to her Uncle Orrin not long after her family's move in which she noted that "no Colbys" were left in Cherry Valley. This note was true, for the most part. Orrin Colby had left Cherry Valley years back and ended up in Nebraska. David and Emily Colby (Annie's parents) separated some time after Annie's 1861 death. Emily Colby remained in Cherry Valley—living alone, as all three of her children died early deaths—until her death in 1875. Vine's letter noted that "uncle David" had moved to Madison, Ohio. This relocation is confirmed by the 1880 census, which also shows that he had remarried and was the father of a ten-year-old son. Ned Colby remarried after Annie's death, and he and his family, as well as his parents, Rowell and Abigail Colby, remained in Silver Creek, Illinois, in Stephenson County, which is some eighty miles west of Kane County. At some point after the war, Lewis's "crippled" Uncle Cyrus also moved in with them. Not long after the Civil War's end, Colby and her family left Ohio and joined these Illinois transplants. By the spring of 1866, the Colbys had settled in Freeport, also in Stephenson County, and begun the next stage of their lives.[5]

Freeport, Illinois, is perhaps best known as the site of the famous Lincoln-Douglas debate in which Stephen Douglas proposed the so-called "Freeport Doctrine," regarding slavery and territories' rights. The area was, in many ways, not unlike Cherry Valley: a dairy-producing region with a rural landscape not that different from northeastern Ohio. Despite these similarities, the Colbys' lives in Illinois actually differed considerably from the ones they had led in Ohio. The most significant changes resulted from the fact that the family no longer engaged in farming. The family also lived within the city itself, which would have meant a realignment of daily practices. Lewis operated his own business as a lightning rod salesman, and Colby's presumed duties centered on the private home. Their location and Lewis's job likely required increased immersion in the market and cash economy. His business venture must have been at least moderately successful because by 1870 the family had a live-in housekeeper. Another rather important difference, for Rose and Colby in particular, was that all three children attended public school. Up to this point, likely as a result of Rose's prolonged illness, Colby had taught her at home.[6]

Despite the fact that her children attended school and that Colby no longer engaged in the arduous and time-consuming farm tasks, her life as a middle-class housewife was not one of leisure, even with additional household assistance. Catharine Beecher's expanded version of her domestic advice book, published initially in 1869, made clear that even with domestic help and modern conveniences, such as cook stoves, furnaces, and indoor piped water, the American women's responsibilities were still immense. In addition, the expectations for managing a "city" household as well as maintaining the social obligations of the "middle-class wife" represented a new aspect of woman's sphere to which Colby would not have been completely accustomed. The subtitle of Beecher's book goes a long way in articulating the prevailing ideas about what a "housewife's" duties should encompass. It was quite an expectation: *Principles of Domestic Science: Being a Guide to the Formation and Maintenance of Economical, Healthful, Beautiful and Christian Homes.*[7]

Regardless of this pressure to comply with societal standards, she had shed at least some of the more arduous farm tasks. Thus, if Colby still had a passion for the pursuit of intellectual endeavors and reform interests, then compared to farm life, she surely had more available time. Despite this change in lifestyle and the removal of some of the drudgery, no clear evidence demonstrates that her retreat into apathy, so apparent while still in Ohio, had lessened. The Colbys remained in Freeport until late in 1870, and for the majority of this stay no personal correspondence, only a few scraps of manuscript writing, and no additional publications can be located. If Colby was writing for private or public purposes, then she did so only very sparingly. In early 1870, this hiatus came to a brief end, and she wrote a flurry of pieces focused on varied subjects. This series of publications apparently represented only a temporary burst of writing energy; they are the only publications located from this decade. Although she focused on other topics, such as temperance, many of these pieces—like her work from a half-decade prior—were children's stories. Contrary to the majority, several essays were reminiscent of her earlier strong-minded work.[8]

A letter to the editor of the *Ashtabula Sentinel* in February of 1870 articulated her thoughts on her home of four years. According to Colby, although Freeport had positive attributes, it was not entirely the community she had hoped. She highlighted some positive qualities. Freeport had a good high school that prepared children for college. It also offered somewhat adequate cultural opportunities, such as theater and lectures. In contrast, she complained about the lack of organized reform opportunities. In regard to temperance, she noted that while there were sixty saloons, the town had only two badly organized temperance societies, which were "little more than names." She was especially disappointed that no organized suffrage movement existed. "Well, this is not a progressive atmosphere, not an atmosphere in which such heresies as woman's rights dare strike root, or could flourish." Colby noted her frustration that Anna Dickinson (a women's rights speaker who was touring Illinois) had not dared to enter the "unfriendly atmosphere of Freeport, and has never stopped to lecture." In another piece, she spoke on the lack of support for the supposed benevolent duties of the "Daughters of Rebekah," which was the female group—made up primarily of wives—affiliated with the Odd Fellows, a fraternal service organization. In a sarcastic tone, she asked, "But seriously, what are the privileges and duties of the Daughters of Rebekah? Are we only silent partners . . . or have we 'rights' that Odd Fellows 'are bound to respect'?"[9] Little evidence exists from this half-decade in Freeport, so it is difficult to describe with certainty the state of mind that prompted the reassertion of public views, but perhaps knowledge of their next destination gave her a renewed sense of hope.

On the horizon was a change in circumstances that definitely would have pleased Colby. In January of 1870, after fifteen years of considerable battling and three years after the state legislator advised them to do so, the University of Michigan finally altered its policies to allow women to enroll as equal students. The first woman entered the University of Michigan immediately after this decision in January of 1870, and in September of 1870, thirty-three women were added to the class. These women represented just 3 percent of total enrollment. Although the University of Michigan was not the first college to allow women or even the first state school to do so, it was the largest and arguably the university with the "highest prestige" west of New England to alter its policy. Vine Colby graduated from high school in Freeport in June of 1870, and soon afterwards the Colbys moved to Ann Arbor, Michigan, where Vine entered as a freshman at the University of Michigan.[10]

Colby had long emphasized the importance of education, for her daughters as well as her son, as a means to attain personal fulfillment and become productive citizens. Her own lack of education was a subject of constant distress to her, and she repeatedly remarked on her wish that all her children would have better opportunities. Her eldest daughter's attendance at a major university must have given her great joy. This joy was not universal. The Ann Arbor community, which surrounded the school, was not in complete acceptance of this notion of female college students in their midst. A history of women at the University of Michigan notes that those early attendees "had to possess exceptional ability, exceptional motivation, for all of them remembered meeting discrimination and prejudice in the first years." One of those prejudices manifested as a difficulty to find lodging, which was likely one of the reasons the entire family moved to Ann Arbor when Vine began school. Another reason, no doubt, was anticipation that Branch and eventually Rose would attend as well, which they did. All three children graduated from the University of Michigan.[11]

Vine entered school at the University of Michigan in 1870. She married a fellow student, Sidney Foster, on December 19, 1873—Colby's forty-sixth birthday—but contrary to what would have been a common occurrence for many nineteenth-century newlyweds, their marriage did not signify the end of her education. Interestingly, her decision to marry was actually an uncommon choice for University of Michigan female students. Before 1900, only slightly more than half of Michigan female graduates married as compared to almost three-quarters of women in the general population. Vine and her husband both continued with school; Sidney Foster graduated in 1874 and Vine graduated from the College of Literature, Science and the Arts with her B.Ph. in 1876. The couple then moved to Keokuk, Iowa, where they both graduated from medical school in 1877. This accomplishment placed her at the forefront of the pioneering surge of women who earned medical degrees between 1870 and the mid-1880s. During the mid- to late nineteenth-century, medicine offered one of the most accessible professions for women to enter. Physicians' status as professionals still was a bit doubtful; consequently, their professional organizations were less rigid, unlike, for example, attorneys, who required a state's approval to legally practice law. Therefore, it was easier for women to establish medical practices. After Vine and Sidney graduated, the couple moved to northern New York, just south of the Canadian border, where they operated a joint medical practice in Moira, until Vine's untimely death in March of 1878 from pelvic peritonitis. She was only twenty-five years old.[12]

Branch was the next to enter the University of Michigan, and he graduated with his B.S. in 1877. After graduate-level training, he then embarked on a career in engineering that spanned over forty very successful years. Almost immediately after graduation, he was named United States Assistant Engineer with the Mississippi River Commission. This position required that he work in the field quite a bit, but he made his home base in Flint, Michigan, where his family lived in the early 1880s. While living in Ann Arbor, Branch had met a "school

Vine Colby Foster's student portrait from the University of Michigan, c. 1876. She was the first of Colby's children to graduate from college and went on to become a doctor before passing away at age twenty-five. Used by permission University of Michigan Student Portrait Collection, Bentley Historical Library, University of Michigan, Ann Arbor, Michigan.

chum" of Rose's, Minnie Bary, who, after her own graduation from the University of Michigan, worked as a Latin and Greek teacher in Detroit, Michigan. On June 28, 1883, Branch and Minnie Bary married. The couple settled in St. Louis, Missouri—although Branch still traveled quite frequently—and within several years were the parents of two daughters: Vine and Dorothy. Whether Minnie continued to teach in the early years after their marriage is unclear, but unlikely as many school systems did not allow or strongly discouraged married teachers, especially women with children. In 1889, Branch was appointed to a special project by the sewer commissioner of the City of St. Louis—the position he advanced to himself in 1895. The family remained in St. Louis until the United States entered the First World War, when Branch was recruited to work for the government as a civilian civil engineer. This service took him to various locations where he supervised engineering projects. While stationed at his final wartime location, Jacksonville, Florida, Minnie fell ill and died in April of 1919. At the close of the war, Branch took an engineering position in Alabama where he suffered an almost fatal heart attack in 1920 from which he never fully recovered. This attack marked the end of his career. He moved to Normal, Illinois, in the autumn of 1920 and spent the remainder of his life living with his sister, Rose, before succumbing to his weak heart in January of 1933.[13]

Branch Harris Colby's student portrait from the University of Michigan, c. 1877. After graduation, Branch went on to have a very successful career in engineering. Used by permission University of Michigan Student Portrait Collection, Bentley Historical Library, University of Michigan, Ann Arbor, Michigan.

Rose graduated from Ann Arbor High School and entered the University of Michigan in 1874. She graduated in 1878 with her A.B. degree and then taught high school in Ann Arbor for a brief time. The family then moved to Flint, Michigan, where she taught high school from 1880 through 1883. In 1883, she returned to school, first at the Harvard Annex (Radcliffe's precursor) and then back to the University of Michigan where she received her A.M. degree in 1885. In 1886, she earned one of the first Ph.D. degrees awarded to a woman by the University of Michigan. Unable to initially obtain a professorship, she again taught high school, this time in Peoria, Illinois. In 1892, the Illinois State Normal University (ISNU) in Normal, Illinois, offered her a position as a professor of literature—only the third female professor in the school's thirty-five-year history. She spent the remaining years of her career as a highly popular and successful English literature professor as well as the preceptress, or the Dean of Women, at ISNU. Rose also inherited her mother's passion for social justice. As an active participant in the women's suffrage movement, she worked in Michigan and Illinois

June Rose Colby's student portrait from the University of Michigan, c. 1878. Rose eventually became one of the first women to earn her Ph.D. from the University of Michigan and then spent almost two decades as a professor of literature at the Illinois State Normal University. Used by permission: University of Michigan Student Portrait Collection, Bentley Historical Library, University of Michigan, Ann Arbor, Michigan.

to obtain the vote for women and had a reputation among her students for her strident support for the cause. She officially retired in 1931, but remained a part of the university family until her death in 1941. At the time of her death, she was still so highly regarded in the community at large that the local newspaper devoted a two-column story and picture as well as an editorial celebrating her life and accomplishments. Twenty years after Rose's death, ISNU broke ground on a new residence hall that still bears her name—Colby Hall.[14]

After Lewis and Colby moved to Michigan in 1870, they relocated several times in the next decade as the children's situations changed. They lived in Ann Arbor until Rose relocated to Flint in 1880 to teach, and then the entire family moved there. During the latter half of the 1860s and the 1870s, Lewis worked at several different jobs. The economy of this time afforded the daring with possibilities of "getting rich," and Lewis apparently attempted to achieve this goal primarily through sales. He was a grocery salesman, a meat salesman, a "traveling agent," and a "commercial agent," presumably also some sort of sales job. These jobs kept him on the road for long stretches of time. Perhaps his years traveling, the tension between Lewis and Colby, or events unknown affected his relationship with his children because—similar to their childhood years—it is unclear what sort of role he played within the family. Lewis's name rarely, if ever, appears in any of his children's extant personal documents. In contrast, their regard and love for their mother is obvious; later in life, Branch and Rose both credit their mother as an inspiration. For example, Rose's brief biography in the 1932 Illinois State Normal University's *Index* noted that "her early education was gained at home from her mother, a woman of unusual gifts." Beyond her role as mother to her adult children and the wife of an absentee husband, Colby's activities during the 1870s are unclear. Extant sources provide insight into Lewis's businesses and the children's college years and subsequent careers, but no direct evidence illustrates any details of Colby's life in this decade.[15] In the past, writing served as Colby's primary means of personal enrichment, so this dearth of evidence implies that, similar to the latter half of the 1860s, she devoted little time during the 1870s to cultivating her inner life.

In late 1881, however, an outburst of activity seems to signify a change in circumstance and/or attitude for Colby. The most notable difference was that she was writing again. She produced at least three long essays for publication in the final two months of 1881 alone and continued writing regularly over the next two decades. Evidence of Colby's correspondence from the early 1880s is also abundant. She wrote to friends and family and renewed ties to past reform acquaintances, such as Frances Dana Gage. Gage's response, written to Colby on May 16, 1882, reminisced about her visit to Cherry Valley over twenty years prior and how she could not forget "the night spent at your home or the two bright sweet little girls Vine & Rose, as for our talks I only remember we *talked* and I guess you did me as much good as I did you, maybe more." The Colby household also received three letters from women's rights activist Lucy Stone during the span of 1881 through 1883. Unfortunately, Stone's extremely sloppy handwriting makes it difficult to ascertain whether the letters were addressed to Miss or Mrs. Colby. Suffrage work was the topic, so context does not solve the puzzle, as both Colby and her daughter Rose were interested in women's rights. Rose's early 1882 contribution to Stone's *Woman's Journal* points to her as the possible letter recipient; however, Stone had visited Ohio many times as an antebellum reform speaker, so it is possible that Colby instigated their acquaintance. Colby also reached out to other reform icons. A letter received as a response to a request, also from May of 1882, contains Sojourner Truth's "mark" and a note as to how to purchase her picture and autobiography.[16]

The lives of both children also took big turns during the early 1880s. Rose resumed her education in 1883, and Branch married and moved his home base to St. Louis in the fall of 1883. Interestingly, Colby's reemergence, as well as her children's moves, coincide with Lewis's apparent absence from the family. The Colby Collection offers substantial information, confirmed by other sources, that places Colby and her children in the first half of the 1880s, but by 1882, Lewis's name simply disappears from the family papers. Other sources support the fact that the family apparently was living together in Flint as late as possibly 1882 or even 1883. By the fall of 1884, however, Colby and Rose were living in Ann Arbor on their own, and nothing in the family documents definitively explains Lewis's absence. Interestingly, Colby made out a new last will and testament in November 1883, in which she denoted her two children as sole beneficiaries, but made no mention of Lewis. In addition, subsequent sources—an 1891–92 city directory and the 1900 census—designate Colby's status as a widow, all of which would seem to imply that Lewis died prior to November of 1883. Nevertheless, other evidence counters that interpretation.[17]

Michigan death records show that an eighty-five-year-old man named Lewis Colby died in Livingston County, Michigan, in March of 1913. According to census and marriage records, this Lewis Colby spent the last thirty years of his life in Pinckney, Michigan, which is just south of Flint in Livingston County and slightly northwest of Ann Arbor. On September 5, 1883, he and a widow named Harriet M. Darrow married and settled in her Pinckney home, where Lewis worked as a gardener. Of course, coincidental timing and a corresponding name do not conclusively lead to the conclusion that this Lewis Colby was Colby's husband. Nonetheless, the available vital information regarding this man's birth date (either September or October 3, 1827), birth place (Enfield, New Hampshire), and parents' names (David Colby and [illegible] Johnson) match too closely with the known details about Colby's husband, Lewis—who was born on October 3, 1827 in Enfield to David Colby and Naomi Johnson— to be dismissed. Pre-twentieth-century divorce decrees are often very difficult, if not impossible, to locate, so although no divorce records can be found to corroborate this conclusion, the preponderance of the evidence points to the interpretation that sometime between 1881 and 1883, Lewis and Celestia Rice Colby parted ways.[18]

If this interpretation is correct, what implications could this turn of events have had for Colby as she continued on with her life? Scholarship examining nineteenth-century divorce has increased over the last two decades, but no absolute and overriding consensus regarding its ultimate meaning in women's lives has been reached. Much like thoughts regarding divorce today, difficulty ensues when attempting to narrow interpretations to provide concise conclusions applicable to an individual. However, one aspect of nineteenth-century divorce is clear: the divorce rate was rising, and this rise had people talking. Talk centered on what the rise implied about society and what should be done about it. Reform proponents made their case for both liberalizing and tightening existing laws governing divorce. Culturally, the battle was fought in print; for example, editor and divorce critique Horace Greeley used the pages of the *New York Tribune* to call for reform, and novelists, such as E. D. E. N. Southworth, glorified marriage in her fiction. Legislatively, individual states responded in different ways. Some states eased restrictions, while others made it more difficult to obtain divorces; however, regardless of any cultural pressures to the contrary, by 1888, only South Carolina did not allow divorce.[19]

This nationwide debate also prompted a government-sponsored study. In 1889, the first phase of this research concluded that between 1870 and 1880 the divorce rate grew one and a half times faster than the rate of population. Between 1877 and 1881, the absolute number of divorces nationwide increased 30 percent over the previous five-year span. By 1886, the annual number of divorces in America numbered over 25,000, up from 10,000 only twenty years prior, and women made up the majority of petitioners. The rising numbers fueled the divorce debate, and regardless whether reformers wanted divorce laws tightened or liberalized, their rationales often were grounded in ideas about what was "best" for families. This type of thorny conundrum also grounds differences in historical interpretations regarding divorce and women. Statistics, although helpful, cannot fully answer the more intuitive uncertainty of why so many people chose divorce as an option. Did divorce—for women in particular—reflect raised expectations regarding marriage in which divorce freed women from the "endless pursuit of the perfect marriage" in order to consider their own needs? Or did it merely reflect society's grudging acceptance of acts—for the most part by men—of desertion: economically, physically, or emotionally? As one historian notes, "as men created de facto divorces, women sought out legal ones."[20]

The fact that most nineteenth-century divorce requests—two-thirds nationally—came from women is often cited as strong support for the notion that women left unsatisfying but intact marriages in order to find individual fulfillment. The argument is grounded partially in the view that when a society embraces the idea that marriage is based on love and mutual respect, then the lack of those ideals should be sufficient cause for societally sanctioned marriage dissolution. This ideal, however, is not evident in the reasons most often cited for nineteenth-century separation. Legal justifications for divorce had little to do with notions of love; instead, they were grounded in societal ideas about proper roles. In addition, studies show that the official reasons for separation varied based on gender. Women most often filed for divorce on the grounds that their husbands had in some way abandoned them. These decrees cite that husbands had failed to monetarily support them, forced them into the labor force, or indulged in nonsocially sanctioned activities like excessive drinking or gambling. Men's complaints more often centered on either proof of premarital sex or a woman's failure to adequately satisfy a husband's perception regarding conjugal, maternal, or domestic obligations. Of course, the use of the available legal remedies does not preclude the notion that women's underlying reasons for seeking divorce did not ultimately lay in greater expectations regarding companionate marriage. Abundant historical scholarship supports this inter- pretation. However, some recent studies conclude that in reality, women often were acting to terminate marriages already informally dissolved by husbands who had abandoned them in pursuit of another woman or economic opportu- nities. In essence, this interpretation finds that the decision to seek a remedy for a detrimental marriage more often was grounded in pragmatic reasons than it was based on higher ideals about personal fulfillment.[21]

The lack of direct evidence illustrating even the basic facts regarding the Col- bys' separation renders it difficult to determine how Colby fits into the broader context of interpretations concerning nineteenth-century divorce. In reality, they may not have been even legally divorced. The practice of "self-divorce" was not uncommon in the nineteenth century. Lewis could have settled into a long-term relationship and even "married" without the benefit of an actual legal divorce. The idea that Lewis left the marriage is a plausible one. Despite the fact that census records and city directories place him in Flint through 1882, the realities of his day-to-day life are unknown. Family records provide no clear indication as to his living status after the late 1870s, and his 1883 marriage record actually places him in Akron, Ohio, working as a merchant. Over the years, Lewis's sales jobs required him to travel extensively, and he likely stayed in boarding houses while on the road.[22] As a widowed woman with her own home, Harriet Darrow would have been a prime example of a typical boarding housekeeper, so perhaps he met her through his travels and began a relationship. This interpretation is only speculation, but twenty years prior to this point, Colby had hinted at in- fidelity on his part, so the idea that Lewis may have sought satisfaction away from home is not without precedent.

Regardless whether Lewis left first, if the couple legally divorced, then sta- tistics support the idea that Colby initiated it. Nationally, women filed two- thirds of nineteenth-century divorce petitions, but in the west and north cen- tral United States, which included Illinois, Indiana, Michigan, and Ohio, that rate was considerably higher. Nonsupport was the most common ground, and Lewis leaving her for another woman certainly would have qualified in that regard. However, cruelty—which was an extremely flexible ground—was the fastest-growing reason, and under that umbrella the idea that Colby chose to divorce him, for reasons other than abandonment or infidelity, is plausible. Her

personal frustration may have grown to a point where she could no longer justify staying in a dissatisfying marriage. Her earlier private words certainly could
be used as evidence to support the interpretation that she left the marriage in
order to find individual fulfillment. Possibly also of great significance is that
Branch and Rose may have reached a point where they had sufficient means
to provide financial support; consequently reducing what may have been an
important consideration in Colby's life—worries about money. Alimony, if
awarded—and that happened only very infrequently—most often came in the
form of a one-time, lump-sum payment. Therefore, much like the present, unless a woman had independent means, divorce in the 1880s often negatively
impacted women's financial situations.[23]

Despite the rise in sheer numbers of divorces in the latter half of the nineteenth century, it was still relatively rare. During the 1880s, only one in fourteen
to sixteen marriages ended that way. In addition, the national debate over its
status ensured that divorce remained a subject of considerable social stigma.
One historian states that women's willingness to sue for divorce within this social milieu reflected their "quest for identity, order, and respectability generated
by the penetration of state law into . . . family life once regulated by religious
and community norms." However, this same historian also notes that divorce's
negative cultural connotations led many women to opt for "passing" as spin-
sters or widows. Colby apparently did "pass" as a widow and this confounds
attempts to offer interpretations regarding her situation. Unfortunately, only
speculation can be made regarding the true termination of their marriage, and
all interpretations have a primary weakness—why, after more than thirty years
together, did one of them make the decision to leave? Without personal documents, or at least a divorce filing case, the exact sequence of events and emotions may well be lost, but what is known for sure is that after Lewis's removal
from her life, Colby's course continued on a new path and in many ways joined
Rose's journey.[24] The fact that she remained with Rose should not lead to an
interpretation that Colby did not also live her own life. In fact, in many ways
she seems to have blossomed after the early 1880s.

This "blossoming" contributes to the notion that whether Colby chose to
leave her marriage or not, she achieved a sense of growing satisfaction as a
single woman. This satisfaction may have been rooted in her ability to finally
embark on a personal "quest for identity" and live in the outward world as her
inner life dictated. Nevertheless, as noted, despite this emergence of activity,
Colby may have felt a sense of social stigma regarding her status. Colby, or even
possibly Rose, apparently provided misleading information while living in Peoria and later in Normal by designating Colby a widow. Perhaps after moving

to Illinois—a state Colby previously had declared not a progressive one—she wished to avoid possible ignominy, not only for herself but also for her daughter and simply allowed the implied conclusion to endure: a woman over sixty who lived with her unmarried daughter was likely a widow. It also must be noted that records, such as directories and census returns, often contain errors—contributed by both those reporting data and those collecting it—so it is difficult to ascertain how much intent to actually deceive existed.

It is also difficult to ascertain what Colby's friends and family knew or thought about the situation. Correspondence with the extended Colby clan is noticeably absent after 1880. Whether this absence signifies that no correspondence ever existed or that Colby chose not to keep it is unknown; however, either scenario easily can be interpreted as a sign of less than amicable relationships. She did keep in close touch with many extended Rice family members, as well as friends, but discussions regarding Lewis are absent in these letters, including those between Colby and her son. Lewis's name is also noticeably absent from family papers, such as genealogical notes and private essays. For example, Rose's family tree lists her father's name and her parent's marriage, but gives no indication of his death. Consequently, personal papers add little to the understanding of the family's view of Colby's status, except the obvious fact that they remained part of her life. What the evidence does imply is that Colby's family life had evolved into a happier and more supportive network.

Colby received regular letters from both Branch and his wife Minnie. These letters are filled with the usual news about the family's health and activities, including assurances regarding visits and correspondence. As a former teacher, Minnie especially was concerned about her children's education and—like her mother-in-law had done years earlier—taught them at home for a time. Also like Colby, the love of literature clearly had passed to a new generation if the following note regarding Colby's then seven-year-old granddaughter Vine serves as an accurate indicator. Minnie observed that Branch was reading *The Odyssey* out loud "to his, Vine's & my great enjoyment." Correspondence also shows that despite the distance between them, Colby valued herself as a regular part of Branch's family. They saw each other as much as possible, and a letter written to "my dear little Vine" after one of these visits illustrates Colby's strong feelings for her granddaughters. "I think of you every hour of the day and sometimes dream of you at night. . . . I love you and Dorothy too. . . . Good night my darling and kiss little Dorothy on both cheeks and both lips and on every one of her ten fingers and toes for me—and I wish I could give you as many."[25]

During the 1880s and 1890s, Colby still centered much of her life on her children and grandchildren, and she was also involved in the outward world in a more direct fashion. Although her family correspondence often was filled with typical family update material, these letters also show Colby's interest in issues beyond births and deaths, especially the letters between Colby and Cordelia, who had relocated back to Cherry Valley by this point, and Colby and her niece, Eva Davis (Cordelia's daughter). These letters contain occasional references to women's issues, such as the importance of equality of the sexes and the existence of double standards. In 1892, Eva wrote Colby a letter in which she discussed voting rights. Eva noted that she had received a "letter from Aunt Flavia [Colby's sister] to day. She also is ready for the ballot and has political ideas as well as any men." Apparently, time had brought Colby's sisters in accord with many of her views regarding women's issues. Colby's correspondence also indicates that she was able to travel some during the 1880s, although she never made it to Europe to see the sites that her earlier reading had inspired her to imagine.[26]

As noted, Colby also resumed writing for publication after 1881. Numerous draft manuscripts of material written in the years she lived in Flint, as well as her later years spent in Ann Arbor, Peoria, and Normal, survive. Like her writing in the mid-1860s, these manuscripts were, for the most part, children's stories, as well as rebuses and enigmas aimed at children. She also frequently focused on topics in nature. Also similar to prior decades, she resumed the practice of trading her writing for subscriptions. Her efforts appeared to be relatively successful; for example, in February of 1888, she was given a one-year subscription to the *New York Tribune* as payment for one of her children's stories. Unfortunately, either she no longer kept scrapbooks of her publications or they do not survive, so it is difficult to ascertain the scope or depth of her public writing beyond those surviving manuscript drafts and notes.[27]

Beyond writing, Colby also engaged in numerous activities that allowed her to stretch her mind. Like many women of this era, she became involved with the club movement. In a lot of ways, these clubs provided women a substitute for the higher education to which their daughters had gained access. Colby's memberships in history clubs in Ann Arbor and Normal certainly indicated a continuation of her lifelong quest for knowledge. A brief, organizational self-history in 1974 of the Normal History Club states that the group formed in 1894 "dedicated to the proposition that women are created the intellectual equals with men; that they are not to be regulated to a lifetime of serving their husbands, rearing their children, and performing all the menial tasks related thereto while minds and spirits atrophy; that they have minds that are capable of the acquisition of knowledge, and have ideas and initiative that can contribute to the quality of life in the community and beyond." This principle certainly echoed Colby's own sentiments about womanhood. Women's clubs also could mirror the college experience in another important way: they were often exclusionary. Who was let in was frequently as important as who was kept out. Although no direct evidence illustrates that the Normal History Club actively acted to exclude anyone, the club's membership roster certainly reflected that attitude. Among the nineteenth-century club participants were the wives and daughters of influential Normal male citizens—ISNU professors, Town of Normal business owners, and professionals. The club's organizer and first president, Auta Stout Felmley, was married to David Felmley who served as ISNU's president for thirty years. Fear that her status may have limited her access to clubs such as this one may further explain Colby's apparent reticence about revealing her divorce.[28]

In the past, Colby sometimes had defied role prescriptions and engaged in the public sphere in ways that were not socially sanctioned, but she always had displayed her desire to share her experiences with women who were like-minded. The club movement offered that path. Clubs created separate, but socially acceptable, space for women in public life. These clubs were typically led by women, very often secular in nature, and devoted to intellectual or cultural enrichment—ideas Colby would have found appealing. In addition, the club movement was huge. In 1892, the General Federation of Women's Clubs was established with over 100,000 members and by 1900 boasted 160,000 members. The history clubs to which Colby belonged mirrored many other clubs in that they were highly organized and structured. The clubs each held weekly meetings in which one woman delivered a presentation on a topic she had researched. The schedule of topics and presenters was predetermined for an entire season. The 1884–85 season of the "Tuesday Club" of Ann Arbor focused on "studies in French history," and Colby's presentation centered on Napoleon's invasion of Italy in 1796. During her active membership in the Normal History Club from 1894 through 1899, the club focused on topics such as "Studies in English Literature" and "Studies in American History," where Colby spoke on diverse subjects, such as Edward Hyde, the first Earl of Clarendon's history of England, as well as the history of the Carolinas.[29]

Evidence implies that throughout the 1880s and 1890s Colby led a relatively happy and somewhat fulfilled life. Her foremost interests during this period mirrored those facets she had deemed vital for a fulfilled life during the antebellum years—reading, writing, education, women's issues, and her family—and she had at least some limited opportunity to enjoy them all. Evidence, from 1865 through 1880, which can be used to determine her state of mind for the approximately fifteen years after the move from Ohio, is more ephemeral. As we have seen, Colby had expressed clearly her feelings that her own opportunities

Colby is shown here in the mid-1890s as part of the prestigious Normal History Club. This women's club was "dedicated to the proposition that women are created the intellectual equals of men." Used by permission Normal History Club Collection, Illinois State University Archives, Illinois State University, Normal, Illinois.

to achieve her aspirations were quite limited. Contrary to this attitude, she must have projected an entirely different message to her children that counteracted the possible negative implications of her own stymied ambitions. Colby's children showed no signs that they felt inhibited by their circumstances. Their graduations from high school in the early 1870s, as well as the fact that each of them obtained college degrees before 1878, placed them on the leading edge of the rush to higher education that would occur as the century closed. In addition, both her daughters worked at professional careers dominated by men—medicine and college-level teaching. Her son married a woman with a college degree and a career at a time when society was portraying women of that "type" in an increasingly negative light. All of this spoke to Colby's ability to inspire confidence and trust in their own abilities.

Colby had ceased using her journals for self-analysis in the mid-1860s when her youngest child, Rose, was only ten years old. As we have seen, at that time, she had surrendered to an apathy that, quite frankly, was at odds with this apparent influence on her children. Colby's own thoughts about her life during the years after the war are not available, but because of the love of words that Colby clearly passed to her daughter, Rose, we do have a secondhand interpretation. Rose wrote a lengthy essay that essentially tells the story of her mother's life. Obviously, details about Colby's early life were based on her mother's memories and perspectives and then additionally colored by Rose's perceptions. Nevertheless, the basic facts in the essay coincide with known historical facts and interpretations, although the timing and scope were somewhat foreshortened—a not uncommon occurrence when reminiscing on the past. Most importantly, it serves as an indication of how Colby's children perceived her.

Interestingly, Rose focused much of her essay on her mother's youth and the "spiritual transformation" that she perceived made Colby the woman she so obviously admired. We have seen compelling evidence that during Rose's childhood, Colby still searched for spiritual answers that explained her place in the world. Nevertheless, Rose's description illustrates that in her eyes, her mother's spiritual journey was completed prior to Colby's marriage and children. The fact that Rose's perception did not incorporate the angst of Colby's struggle to bring together her inner life and her outer world indicates that Colby displayed a more confident attitude than she felt. In Rose's descriptions of how her mother reached her sense of the world, she pushed the culmination of Colby's struggle backward in time and foreshortened the actual struggle. Rose also presumed that Colby realistically achieved a balance, with which Colby herself would have not necessarily agreed.

> Little by little the unity of mankind was dawning on her. Gradually the conscience grew of the inextricable tie that binds, each to each and one to all, the parts of this wonderful race, apparently so widely sundered, of that marvelous tie which makes the good of one depend upon the good of all, the fate of all upon the will of one. . . . Face to face with this persistent, enduring fact of the interdependence of all parts of the race, the life of an individual becomes a serious thing. Carelessness may shrug its shoulders, humility disclaim all powers yet the eternal law will be fulfilled; we may not escape our individual responsibility by throwing the burden upon a remote and mysterious Providence, the religion of Faith is incomplete until there is added to it the religion of Duty and Righteousness. A new awe of life came upon the girl . . . as the new religion displaced the old.[30]

According to Colby's own words, the type of spiritual transformation to which Rose referred as one based on the equality of humanity did not have its true conscious beginnings until well into the 1850s. In addition, her choice to act on this belief was compromised by her doubts. It is interesting that, in Rose's mind, her mother had come to this peace easily.

Rose also described her mother's growing interest in the abolition movement. She claimed this interest was spurred forward by the death of Elijah Lovejoy. Lovejoy published an abolition newspaper in Alton, Illinois, and after his presses were destroyed on three previous occasions by mobs, he chose to stand up to the next mob. This action resulted in his death, and as the only known abolitionist murdered by an anti-abolition mob, he was afforded martyr status and significant news coverage. However, Lovejoy's death occurred in 1837, so how much it actually affected Colby, who would have been only ten years old at the time, was perhaps embellished with time. Rose's account also spoke of Abby Kelley Foster's influence on Colby's attitude. Foster did influence Colby's thoughts in the late 1850s, but as previously discussed, Colby herself wrote that when Abby Kelley visited Ohio in the 1840s, Colby considered her to be an "infidel." Clearly, Colby had chosen to downplay her early doubts and frustration and picture herself in a way that her children, especially her daughters, could find inspiration—even if she felt her own hopes were dead.[31]

The last section of Rose's essay focused on the next stage of Colby's life. "Proud and humble, eager and reluctant, with lingering backward glance, and flushed longing for the future, she passed the portal of girlhood and entered the realm of womanhood." Rose wrote about the births of Colby's children and the deaths of both her oldest son, "the empty arms ached for the dear burden," and her oldest daughter, "and once again life turned its mournful eyes upon her, unclasping love's clinging finger." Rose emphasized that the birth of Colby's children renewed her spirit of justice. "Still closer pressed the problems of the world's struggle now that their little feet must follow its weary paths." Rose never directly mentioned her father in this essay, but the final paragraph made her feelings about her mother abundantly clear. "Who can tell the sweetness of that life, love-nourished sorrow crowned? I see today that white haired, gracious womanhood, the sweet lips and solemn eyes. I see her children's reverencing love. I catch the echoes of gratitude from lives better, purer, for her life."[32]

This essay serves to highlight Rose's perception of her mother as an intelligent, strong-minded, moral woman who believed in acting for what was right. This view clearly had influence on Rose's life choices as it must also have for her other children. Hard evidence that outlines Colby's actions or feelings, especially from 1865 through the early 1880s, is scarce. However, her children's lives illustrate that Colby ensured that *they* felt the ideals embodied in her inner life could be manifested in *their* actual lives. As for Colby's own life, her satisfaction is less clear. In July of 1900, at the age of seventy-two, following a brief illness, Celestia Rice Colby passed away at her home in Normal. At this time, her death was noted in the "Normal News" section of *The Pantagraph*. "Mrs. Colby was a woman of remarkable attainments of mind. She was a hard working student all her life, and her literary tastes were thoroughly cultivated. Her papers were among the most scholarly productions heard by the Normal History Club during its existence. Mrs. Colby was highly esteemed as a neighbor, and her death causes general regret in Normal."[33]

The tenor of this notice can be interpreted as a sign that at the end of her life at least, she had negotiated a space that allowed for the pursuit of her inner life's aspirations. In addition, the focus on her role as scholar and writer implies that she had reached a level of respect among her community as an accomplished person who was also a woman, rather than a woman who was then necessarily a wife, mother, or grandmother. The question of whether this tenor accurately reflected Colby's thoughts about her life or once again served as further evidence of Rose's respect cannot be answered. Nonetheless, Colby clearly aspired to reach this level of respect, so its place as part of her legacy serves—at the very least—as a tribute to that aspiration.

Conclusion

CELESTIA RICE COLBY's life story defies attempts to place her within an easily labeled category for the sake of a tidy historical "summing up." Her biography, if examined without the benefit of her own words, reveals a rather typical, Northern, white, antebellum woman. While the portrait achieved with the addition of her words changes this assumption, it is neither clear nor unambiguous. Although her publicly articulated words on women's roles were similar to what she privately imagined her role should be, those words differed significantly from her descriptions and perceptions of what her actual role consisted. Obvious dichotomies existed in her life—broad differences are apparent between her public persona and her private one, her "inner" life and her "outward" actions, and society's expectations compared to her own desires. For most of her life, Colby's outward world—the duties to house, children, family, and community as prescribed by woman's sphere and necessity—demanded most of her time. These duties intertwined to form the social space that acted as the framework, or perhaps more accurately the boundary, from which Colby made decisions concerning her life. Her diary entries, which reveal her private thoughts or inner life, demonstrate that she felt these time-consuming tasks should not solely define her as a woman. To complicate matters further, not only did her day-to-day life differ from the world as she imagined it, it also differed from life as the popular culture of the time idealized it. Her desires, society's prescriptions, and the obligations of everyday life all exerted a force that affected her actions and attitudes. From Colby's perspective, regardless of what her daily "multitude of little chores" actually consisted, she fell short of achieving success as defined by any one of those forces. This perceived failing is evident in the examination of her inner conflicts, and it manifested itself in her everyday life.

The fact that Colby's inner life and outward world were often at odds with each other contributed to a state of constant negotiation. She took sporadic steps toward her progressive goals, but more often in her daily life she felt compelled to perform her "duties" as prescribed by society, regardless of private hopes. The energy that she gave to actions in the outer world that were contradictory to

220

her inner thoughts provides strong evidence as to the dominant position that society's message, in the form of prescribed norms, laws, political options, and economic opportunities, played in this negotiation. By mid-nineteenth century, women's realistic opportunities to wield societal power were lessened by the strong hold of this gender ideology. In particular, women whose aspirations took them beyond societal norms, who were also wives and mothers, were frequently and harshly vilified as immoral and unfit mothers, among other heresies. By the 1860s, Colby publicly promoted the notion that expanded and varied roles should be afforded women, but her private words reveal that she did not feel those options translated into her own life. Instead, her private reflections showcase the strong effect that the ideal of separate spheres had in her daily life in regard to the ultimate direction she felt possible for herself.

Perhaps if Colby had consistent support for her more progressive views, she would have been less conflicted in her daily life, but in reality, she was a contradiction. She chose, in many instances, to follow society's expectations regarding her proper role instead of following her aspirations as articulated in her writings. Ironically, although she felt consistently at odds with her prescribed role, as well as essentially apart from her available community, her life in many ways actually provides a truthful illustration of women's contentious position in northeastern society as a whole. Her location in a region that was a cultural extension of New England in the mid-nineteenth century placed her in a time and place in which opposing historical processes were intersecting. Because we are privy to Colby's internal dialogue, her public declarations, and her descriptions of actual daily life, we are granted a rare look at the actual, day-to-day struggle of one woman in her place and time. Of course, this picture cannot be transferred out of whole cloth to all women, and the importance of the inadvisability of generalizing to the whole from one woman's experience is important to keep in mind at this time. However, Colby's words make clear that one hundred years before Betty Friedan defined "the problem that has no name," ordinary women struggled with the notion of personal identity.[1] Therefore, any addition of details, like those details found in Colby's writings, support efforts to draw truthful conclusions about the past that can be applied to a broader picture of the present or future.

The details of Colby's struggle are grounded in her particular location in both place and time. Her generation received the full brunt of the message that defined the proper female sphere. This societal force had its beginnings before her birth, but achieved full strength as she matured. She also was a member of the generation of women who, as they embarked on their adult lives, began receiving new competing messages that spoke of female equality. In 1848, Colby married, and in that same year, less than fifty miles to the northeast, in Seneca Falls, New York, a vocal call for women's rights rang out. The Seneca Falls Convention was a seminal event in the growing movement for female equality. Although this convention did not represent the first voice for female equality, it perhaps did symbolize the loudest voice up to that time with its bold public declarations, standard of demands, and the impetus it provided for the women's rights conventions that followed it. The influence of its radical ideas of equality spread slowly throughout the northeast and into the northwest over the next few years. A decade after Seneca Falls, the ideas espoused by those women's rights advocates are obvious in Colby's writings, but the influence of the "cult of true womanhood" is also evident. The seemingly uncompromising struggle between true womanhood and a new type of woman is obvious in Colby's descriptions of her life. The realistic depiction of this dichotomy is what makes her story an important illustration of the intersection of historical forces. These diverse influences, and how women reacted to them, as well as how history illustrates this dynamic, continue to have an effect on the way women are viewed today.

This examination shows that although gender roles were strongly defined by societal norms and legal boundaries, much of the power that the ideal of separate spheres held in Colby's life was due to the dominant position she afforded it. This allowance then strongly affected the direction she chose when it was within her power to do so. In short, its effects were most evident in the manner in which she constructed her own identity based on what she deemed possible. Colby's public words offered an image of a progressive ideal in which she perceived cooperation and interconnection between male/female and public/private spheres. Her private words, conversely, display the strong effect that the ideal of separate spheres had in actually managing her day-to-day life. The ultimate direction Colby's antebellum life took illustrates the power of the ideal in her mind as well as society. Colby's life shows the reality of separate female spheres not as a complete physical reality, but as a very real component that affected her choices as she struggled to define her own sphere—socially, economically, politically, and culturally.

As noted, it is difficult to draw any firm conclusions about the last thirty years of Colby's life or her life as a whole. In the last twenty years of her life—after her children were grown and her husband was removed from the picture—she finally was able to experience a less duty-bound life. The passage of time, however, may have served to dull the urgency of some of her earlier ideals, as reality showed how little and slowly societal change actually occurred. At the time of her death, many of her personal, as well as societal, goals remained unfulfilled. It would be another twenty years before universal female suffrage finally was achieved throughout the nation; the continued lack of female equality, however, can be easily argued: temperance as a national measure did not materialize for twenty years, female educational and career opportunities actually experienced a decline after some breakthroughs in the nineteenth century, and the goal of legal and social equality for African Americans rapidly disappeared after Reconstruction ended. Personally, Colby continued until her death to take opportunities to raise her own level of knowledge, but she never achieved any level of formalized higher education; the perceived disability that caused her to distrust her own intelligence so much in her earlier life endured. She witnessed her three children achieve the higher education that she stressed as invaluable. Two of them survived her death and lived long lives of purpose made possible by that education. However, for a woman who often had articulated privately that her children should not solely define her life, this success was perhaps bittersweet.

Colby's life story illustrates the struggle that many women of the nineteenth century faced—the balance between society's expectations of the idealized role for women, which excluded the public world and always placed house and home first, and realistic roles, which varied as much as the real women who played them and were molded by forces from the inside and the outside. In Colby's case, this balance was a precarious one in which her love of family consistently competed with her personal needs, as a citizen and a woman, to be intellectually fulfilled and make a difference with her life. Whether she considered her life a success or failure is unknown, but through the lens of time it is possible to view her struggle in a new perspective, which incorporates both an individual "story" and broader historical interpretations.

This struggle translates to the present as an inability to apply a single interpretation to her experiences. She was not simply a typical antebellum housewife who happily tended the home fires, but she also was not a radical who completely or consistently defied societal conventions. Like many women, she was alternatively, and sometimes simultaneously, compliant and brave. Whether her efforts ultimately define her as ordinary or extraordinary, her ability to so vividly reflect her emotional struggles on paper makes her special. It is those words that make her difficult to label, but it is also those words that provide a truthful legacy of her life. Perhaps, most importantly, her words contribute to our understanding of not only a particular time and place in women's history, but also help to illuminate the effect that assumptions about those women's lives have on present as well as future interpretations regarding women's roles. My hope is that Colby would have viewed her contribution to this illumination as "useful" to the ongoing effort "to elevate and redeem woman"—past, present, and future.

Abbreviations

Notes

1. CRCD, Oct. 24, 1857, in CC available at Illinois State University Archives, Illinois State University, Normal.

2. CRCD, Feb. 5, 1860.

3. For an in-depth examination of the consequences of this "pastoralization of housework," see Jeanne Boydston, *Home and Work: Housework, Wages, and the Ideology of Labor in the Early Republic* (New York: Oxford Univ. Press, 1990).

4. The sheer amount of scholarship that informs this study makes listing it separately in a note unwieldy. For the complete list, see Secondary Sources in the Bibliography.

5. CRC, "Aurora Leigh," *MF,* March 1, 1862; CRC, "An Essay Read Before the Cherry Valley Literary Society," *MF,* Aug. 1, 1861; CRCD, Dec. 23, 1858, Oct. 24, 1857.

6. For interesting discussions on the challenges and benefits of the use of ordinary women's private writings for the purpose of research, see Elizabeth Hampsten, *Read This Only to Yourself: The Private Writings of Midwestern Women, 1880–1910* (Bloomington, Ind.: Indiana Univ. Press, 1982), 1–16 and Judy Nolte Lensink, *"A Secret to Be Burried": The Diary and Life of Emily Hawley Gillespie, 1858–1888* (Iowa City: Univ. of Iowa Press, 1989), xii–xxvi.

1. 1827–1848

1. CRCD, Feb. 17, 1865.

2. CRC, partial manuscript essay with alternative titles listed; for example, "Memories of my Childhood" and "Memories of Susie Lee," c. 1850s, CRCMM in CC, available at Illinois State University Archives, Illinois State University, Normal, Illinois.

3. Genealogical notes contained in CRCMM and JRCNB in CC, available at Illinois State University Archives, Illinois State University, Normal, Illinois (hereafter GN); CRCD Dec. 19, 1849; CRC, "Memories," c. 1850s.

4. CRC, "Memories," c. 1850s; GN; *Census for Ohio,* 1830. Colby's father, Joel Rice, was the grandson of a Welsh immigrant, Peter Rice, who came to the New World sometime before his children were born. Peter's son, Joel Rice Sr., apparently made his living as a peddler. This job eventually led him to New York, where he met his future wife, Cirlissa Baker. Joel Sr. and Cirlissa married and eventually settled in Granby, Connecticut, where Joel Rice was born in 1796. At some point after his birth, Cirlissa Rice died in New York City of "yellow fever." Colby's mother, Flavia Bradley, was born in December of 1799, one of two daughters born in the "Bay State," specifically in North Haven, Massachusetts, to Caleb and Resign Bradley née Barker. The details of how and where Joel Rice and Flavia Bradley were brought

together are not known, but their meeting was likely a result of proximity. Resign Bradley's childhood home was Agawam, Massachusetts, and Flavia and Cordelia were also born there. At some point the Bradley family settled in Southwick, Massachusetts. Both of these towns are southeast of Springfield, Massachusetts, and are less than ten miles from Granby, Connecticut—Joel Rice's birthplace.

5. Williams Brothers, eds., *History of Ashtabula County, Ohio with Illustrations and Biographical Sketches of its Pioneers and Most Prominent Men* (Philadelphia, Pa.: J. B. Lippincott and Co., 1878), 24–25; *Atlas of the State of Ohio: From Surveys under the direction of H. F. Walling* (New York: Henry S. Stebbins, 1867–68), 6–7.

6. Williams Brothers, *History of Ashtabula County,* 24.

7. CRC, "Memories," c. 1850s; Williams Brothers, *History of Ashtabula County,* 236–37.

8. Williams Brothers, *History of Ashtabula County,* 25–26, 237; *Atlas of Ohio,* 6–7; Henry Howe, *Historical Collections of Ohio* (published by author, 1898); Ashtabula County Genealogical Association, *Ashtabula County History: Then and Now* (Dallas, Tex.: Taylor, 1985), 55; Moina W. Large, *History of Ashtabula County, Vol. 1* (Topeka-Indianapolis: Historical Publishing, 1924), 243, 254; *Census for Ohio,* 1820, 1830; *United States Historical Web Browser, 1790–1970* available at http://fisher.lib.Virginia.edu/census. From 1830 through 1870, Ashtabula County had a consistent male to female ratio of just over 51 percent; the number of "free blacks" in the county never rose above forty-five individuals; there were no slaves, and even in 1860, at the zenith of immigration, only 1,700 residents were of foreign birth.

9. Large, *Ashtabula County,* 253–56; Kathryn H. Talcott, "Cherry Valley," *Ashtabula County Historical Society Quarterly Bulletin,* vol. 6, no. 4 (Dec. 15, 1959).

10. *Census for Ohio,* 1820–70. A comparison of census data from 1850 to 1860 demonstrates that those families, like the Rices, who owned land in 1850, still remained in Cherry Valley in 1860, but those men who were nonlandowning laborers in 1850 had moved on by 1860, with relatively few new names added to the population. The 1840 population was composed of 219 "heads of household": 189 farmers and 29 professionals, manufacturers, or tradesmen. The remaining population was made up of 255 "scholars" [pupils]; two people who were designated as deaf, "dumb," or blind; and approximately 245 residents who were likely women, or children too young to attend school. Large, *Ashtabula County,* 256; *United States Census Bureau 2000 Population Summary* available at http://factfinder.census.gov/home/datanotes/.

11. Ashtabula Genealogical, *Then and Now,* 15–16; Williams Brothers, *History of Ashtabula County,* 7 (map), 28, 236–37. The first county rail line was completed in 1851. This east-west route ran roughly parallel to Lake Erie. In 1854 a north-south line was added, but neither line entered into the southeastern end of the county.

12. GN; Williams Brothers, *History of Ashtabula County,* 237; *Census for Ohio,* 1830–50.

13. Williams Brothers, *History of Ashtabula County,* 24.

14. GN; JRC, "A Study," in JRCNB, c. 1880–90s. According to genealogical information and grave records, Evelina Johnson Rice was Resign Morley's daughter. Resign Morley was possibly the widow of Caleb Bradley, thus Flavia Bradley's (Colby's mother) mother and Evelina's sister or half-sister. This connection is not established as an absolute fact, but the 1850 census records show Resign Morley as living in Fayette Johnson's household and designated as his mother-in-law. Fayette Johnson was married to Flavia's sister Cordelia, thus as Cordelia's mother she would be Flavia's mother as well. Joel Rice's third wife, Dorcas Barker,

was also related, as she was Resign Bradley née Barker's niece, thus Flavia Rice's cousin. Joel Rice (d. 1881), all three of his wives, Flavia (d. 1829), Evelina (d. 1863), and Dorcas (d. 1873), plus Resign Morley, and Joel and Flavia's first daughter, Celestia Resign, are all listed on one stone in the cemetery behind the Congregational Church of Andover, Ohio.

15. Dorothy Sterling, *Ahead of her Time: Abby Kelley and the Politics of Antislavery* (New York: W. W. Norton, 1991), 85–86; JRC, "A Study," c. 1880–90s (quote); Stacey M. Robertson, *Parker Pillsbury: Radical Abolitionist, Male Feminist* (Ithaca, N.Y.: Cornell Univ. Press, 2000), 10.

16. Williams Brothers, *History of Ashtabula County*, 35–37; Large, *Ashtabula County*, 245; "Early church life in Cherry Valley: Extracts from the record book, Regular Baptist Church in Cherry Valley, Ashtabula County, Ohio, Feb. 13, 1830–Jan. 12, 1878" (transcribed from handwritten original manuscript).

17. "Early church life."

18. David Chesebrough, *Charles G. Finney: Revivalistic Rhetoric* (Westport, Conn.: Greenwood Press, 2001), 48–52; "Early church life."

19. Stephane Elise Booth, *Buckeye Women: The History of Ohio's Daughters* (Athens: Ohio Univ. Press, 2001), 3–5; Robert Fuller, *Underground to Freedom: An Account of the Anti-Slavery Activities in Ashtabula County Prior to the Civil War* (Jefferson, Ohio: Gazette Printing 1977), 3. For a thorough examination of the antislavery movement and specifically the sometimes controversial thoughts regarding women's involvement, see Nancy Hewitt, *Women's Activism and Social Change: Rochester, New York, 1822–1872* (Ithaca, N.Y.: Cornell Univ. Press, 1984), 104–13; Lori Ginsberg, *Women and the Work of Benevolence: Morality, Politics, and Class in the Nineteenth-Century United States* (New Haven, Conn.: Yale Univ. Press, 1990), 85–110; Sterling, *Ahead of Her Time*, 94–106.

20. *Census for Ohio*, 1830–50; Williams Brothers, *History of Ashtabula County*, 38, 237; Large, *Ashtabula County*, 255; Talcott, "Cherry Valley"; *Historical Sketch: Grand River Institute* (Austinburg, Ohio: Grand River Institute, 1924).

21. *Catalogues of the Officers and Students of Grand River Institute* (Ashtabula, Ohio: Sentinel Office, 1846, 1848, 1849); *Catalogue of the Officers and Students of Grand River Institute* (Cleveland, Ohio: Smead & Cowles', 1850).

22. *Historical Sketch, GRI* (quote); *Catalogues of GRI*, 1846, 1848, 1849, 1850.

23. *Historical Sketch: GRI*; Sterling, *Ahead of Her Time*, 214–17.

24. Sally Ann McMurry, *Transforming Rural Life: Dairying Families and Agricultural Change, 1820–1885* (Baltimore, Md.: Johns Hopkins Univ. Press, 1995), 101, 118–22; CRCD, May 25, 1849; GN.

25. GN; Joel Rice math notebook, CC; McMurry, *Transforming Rural Life*, 110, 138–39.

26. *History of Ohio, Vol. 4* (Chicago: American Historical Society, 1925), 251–52, 258–59; Nancy Woloch, *Women and the American Experience*, 3rd ed. (Boston: McGraw-Hill, 2000), 281; *Atlas of Ohio*, 16.

27. *Atlas of Ohio*, 14; *Historical Sketch: GRI*.

28. *Catalogues of GRI*, 1846, 1848; CRCD, "On the Death of Cynthia Weeks," August, 1847; "My Sister's Grave," undated; "Mother," March, 16, 1847. An acrostic is a poem in which the beginning letter of each line spells out a word, for example, MOTHER.

29. *Catalogue of the Instructors and Students of the Ashtabula County Teachers' Institute* (Cleveland, Ohio: Younglove's Steam, 1846); *Catalogues of the Instructors and Students of the Ashtabula County Teachers' Institute* (Ashtabula, Ohio: Sentinel Office, 1847, 1849, 1851); *Catalogue of the*

Instructors and Students of the Ashtabula County Teachers' Institute (Conneaut, Ohio: D. C. Allen, 1848); *Catalogue of the Instructors and Students of the Ashtabula County Teachers' Institute* (Ashtabula, Ohio: N. W. Thayer, 1850); Booth, *Buckeye Women*, 173; *Atlas of Ohio*, 15.

30. *Catalogue of the Instructors and Students of the Ashtabula County Teachers' Institute*, 1846, 1847, 1848, 1849, 1850 (quote), 1851.

31. CRCD, "Ever dear Nette," April 23, 1848.

32. CRCD, Aug. 1, 1851; CRC, "Lewis," Aug. 1847, CRCMM; CRCD, miscellaneous writings, 1847–48.

33. Mary P. Ryan, *Womanhood in America From Colonial Times to the Present*, 3rd ed. (New York: Franklin Watts, 1983), 134–50.

34. Catherine Kelly, *In the New England Fashion: Reshaping Women's Lives in the Nineteenth-Century* (Ithaca, N.Y.: Cornell Univ. Press, 1999), 14, 107; Lewis Colby and Celestia M. Rice Marriage Record, July 1848, Ashtabula County Marriage Records, Volume B, available from the Ohio State Historical Society, Columbus, Ohio.

2. 1848–1853

1. CRCD, Aug. 19, 1851, Aug. 15, 1851, Oct. 9, 1851.

2. CRCD, Oct. 17, 1850, May 25, 1849; Lewis Colby and Celestia M. Rice application for marriage, July 1848, Ashtabula County Marriage Application Records available from the Ohio State Historical Society, Columbus, Ohio; *Census for Ohio*, 1850–60.

3. CRCD, Aug. 6, 1850.

4. Karen Lystra, *Searching the Heart: Women, Men and Romantic Love in Nineteenth-Century America* (New York: Oxford Univ. Press, 1989), 28–32; Glenda Riley, *The Female Frontier: A Comparative View of Women on the Prairie and the Plains* (Lawrence: Univ. Press of Kansas, 1988), 149–50. Riley notes that women's notions about what "civilization" meant, which they attempted to recreate as they moved west, were rendered in part from fictional idealization of home life.

5. Riley, *The Female Frontier*, 2–4, 148–51; Boydston, *Home and Work*, 142–63.

6. Frances Trollope, "Domestic Manners of the Americans," excerpts available at *Women in America, 1820–1842*, accessed at *http://xroads.Virginia.edu/~hyper/detoc/fem/home.htm*. For an informative description of women's lives and hardships on the prairie, see John Mack Faragher, *Sugar Creek: Life on the Illinois Prairie* (New Haven, Conn.: Yale Univ. Press, 1986), 110–18; CRCD, Dec. 19, 1859.

7. David Colby's death notice, *AS* (Jefferson, Ohio), March 22, 1855; *Census for Ohio* 1830–50; *Catalogue of Ashtabula County Teachers' Institute*, 1846.

8. Kelly, *In the New England Fashion*, 98, 107, 115, 123.

9. *Census for Ohio*, 1850.

10. CRCD, Oct. 21, 1850; Kelly, *In the New England Fashion*, 107–9. Colby's angst—at this early stage of her marriage—corroborates Kelly's observations that rural antebellum women's fears about marriage were based more on competing ideas about who rightly claimed their time and energy, rather than a fear of losing self-determination, that is, Nancy Cott's "marriage trauma." Later in her married life, however, Colby's attitude shifts dramatically toward despair that she had indeed lost any sense of self-determination. Nancy F. Cott, *The*

Bonds of Womanhood: "Woman's Sphere" in New England, 1780–1835 (New Haven, Conn.: Yale Univ. Press, 1977), 74–84.

11. Carroll Smith-Rosenberg, "The Cross and the Pedestal: Women, Anti-Ritualism, and the Emergence of the American Bourgeoisie," in *Disorderly Conduct: Visions of Gender in Victorian America* (New York: Alfred E. Knopf, 1985), 129–64.

12. CRCD, Oct. 9, 1849, Jan. 24, 1850, March 29, 1849, June 4, 1849.

13. Cott, *Bonds of Womanhood,* 15; CRCD, April 9, 1849; untitled poem, c. Nov. 1847.

14. CRCD, Aug. 1, 1849, April 2, 1849.

15. CRCD, April 12, 1849, May 11, 1849, Aug. 16, 1849, July 5, 1851.

16. CRCD, June 6, 1849, June 26, 1849, Oct. 5, 1849.

17. CRCD, March 29, 1849, May 11, 1849, July 30, 1850; Chesebrough, *Charles G. Finney,* 77–91.

18. CRCD, March 31, 1849, Feb. 19, 1852, Aug. 3, 1851, June 25, 1851.

19. For the in-depth discussion regarding evangelism and women's resistance to conformity in which my interpretation is grounded, see Smith-Rosenberg, "Cross and the Pedestal," 129–64.

20. Smith-Rosenberg, "Cross and the Pedestal," 129–59.

21. Elizabeth Hampsten, *Read This Only to Yourself,* 111–18 (quote); CRCD, Jan. 15, 1850, Jan. 20, 1850.

22. CRCD, April 10, 1849, May 26, 1849, March 28, 1850, June 25, 1849, May 2, 1850; CRC, "Little Montie," c. Jan. 19, 1861, *ASB* in CRCPSB3. Colby always referred to her son as Plummer, but several sources indicate his full name was Montie Plummer. His apparent gravestone is marked M. P. Colby. Colby frequently also used her children's middle or unused first names when writing about them for publication, as in Cynthia for Vine, June for Rose and Harris for Branch; the aforementioned poem, which was written about her son's death, refers to him as "Montie."

23. CRCD, March 31, 1850, April 19, 1850, June 1, 1850.

24. CRCD, March 9, 1850, April 21, 1850.

25. "Flowers," written under pen name "Flora," *The Ladies Repository* (Cincinnati, Ohio), June 1851; Booth, *Buckeye Women,* 179; CRCD, June 1, 1851. For reasons unknown, Colby occasionally used the names "Flora Vernon," "Susie Vernon," and "Susie Lee" in place of her own name in the text of autobiographical-styled material for publication, particularly in her children's stories. This instance is one of the only known uses of one of those names as an author pseudonym.

26. CRCD, May 9, 1851, Sept. 5, 1851; Carroll Smith-Rosenberg, "The Female World of Love and Ritual: Relationships between Women in Nineteenth-Century America," in *Women's Experience in America: An Historical Anthology,* ed. Esther Katz and Anita Rapone (New Brunswick, N.J.: Transaction Books, 1980), 259–91.

27. CRCD, Aug. 30, 1849, May 16, 1849; Ann Lee Bressler, *The Universalist Movement in America 1770–1880* (New York: Oxford Univ. Press, 2001), 97–110.

28. CRCD, Nov. 3, 1850; CRC, "To Vine," *DN,* 1854 in CRCPSB1 in CC, available at Illinois State University Archives, Illinois State University, Normal, Illinois.

29. CRCD, Nov. 21, 1851, Feb. 19, 1852, Aug. 14, 1852.

30. CRCD, March 13, 1853.

3. 1853–1857

1. CRCD, Nov. 15, 1853, Nov 26, 1853, Jan. 29, 1854, April 23, 1854.

2. CRCD, July 20, 1858, July 16, 1854, Aug. 24, 1854.

3. CRCD, June 4, 1858; *Census for Illinois,* 1900; GN.

4. David Colby's death notice, March 22, 1855; Naomi Colby's death notice, *AS,* Oct. 14, 1863; CRCD, Nov. 14, 1849; *Census for Ohio,* 1850, 1860.

5. *Atlas of Ohio,* 13; McMurray, *Transforming Rural Life,* 1–5.

6. McMurry, *Transforming Rural Life,* 72–75.

7. McMurry, *Transforming Rural Life,* 75–77; CRC, "Cheese," *DN,* c. 1854 in CRCPSB1.

8. McMurry, *Transforming Rural Life,* 84; CRC, "Cheese," c. 1854 and "Cheesemaking," *AS,* Dec. 2, 1857 in CRCPSB1.

9. For changing technology and the cheese industry, see McMurry, *Transforming Rural Life,* 85–92, 73 (quote). For an interesting look at how changes in technology, the economy, and societal views regarding women affected rural women engaged primarily in market butter production, see Joan Jensen, *Loosening the Bonds: Mid-Atlantic Farm Women, 1750–1850* (New Haven, Conn.: Yale Univ. Press, 1986).

10. McMurry, *Transforming Rural Life,* 94; CRC, "Our Fair, its Past, Present, and Future," *AS,* Sept. 2, 1854, and "Rainy Days," *DN,* c. 1853 in CRCPSB1. Colby frequently wrote about the intellectual side of farming and the superior nature of rural life. For example, see CRCPSB1 for "Clara Vinlay," *AS,* June 1854; "The Farmer's Holiday," *AS,* Aug. 29, 1854; "Winter Evenings at Home," *DN,* c. 1854; "The Poetry of Farming," unknown publication, c. 1853.

11. Sally McMurry, *Families and Farmhouses in Nineteenth-Century America: Vernacular Design and Social Change* (New York: Oxford Univ. Press, 1988), 69–70, 77–80.

12. Hampsten, *Read This Only to Yourself,* ix, 111, 118; Lyde Cullen Sizer, *The Political Work of Northern Women Writers and the Civil War, 1850–1872* (Chapel Hill: Univ. of North Carolina Press, 2000), 27–28.

13. Hewitt, *Women's Activism,* 104–13; Ginsberg, *Work of Benevolence,* 85–110; Sterling, *Ahead of Her Time,* 94–106.

14. For reactions at the Ashtabula County level see Fuller, *Underground to Freedom,* 3 (quote), 8, 21–22; for a statewide view, see Booth, *Buckeye Women,* 94; for an even broader view, see Sterling, *Ahead of Her Time,* 287–311.

15. Fuller, *Underground to Freedom,* 22, 24–32; Williams Brothers, *History of Ashtabula County,* 33–36, 100–101; *Historical Sketch: GRI.* Foster, Kelley, and Pillsbury were all active participants in what was arguably the most radical faction of abolitionists: the Garrison-led American Anti-Slavery Society. Colby noted the visit of "Mrs. John Brown" on April 25, 1860.

16. Williams Brothers, *History of Ashtabula County,* 34, 40, 100; *AS,* 1850–60. Congregationalists opposed radical abolition and women in public roles. For example, the General Association of Congregational Ministers issued the infamous July 1837 Pastoral Letter that condemned the Grimke sisters for not only speaking in public, but also for addressing subjects that were unwomanly.

17. Mary Kelley, *Private Women, Public Stage: Literary Domesticity in Nineteenth-Century America* (New York: Oxford Univ. Press, 1984; Chapel Hill: Univ. of North Carolina Press, 2002), 181–214; Ryan, *Womanhood in America,* 142–43.

18. Catharine Beecher, *A Treatise on the Domestic Economy* (New York: March, Capen,

Lyon, and Webb, 1841; Schocken Books, 1977), 13; Kathryn Kish Sklar, *Catharine Beecher: A Study in American Domesticity* (New Haven, Conn.: Yale Univ. Press, 1973), 156–60.

19. CRC, "I Have No Time to Read," *OC,* 1853 in CRCPSB1.

20. Blanche Glassman Hersh, *The Slavery of Sex: Feminist-Abolitionists in America* (Urbana: Univ. of Illinois Press, 1978), 47; Ann Russo and Cheris Kramarae, eds., *The Radical Women's Press of the 1850s* (New York: Routledge, 1991), 300–302; CRC, "The Ladies Department of the Cultivator," *OC,* c. 1853 in CRCPSB1.

21. CRC, "A Happy Home," *OC,* c. 1854 in CRCPSB1.

22. CRC, "Reading for Children," *OC,* October 1853; "Winter Evenings at Home, *DN,* c. 1854; and "A Wholesome Moral Influence at Home," *OC,* c. 1854 in CRCPSB1.

23. CRC, "The Slave Mother," *AS,* Sept. 16, 1854, in CRCPSB1.

24. CRC, "The Slave Mother," *AS,* Sept. 16, 1854, in CRCPSB1.

25. CRC, "The Daughter's Appeal," *AS,* c. June 1854 in CRCPSB1.

26. Hersh, *Slavery of Sex,* 45; Sterling, *Ahead of Her Time,* 214–15, 330.

27. CRC, "The Sisters: A Tale of the Sunny South," *ASB,* Jan. 17, 1857, Jan. 24, 1857.

28. CRC, "Tobacco v. The Gospel," *ASB,* Jan. 10, 1857.

29. CRC, "The Ladies Department of the Cultivator," *OC,* c. 1853 in CRCPSB1.

4. OCTOBER 1857–JANUARY 1858

1. CRCD, Oct. 16, 1857.

2. CRCD, Oct. 1, 1857. The nineteenth-century sewing machine was a particularly pernicious machine, and contemporaries often noted it was difficult to master because it often seemed to have a will of its own. In addition, and perhaps most important, new technology frequently raised household clothing expectations, thus rather than provide extra freedom from the "drudgery of the needle," it actually increased time and labor input. For discussions on the advantages and disadvantages of new technology such as the sewing machine, see Boydston, *Home and Work,* 106–13 and Ruth Schwartz Cowan, *More Work for Mother: The Ironies of Household Technology from the Open Hearth to the Microwave* (New York: Basic Books, 1983), 64–65, 74.

3. CRCD, Oct. 1, 1857; Kelly, *In the New England Fashion,* 54, 64–92.

4. CRCD, Oct. 4, 1857, Oct. 11, 1857. Annie Colby's genealogy is compiled from the following: marriage announcement for Edward L. Colby and Annie Colby, *AS,* Nov. 11, 1858; Annie Colby's death notice, *AS,* Sept. 19, 1861; Annie Colby's gravestone located in the Cherry Valley cemetery as well as inferences drawn from various diary entries.

5. CRCD, Jan. 15, 1858.

6. CRCD, Jan. 26, 1858, Nov. 11, 1857, Oct. 5, 1858; CRC to Emily Sanborn (draft copy of letter), Oct. 4, 1858 in CRCMM.

7. Marilyn Ferris Motz, *True Sisterhood: Michigan Women and Their Kin 1820–1920* (Albany: State Univ. of New York Press, 1983), 2, 14, 128–29; CRCD, Nov. 6, 1857.

8. CRCD, Dec. 20, 1857; Sterling, *Ahead of Her Time,* 39.

9. CRCD, Jan. 20, 1857, Jan. 28, 1857 (quote); Hewitt, *Women's Activism,* 184.

10. CRC, "A Mother's Kiss," *The Instructor,* c. July 1855 in CRCPSB1; CRC, "My Mother," *ASB,* Jan. 9, 1858; CRCD, Jan. 3, 1858, Jan. 21, 1860, Aug. 6, 1858.

11. CRCD, Jan. 29, 1858.

12. Kelly, *In the New England Fashion,* 90–92; Smith-Rosenberg, "Female World," 259–91. For other research that notes the importance of female networks, see Hersh, *Slavery of Sex,* 32; Hewitt, *Women's Activism;* Julie Roy Jeffrey, *Ordinary Women in the Antislavery Movement* (Chapel Hill: Univ. of North Carolina Press, 1998); Cott, *Bonds of Womanhood;* Motz, *True Sisterhood;* Pamela Riney-Kehrberg, "The Limits of Community: Martha Friesen of Hamilton County, Kansas," in *Midwestern Women: Work, Community, and Leadership at the Crossroads,* ed. Lucy Eldersveld Murphy and Wendy Hamand Venet (Bloomington: Indiana Univ. Press, 1997), 76–91.

13. Smith-Rosenberg, "Female World," 265–66; Motz, *True Sisterhood;* CRCD, Nov. 1, 1858.

14. Mary Kelley, "Reading Women/Women Reading: The Making of Learned Women in Antebellum America," *Journal of American History* 83 (1996): 401–24.

15. CRCD, Oct. 16, 1857.

16. Bernard Rosenthal, "Introduction," in Margaret Fuller, *Woman in the Nineteenth Century* (New York: W. W. Norton, 1971), v–ix; CRCD, Oct. 25, 1857.

17. "Catharine Maria Sedgewick," in *Notable American Women, 1607–1950: A Biographical Dictionary,* ed. Edward T. James et al. (Cambridge, Mass.: Harvard Univ. Press, 1971); CRCD, Oct. 27, 1857, Nov. 8, 1857.

18. CRCD, Oct. 4, 1857; Ryan, *Womanhood in America,* 143.

19. CRCD, Oct. 17, 1857 or Oct. 19, 1857 (date blurred).

20. CRCD, Dec. 4, 1857.

21. CRCD, Oct. 13, 1857.

22. CRC, "Tobacco v. Gospel," *ASB,* Jan. 10, 1857.

23. Barbara Welter, "The Feminization of American Religion," in *Clio's Consciousness Raised: New Perspectives on the History of Women,* ed. Mary Hartman and Lois W. Banner (New York: Harper Torchbooks, 1974), 138–45; Barbara Leslie Epstein, *The Politics of Domesticity: Women, Evangelism, and Temperance in Nineteenth-Century America* (Middletown, Conn.: Wesleyan Univ. Press, 1981), 1–3.

24. Hewitt, *Women's Activism;* Jeffrey, *Ordinary Women,* 153.

25. CRCD, Dec. 10, 1857, Jan. 17, 1858, Jan. 24, 1858.

26. CRCD, Jan. 14, 1858, Jan. 2, 1858, Aug. 22, 1858; Robertson, *Parker Pillsbury,* 17.

5. December 1857–May 1858

1. CRCD, Dec. 19, 1857.

2. CRCD, Dec. 28, 1857, Dec. 20, 1857.

3. Kimberly K. Smith, *The Dominion of the Voice: Riot, Reason, and Romance in Antebellum Politics* (Lawrence: Univ. of Kansas Press, 1999), 125–26; Hersh, *Slavery of Sex,* 45.

4. CRCD, Oct. 1, 1857; *AS,* Jan. 15, 1857, April 2, 1857.

5. Sterling, *Ahead of Her Time,* 311–12.

6. Ginsberg, *Work of Benevolence,* 99–100; Jeffrey, *Ordinary Women,* 172.

7. For detailed information about women and professional reform work, see Sterling, *Ahead of Her Time.*

8. Hewitt, *Women's Activism,* 219, 223–25, 231, 241.

9. Hewitt, *Women's Activism*, 63, 223–26, 231–32, 241–42.

10. Jeffrey, *Ordinary Women*, 135–36, 172, 214; Hewitt, *Women's Activism*, 40, 104–6, 123, 138; Sizer, *Political Work*, 52–73.

11. CRC to editor "Friend Robinson," *ASB*, Jan. 2, 1858.

12. Ibid.

13. CRC, "Political Backsliding," *ASB*, Jan. 23, 1858.

14. Ibid.

15. Ibid.; CRC, "The Unpardonable Sin," *ASB*, Jan. 30, 1858.

16. CRC, "Slavery at the North," *ASB*, Feb. 6, 1858.

17. Joseph Howland quoted in Sterling, *Ahead of Her Time*, 311.

18. CRCD, Jan. 10, 1858; CRC to editor "Friend Robinson," *ASB*, Feb. 27, 1858; Jeffrey, *Ordinary Women*, 135, 148, 153.

19. CRCD, April 13, 1858.

20. Kelly, *In the New England Fashion*, 190–99; CRCD, Jan. 10, 1858, Jan. 11, 1858, Jan. 12, 1858, Jan. 31, 1858, Feb. 5, 1858 (quotes), Feb. 19, 1859, Feb. 21, 1858, Feb. 28, 1858, April 4, 1858.

21. Hewitt, *Women's Activism*, 135, 141, 184, 190.

22. CRCD, Feb. 28, 1858, March 3, 1858, March 23, 1858; "Early Church Life," 1830–1878.

23. CRCD, Feb. 7, 1858, March 4, 1858.

24. CRCD, Jan. 7, 1858, Jan. 12, 1858, Jan. 9, 1858; CRC, "The Unpardonable Sin," *ASB*, Jan. 30, 1858.

25. CRCD, Feb. 24, 1858, Feb. 5, 1858.

26. CRCD, April 1, 1858.

27. CRCD, March 14, 1858.

6. June 1858–December 1858

1. *Map of the State of Ohio* (New York: J. H. Colton, 1855); advertisement for the C & E Railroad passenger train in the *AS*, June 17, 1858; CRCD, June 11, 1858.

2. CRCD, June 16, 1858.

3. CRCD, June 18, 1858, June 21, 1858.

4. CRCD, June 20, 1858.

5. CRCD, June 22, 1858; Kelly, *In the New England Fashion*, 2–4, 186–87.

6. CRCD, June 24, 1858, June 27, 1858.

7. CRCD, June 29, 1858, July 11, 1858; McMurry, *Transforming Rural Life*, 50, 57–61.

8. CRCD, June 17, 1858, June 23, 1858.

9. For an analysis of nineteenth-century marriages and women's roles within the context of radical abolitionists, including Grimke, Garrison, Kelley, and Stone, see Chris Dixon, *Perfecting the Family: Antislavery Marriages in Nineteenth-Century America* (Amherst: Univ. of Massachusetts Press, 1997), 83–125. For a detailed look at Abby Kelley Foster's marriage, see also Sterling, *Ahead of Her Time*.

10. Kelly, *In the New England Fashion*, 25–27; CRCD, Sept. 10, 1858; *Census for Ohio*, 1850, 1860.

11. CRCD, July 5, 1858, July 19, 1858, July 22, 1858, July 23, 1858, Aug. 2, 1858, Aug. 6, 1858, Aug. 8, 1858, Aug. 15, 1858, Aug. 22, 1858, Sept. 19, 1858, Oct. 14, 1858.

12. CRCD, Oct. 16,1859, July 11, 1858.

13. Boydston, *Home and Work,* 132–33.

14. CRCD, June 30, 1858.

15. Boydston, *Home and Work,* 106–7; Cowan, *More Work for Mother,* 64–65; Riley, *Female Frontier,* 3; CRCD, Dec. 6, 1858, July 19, 1859, July 28, 1859.

16. CRCD, July 27, 1858, Oct. 26, 1858.

17. Beecher, *Treatise,* 136.

18. Ibid., 149.

19. Cowan, *More Work for Mother,* 64; Boydston, *Home and Work,* 85; Beecher, *Treatise,* 308–26, 310–11 (quote).

20. Susan Strasser, *Never Done: A History of American Housework* (New York: Pantheon, 1982), 104–24; Cowan, *More Work for Mother,* 65.

21. CRCD, Feb. 7, 1858, April 6, 1858.

22. CRCD, July 16, 1858.

23. CRCD, Aug. 11, 1858.

24. CRCD, Aug. 12, 1858, Aug. 15, 1858.

25. CRCD, July 12, 1858; John D'Emilio and Estelle B. Freedman, *Intimate Matters: A History of Sexuality in America* (New York: Harper & Row, 1988), 59–61. Contrary to some women's private journals, Colby made no obvious markings that would indicate that she was keeping track of her menstrual cycles—a method often used by women to track fertility and possible pregnancy.

26. CRCD, July 13, 1858, July 27, 1858.

27. Partial manuscript of "'Brookville Home' or The Still Silent Influence of Woman," c. 1858 in CRCMM.

28. CRCD, Oct. 29, 1858; Christina Hardyment, *From Mangle to Microwave: The Mechanization of Household Work* (Oxford, U.K.: Polity, 1988), 42–46; CRC, "My Sewing Machine Drawer," *Ohio Farmer,* c. 1859–60 in CRCPSB2. Interestingly, no testimonial for West & Wilson was located, but approximately a year later she wrote a glowing review for a competitor, Grove and Baker. As one of the best-selling sewing machines of the antebellum era, perhaps it offered a better exchange.

29. CRCD, Dec. 28, 1858, Nov. 2, 1858, Nov. 3, 1858.

30. CRCD, Dec. 6, 1858, Dec. 11, 1858.

31. CRCD, Sept. 25, 1858, Oct. 1, 1857.

32. CRCD, Aug. 29, 1858, Sept. 17, 1858.

33. CRCD, Aug. 21, 1858, Aug. 13, 1858.

7. NOVEMBER 1858–NOVEMBER 1859

1. CRCD, Nov. 6, 1858, Jan. 9, 1859; marriage announcement for Edward L. Colby and Annie Colby in *AS,* Nov. 11, 1858. Edward L. Colby was "brother Ned"—the son of Lewis's older brother, Rowell, which made Annie and Ned first cousins. However, at this time marriage between first cousins was legal, and also not viewed in the same light as today.

2. CRCD, July 28, 1858, May 17, 1859.

3. Bressler, *Universalist Movement,* 37–40; CRCD, April 24, 1859, May 9, 1859.

4. Bressler, *Universalist Movement,* 97–121.

5. Ibid., 98–125; R. Lawrence Moore, "The Spiritualist Medium: A Study of Female Professionalization in Victorian America," 145–56.

6. CRCD, Oct. 29, 1858, Dec. 4, 1859, Dec. 11, 1859.

7. CRCD, May 2, 1858, Oct. 24, 1858, Aug. 2, 1858; Hewitt, *Women's Activism,* 142.

8. CRCSB in CC, available at Illinois State University Archives, Illinois State University, Normal, Illinois; CRCD, Oct. 14, 1857, Aug. 22, 1858. Colby's clippings scrapbook, which contains material from the 1850s to the late 1860s, demonstrates an extremely diverse range of interests—poetry, history, astronomy, politics, geology, weather, current events. The totality illustrates her desire to better understand her world: naturally, supernaturally, and culturally.

9. CRCD, March 1, 1859.

10. CRCD, Oct. 3, 1859, Nov. 27, 1859.

11. CRCD, Oct. 16, 1959.

12. CRCD, Jan. 4, 1859; last will and testament of CRC, Jan. 1, 1859, CC; last will and testament of LC, Jan. 1, 1859, CC; Booth, *Buckeye Women,* 58–63. Ohio's inheritance laws in 1850 entitled a widow to only one-third of a deceased husband's estate if no will was left. In addition, in the event of death or divorce, women had no assumed right of custody; guardianship often was granted to another—male—relative in the event of death and almost automatically to the father in the case of divorce. Women had no legal rights to their own earnings or over their own children, as well as no right to vote. It was not until 1861 that the amount of property a widow could keep if her husband died without a will was changed.

13. CRCD, Jan 5, 1859, Nov. 6, 1858.

14. CRC, "Rosalie," *OC,* Dec. 28, 1858 in CRCPSB2.

15. Ibid.

16. Ibid.; CRCD, Dec. 23, 1858.

17. CRCD, May 9, 1859.

18. CRCD, July 7, 1859.

19. CRCD, Aug. 4, 1859. Robinson's identity is unclear. He was a stranger to Colby, which because of the size of the community makes it unlikely that he was a local, thus he was likely a traveling reform speaker.

20. CRCD, Feb. 19, 1859.

21. CRCD, Dec. 5, 1858.

22. CRCD, April 5, 1859.

23. CRCD, Aug. 30, 1859.

24. Ibid.

25. CRCD, April 1, 1859, May 9, 1859.

26. CRCD, Oct. 16, 1859.

27. CRC to Emily Sanborn (draft copy of letter), Oct.4, 1858 in CRCMM; CRCD, July 5, 1859.

28. CRCD, Aug. 4, 1859, Aug. 27, 1859, May 18, 1859.

29. CRCD, Feb. 6, 1859, Feb. 18, 1859.

30. CRCD, Sept. 25,1859.

31. CRCD, Oct. 26, 1859, Nov. 6, 1859.

32. CRCD, Oct. 29, 1859, Nov. 6, 1859, Nov. 8, 1859.

8. NOVEMBER 1859–FEBRUARY 1861

1. CRCD, Dec. 19, 1859.

2. CRCD, July 7, 1859, Aug. 5, 1859.

3. CRCD, Dec. 12, 1859, Feb. 5, 1860.

4. CRCD, May 6, 1860.

5. CRCD Dec. 19, 1859.

6. CRC, "Woman's Work and Teaching," *OC,* c. June 1860 in CRCPSB3.

7. CRCD, Dec. 25, 1859.

8. CRCD, Oct. 29, 1857, Feb. 2, 1860.

9. CRCD, Dec. 7, 1859.

10. Riley, *The Female Frontier,* 148–51; Kelly, *In the New England Fashion,* 14, 197–207; CRCD, Feb. 17, 1861.

11. CRCD, Dec. 10, 1859, Feb. 4, 1860.

12. Smith-Rosenberg, "Female World," 265–70; Kelly, *In the New England Fashion,* 92; JRC, "A Study," c. 1880–90s.

13. CRCD, April 24, 1860.

14. Carol Steinhagen, "The Two Lives of Frances Dana Gage," *Ohio History* 107 (Winter 1998): 22–38. Frances Dana Gage is not as remembered today as much as many early female reformers, but she was an important member of Ohio's female reform movement. Interestingly, Gage's most lasting contribution to the history of female reform movements may have been her 1863 *New York Independent* depiction of the 1851 Akron Woman's Rights Convention, over which she presided. Gage immortalized Sojourner Truth's infamous "Ain't I a Woman" speech in this article. Historian Nell Irvin Painter establishes that this particular quote—although firmly ensconced in the popular vernacular and historical interpretations—was actually "Gage's invention." Nell Irvin Painter, *Sojourner Truth: A Life, A Symbol* (New York: W. W. Norton), 121–31.

15. CRC, "Mrs. Gage and her Lectures," *OF,* April 26, 1860 in CRCPSB3.

16. CRCD, May 7, 1860.

17. CRCD, May 23, 1860.

18. Lystra, *Searching the Heart,* 28–55, 192–206.

19. CRC to "M.C.C." (manuscript draft of letter), Jan. 10, 1860, CRCMM. "M.C.C." was possibly her cousin Mary Colby, as a letter to Annie with the same date also mentions that she was posting a letter to "cousin Mary" that day.

20. CRCD, Dec. 30, 1859, June 17, 1862.

21. "I Wouldn't, Would You?" undated; "We are Two," undated, CRCMM.

22. Lystra, *Searching the Heart,* 194, 206–13.

23. CRC, "Mrs. Weldon's Vigils," *MF,* c. 1861–62.

24. CRCD, Jan. 21, 1860.

25. CRCD, Nov. 24, 1859.

26. CRCD, Nov. 19, 1859.

27. Kelley, "Reading Women/Women Reading," 402, 412; Riney-Kehrberg, "Limits of Community"; Pamela Riney-Kehrberg, "Separation and Sorrow: A Farm Woman's Life, 1935–1941," *Agricultural History* 67, no. 2 (Spring 1993): 185–96; CRCD, Dec. 18, 1860.

28. CRCD, Dec. 23, 1860.

29. CRCD, Dec. 4, 1859, May 16, 1860.

30. CRCD, Jan. 19, 1860, March 10, 1860, June 19, 1860, Feb. 26, 1860, Nov. 3, 1858.

9. FEBRUARY 1861–NOVEMBER 1861

1. *AS,* October, 1857–March 1858.

2. Sterling, *Ahead of Her Time,* 318–23; Fuller, *Underground to Freedom,* 21–22.

3. Sterling, *Ahead of Her Time,* 325–26, 326 (quote).

4. CRCD, Dec. 2, 1859; CRC, "A Morning in December, or a Leaf from my Journal," *ASB,* Jan. 7, 1860.

5. Editorials in *AS,* Jan. 15, 1857, April 11, 1860.

6. CRCD, Sept. 14, 1860; Robertson, *Parker Pillsbury,* 10–84.

7. "A.D.O." to editor, *AS,* Oct. 24, 1860; editorial in *AS,* Sept. 26, 1860.

8. CRC, "A Republican Rejoicing," unknown publication, c. Dec. 1859–Jan. 1860 in CRCPSB3. Colby quotes from Sherman's speech in her essay.

9. Sterling, *Ahead of Her Time,* 328–30.

10. CRCD, Sept. 14, 1860, Oct. 19, 1860, Nov. 26, 1860.

11. CRCD, Oct. 19, 1860, Oct. 28, 1860, Nov. 26, 1860, Dec. 18, 1860, Dec. 23, 1860, Jan. 12, 1861, June 30, 1860.

12. CRC, "Making Little Ladies," *Field Notes,* May 1861 in CRCPSB3.

13. CRC, "Equal Rights—Circulating Petitions &c.," *ASB,* Feb. 9, 1861.

14. Russo and Kramarae, *Radical Women's Press,* 31–324; Booth, *Buckeye Women,* 58–63.

15. Mrs. Betsy Phelps Wadsworth Guild's death notice, *AS,* May 28, 1857; CRC, "Equal Rights—Circulating Petitions &c.," *ASB,* Feb. 9, 1861; CRCD, Feb. 15, 1861.

16. CRCD, Feb. 18, 1861.

17. CRCD, March 20, 1861, May 8, 1861.

18. CRC, "To the Editor," *AS,* Aug. 26, 1861.

19. Advertisements in the *ASB,* December 1860; Russo and Kramarae, *Radical Women's Press,* 294, 325. *The Mayflower* first appeared in Jan. 1861 as a paper "devoted to temperance, chaste Literature, and the general interests of women." It was published in Peru, Indiana, by two women, Lizzie Bunnel and Dr. Mary Myers Thomas, and its contributors included such noted reformers as Amelia Bloomer.

20. CRC, "An Essay: Read Before the Cherry Valley Literary Society," *MF,* Aug. 1, 1861.

21. CRC, "Woman, the 'Stronger Vessel,'" *MF,* July 1, 1861.

22. CRC, "An Essay: Read Before the Cherry Valley Literary Society," *MF,* Aug. 1, 1861; Robin Morgan, *Going Too Far: The Personal Chronicle of a Feminist.* Originally published by the author, 1968; New York: First Vintage Books, 1978.

23. CRC, "An Essay: Read Before the Cherry Valley Literary Society," *MF,* Aug. 1, 1861.

24. Ibid., Aug. 15, 1861.

25. CRC, "An Essay: Read Before the Cherry Valley Literary Society," *MF,* Aug. 15, 1861.

26. Ibid.

27. Sylvia D. Hoffert, *When Hens Crow* (Bloomington: Indiana Univ. Press, 1995), 53–72.

28. These figures come from L. P. Brocket and Mary C. Vaughan's 1867 book *Women's Work in the Civil War* as referenced in Jeannie Attie's *Patriotic Toil: Northern Women and the American Civil War* (Ithaca, N.Y.: Cornell Univ. Press, 1998), 3.

29. Hewitt, *Women's Activism*, 231–32.

10. SEPTEMBER 1861–DECEMBER 1862

1. Annie Colby's death notice in *AS*, Sept. 19, 1861; CRCD, Sept. 29, 1861, Nov. 11, 1861.

2. CRCD, Dec. 28, 1861, Sept. 22, 1861, Oct. 8, 1861, Dec. 15, 1861, March 14, 1862.

3. CRC, "While Darning Socks" and "Silent Heroism," *MF*, c. 1862 in CRCPSB3; CRCD, April 21, 1862.

4. CRC, "To the Editor," *AS*, Nov. 13, 1861.

5. Ibid.

6. Kelly, *In the New England Fashion*, 188–99.

7. CRC, "Treason," *AS*, Nov. 28, 1861.

8. Ibid.; Sizer, *Political Work*, 76–77.

9. Sizer, *Political Work*, 77–79, Attie, *Patriotic Toil*, 1–5.

10. Sizer, *Political Work*, 84–107.

11. CRCD, June 17, 1862, April 24, 1862.

12. CRC, ed. "The Ladies Volunteer," vol. 1, no. 1, November 1861 and vol. 1, no. 5, September 1862, CC; Williams Brothers, *History of Ashtabula County*, 58. *Census for Ohio*, 1850–70; CRCD, Oct. 17, 1861. For Colby's writings on war and politics, see CRCPSB2 and CRCPSB3, 1854–70, and for news she clipped on war and politics, see CRCSB, c. 1860–70.

13. For examples of numerous articles written by CRC that focused on farming, business, and economic issues, see CRCPSB 1–3 for the following: "Our Fair," *AS*, Sept. 2, 1854; "Rainy Days," *DN* (Philadelphia, Pa.), c. 1853; "Raising Calves," *DN*, c. 1853; "Cheese," *DN*, c. 1854; "Girls' Wages—Ohio butter," *OC*, c. 1854; "Our Fair—Labor Misapplied," *OC*, October 1854; "Winter Butter," *DN*, c. 1854; "The Poetry of Farming," *OC*, c. 1853; "Fall Feed and Dairying," *OC*, c. 1854; "Lessons of a Hard Season," *DN*, c. 1856; "Cheese Making," *AS*, December 1857; "Mistaken Economy," *DN*, c. 1858; "Osage Orange Hedges," *DN*, c. 1858; "The Dairy—Essay on Butter," unknown publication, Nov. 12, 1858; "Winter Farming, " *OF*, Jan. 9, 1862; "Cheese Making," *OF*, c. 1862; "Importance of Shelter for Cattle," *DN*, c. 1860; "Be Practical," *OF*, Jan. 4, 1863.

14. Russo and Kramarae, *Radical Women's Press*, 11–16, 95–123; CRC, "A few Queries Answered," *FA*, c. 1862 in CRCPSB3.

15. CRC, "A few Queries Answered," *FA*, c. 1862 in CRCPSB3; Booth, *Buckeye Women*, 173; *Atlas of Ohio*, 15.

16. CRC, "A few Queries Answered," *FA*, c. 1862 in CRCPSB3.

17. CRC, "A Woman's Influence," *MF*, Sept. 1, 1862; CRC, "A few Queries Answered," *FA*, c. 1862.

18. Ruth Bordin, *Woman and Temperance: The Quest for Power and Liberty, 1873–1900* (Philadelphia, Pa.: Temple Univ. Press, 1981), 4–5; Hewitt, *Women's Activism*, 109, 113, 160–64, 162 (quote), 166–67; Norma Basch, *Framing American Divorce: From the Revolutionary Generation to the Victorians* (Berkley: Univ. of California Press, 1999), 68–80. Page number citations are from the 2001 paperback edition.

19. CRC, "Reverie of a Drunkard's Wife," *MF,* c. 1862 in CRCPSB3. For examples of straightforward information dissemination, see CRC, "What are Temperance Society's [*sic*] Doing?" unknown publication, c. 1862, and "The Mission of the Pledge," *Olive Branch,* (Youngstown, Ohio), c. 1862 in CRCPSB3.

20. CRC, "What the Whiskey Did," unknown publication, c. 1861–63 in CRCPSB3.

21. Ibid.

22. CRC, "Essay: Read Before the Cherry Valley Total Abstinence and Literary Society," unknown publication, c. 1862 in CRCPSB3. For an informative discussion regarding women's social accountability within the context of "the divorce question as a battle of competing ideologies whose outcome would reshape both the moral and political contours of the [postbellum] nation," see Basch, *Framing American Divorce,* 80–90.

23. CRCD, March 14, 1862, Jan. 10, 1862.

24. CRCD, Nov. 20, 1862, Feb 3, 1862, Feb. 4, 1862; CRC "Aurora Leigh," March 1, 1862, *MF.*

25. CRCD, June 17, 1862.

26. GN; CRCD, Nov. 20, 1862.

27. CRCD, Aug. 25, 1861.

28. Ibid.

11. SEPTEMBER 1862–APRIL 1865

1. CRCD, Nov. 20, 1862.

2. CRCD, March 11, 1863.

3. CRC, "To ——," Nov. 6, 1864 in CRCMM. For examples of her work during late 1862 through 1863, see CRCSB3. Examples include: A "Letter to Miss Bunnel" about Plummer's death and "Greenworth Home" about happy times in the past with Annie and Jennie, *MF,* c. 1862; and "Bob Tail Grey," "The Faithful Gander," and "Uncle Jess's Old Log Cabin," all children's stories in *LP,* c. 1862–63. Only three essays in CRCPSB3 seem to have been written in 1864: "Madame Brownie's Mourning" for the *LP,* and "Mission of Thought" and "Kind Words" for the *MF. The Little Pilgrim* was one of the nation's first children's magazines. It was published from 1853 to 1875 and had feminist ties, as its publisher—Grace Greenwood, pen name for Sara Jane Clarke—was an abolitionist and women's rights supporter. Abby Kelley Foster gave her young daughter a subscription to *The Little Pilgrim,* which promised "pure morality with pure literature." Russo and Kramarae, *Radical Women's Press,* 303; Ryan, *Cradle of the Middle Class,* 134–35; Sterling, *Ahead of Her Time,* 291.

4. CRC, "Treason." *AS,* Nov. 28, 1861; CRC, "The Slave Mother," *AS,* Sept. 16, 1854 in CRCPSB2; CRCD, Sept. 1, 1862.

5. CRCSB; CRCD, March 11, 1863.

6. Sizer, *Political Work,* 109–14; CRCD, June 26, 1863.

7. CRCSB.

8. Carroll Smith-Rosenberg, "Puberty to Menopause: The Cycle of Femininity in Nineteenth-Century America," in *Disorderly Conduct,* 197–216; CRC, "Patchwork Quilts," *Field Notes,* November, 1861 in CRCPSB3.

9. CRCD, Sept. 1, 1862, *Atlas of Ohio,* 14.

10. CRCD, April 9, 1863; Naomi Colby's death notice, Oct. 14, 1863; GN.

11. CRCD, Feb. 5, 1864.

12. Ibid., Feb. 9, 1864.

13. CRCD, March 2, 1864, March 17, 1864.

14. CRCD, March 24, 1864, March 17, 1864, March 11, 1863.

15. CRCD, Nov. 29, 1857 (quote), Jan. 1, 1858 (quote), March 16, 1858, Jan. 23, 1858 (quote), March 1, 1859 (quote), Nov. 24, 1858, Nov. 28, 1858, May 17, 1859, Sept. 25, 1859, Oct. 16, 1859 (quote), Oct. 27, 1859 (quote).

16. Kelley, "Reading Women/Women Reading," 401–24, 405 (quote); CRCD, Jan. 20, 1860, Nov. 26, 1860, Jan. 19, 1860.

17. CRC, "Aurora Leigh," March 1, 1862, *MF;* CRCD, March 22, 1863.

18. CRCD, March 26, 1864, April 22, 1864, April 3, 1864, March 17, 1864, May 29, 1864. She mentioned reading the *Atlantic Monthly* magazine several times, but only a few books, and only one real critique: Bayard Taylor's *Hannah Thurston,* which she liked "in spite of disliking it."

19. CRCD, July 11, 1864.

20. Sklar, *Beecher,* 156–61, 204–5; Carroll Smith-Rosenberg, "The Hysterical Woman: Sex Roles and Role Conflict in Nineteenth-Century America," in *Women's Experience in America: An Historical Anthology,* ed. Esther Katz and Anita Rapone (New Brunswick, N.J.: Transaction Books, 1980), 315–38.

21. CRCD, Feb. 5, 1865.

22. McMurry, *Transforming Rural Life,* 1–2, 96–101, 127–29.

12. February 1865–July 1900

1. CRCD, Feb. 17, 1865, Feb. 20, 1865.

2. CRC to "Friend Nellie" (manuscript draft of letter), April 11, 1865.

3. CRC, May 20, 1865, May 28, 1865.

4. Flavia Bradley Rice died in 1829, Evelina Johnson Rice died in 1863, and Dorcas Barker Rice died in 1873. Interestingly, but not uncommon for the time, all three women were closely related. Flavia and Evelina were half-sisters, and Flavia and Dorcas were first cousins. Colby's brother, John Bradley Rice, married Susan Adams in December of 1864. In a sad mirror to his own mother's death, he tragically lost his new bride when she and their infant son, Joel Adams Rice, died in December 1865, just two months after Joel's birth. Bradley married Christina August in December of 1868. Gravesite records for Joel Rice, Congregational Church Cemetery, West Andover, Ohio; gravesite records for Jay and Jennie Rice, Cherry Valley Cemetery, Cherry Valley, Ohio; *Census for Ohio,* 1860, 1870, 1880, 1900; *Census for Illinois,* 1870, 1880, 1900; GN; CRCMC in CC, available at Illinois State University Archives, Illinois State University, Normal, Illinois.

5. Vine Colby to "Uncle Orin" (manuscript draft of letter), May 16, 1866, CC; GN; *Census for Ohio,* 1860, 1870, 1880; *Census for Illinois,* 1870, 1880, 1900; *Census for Nebraska,* 1880; Illinois Public Domain Land Tract Records, available at the Illinois State Archives, Springfield, Illinois. Lewis's other known sibling, Converse Colby, was living in Cherry Valley with his wife, Lucinda, in the early 1860s, but is unaccounted for after this point.

6. LCAB, Freeport, Illinois, 1866–70 in CC, available at Illinois State University Archives, Illinois State University, Normal, Illinois; *Census for Illinois,* 1870; *The Index* (Normal: Illinois State Normal University, 1932), 44.

7. Catharine E. Beecher and Harriet Beecher Stowe, *The American Woman's Home or, Principles of Domestic Science: Being a Guide to the Formation and Maintenance of Economical, Healthful, Beautiful and Christian Homes,* ed. Nicole Tonkovich (1869; reprint, New Brunswick, N.J.: Rutgers Univ. Press, 2002).

8. Although this flurry extended only from the beginning of 1870 through March 1870, it totaled approximately seventeen pieces. The temperance writings included, "The Dear Old Spring," *The Prohibitionist,* March 1870, and a poem, "A Summer Scene," unknown publication, c. 1870 in CRCPSB3. The most numerous contributions were children's stories for the *LP,* numbering at least seven.

9. CRC to editor, *AS,* February 1870 and "The Rebekah Degree—What is it?" *Western Odd Fellow,* Feb. 5, 1870 in CRCPSB3.

10. Dorothy Gies McGuigan, *A Dangerous Experiment: 100 Years of Women at the University of Michigan* (Ann Arbor: Univ. if Michigan, 1970), 15–31.

11. McGuigan, *A Dangerous Experiment,* 31–32, quote, 31.

12. VCFNF and SFNF, available at Bentley Historical Library, University of Michigan, Ann Arbor, Michigan; GN; McGuigan, *A Dangerous Experiment,* 78, 88; Woloch, *Women and the American Experience,* 289. The forces of patriarchal professionalization began to gather strength at the turn of the century, and subsequently squashed the female surge of doctors, which peaked around 1910.

13. "Branch Colby, Engineer Dies," *Pantagraph,* Jan. 4, 1944; BCNF, available from Bentley Historical Library, University of Michigan, Ann Arbor, Michigan; *Census for Michigan,* 1880; MBCNF, available from Bentley Historical Library, University of Michigan, Ann Arbor, Michigan; GN.

14. JRCNF and JRCAS, available at Bentley Historical Library, University of Michigan, Ann Arbor, Michigan; *Census for Michigan,* 1880; *Index,* 44; *Historical Encyclopedia of Illinois, Volume II,* (Chicago: Munsell, 1908), 971–72; "Dr. J. Rose Colby Dies at Normal Home," *Pantagraph,* May 12, 1941; editorial, *Pantagraph,* May 13, 1941; "Your News Release from Illinois State Normal University," Feb. 27, 1961.

15. *Census for Illinois,* 1870; *Census for Michigan,* 1880; information from the *Ann Arbor City Directories* 1872, 1874–75, 1878–79 and *Flint City Directory,* 1881–82 provided courtesy of the BHL; LCAB; *Index;* JRC and VCF University of Michigan class notebooks, 1870–86, CC.

16. Numerous partial manuscripts apparently date from the early 1880s, but the following essays are clearly dated from November and December of 1881: CRC, "Sixteen White Cats all in a Row," "My Empty Bird's Nest," and "The Old Woman who lived in a Boot" in CRCMM; CRCMC; JRC, "Silent work for Suffrage," *The Woman's Journal,* Jan. 21, 1882.

17. *Flint City Directory,* 1881–82; CRC, "A Plea for Wild flowers: An essay read before the Genesee County Horticulture Society," Feb. 20, 1883; JRCNF; JRCAS; *Peoria City Directory* (Peoria, Ill.: J. W. Frank and Sons), 1891–92; *Census for Illinois,* 1900; CRC's last will and testament, Nov. 1, 1883, McLean County Clerk Probate and Will Records, available from the Illinois Regional Archives Depository, Illinois State University, Normal, Illinois. The 1881–82 city directory lists Lewis Colby as the head of the Flint household, and Colby appeared before the Horticulture Society in Flint in early spring 1883—both of which imply residency.

18. Lewis Colby's death record, Livingston County Clerk; Marriage Record for Lewis Colby and Harriet Darrow, Livingston County Marriage Records; *Census for Michigan,* 1910. Michigan did not require that counties report divorce proceedings to the state until 1897. Before that date, the counties handled divorce proceedings in various courts, most often

chancery courts. Records from those nineteenth-century courts are often not retained in full, not indexed, and not stored in a way that makes them readily accessible.

19. Glenda Riley, *Divorce: An American Tradition* (New York: Oxford Univ. Press, 1991), 59–61, 72–80, 94–112.

20. Riley, *Divorce*, 79–86; Elaine Tyler May, *Great Expectations: Marriage and Divorce in Post-Victorian America* (Chicago: Univ. of Chicago Press, 1980), 23–48; Carl Degler, *At Odds: Women and the Family in America from the Revolution to the Present* (New York: Oxford Univ. Press, 1980), 144–77, 74 (quote); Statistics are from United States Commissioner of Labor Carroll D. Wright's 1889 report as cited in Riley, *Divorce*, 79–94 and Degler, *At Odds*, 166; Basch, *Framing American Divorce*, 99–109, 117–20, 120 (quote); Nancy Cott, *Public Vows: A History of Marriage and the Nation* (Cambridge, Mass.: Harvard Univ. Press, 2000) 50–51; see also Hendrik Hartog, *Man and Wife in America: A History,* (Cambridge, Mass.: Harvard Univ. Press, 2000). Scholarship regarding divorce has grown steadily and often reflects diverse interpretations. For example, diverging views regarding women and divorce in California in the latter half of the nineteenth century are apparent in the following: Robert L. Griswold, "Apart but not Adrift: Wives, Divorce, and Independence in California, 1850–1890," *Pacific Historical Review* 49, no. 2 (1980): 265–83, and Susan Gonda, "Not a Matter of Choice: San Diego Women and Divorce, 1850–1880," *Journal of San Diego History* 37: 3 (1991): 194–213.

21. For statistics and compelling arguments that the rise in divorce was in many ways grounded in women's rising social status, see May, *Great Expectations*, 27–48; Degler, *At Odds*, 167–77. For an alternative interpretation in which divorce for women is framed around the supposition that in reality the rising rate was not necessarily the function of women's rising expectations, see Basch, *Framing American Divorce*, 99–120.

22. Basch, *Framing American Divorce*, 105; LCAB.

23. Basch, *Framing American Divorce*, 109–14; Riley, *Divorce*, 79–90, 110–11.

24. Riley, *Divorce*, 94, 108–16; Basch, *Framing American Divorce*, 117–18, 118 (quote); *Peoria City Directory* (Peoria, Ill.: David Gould, 1887, 1889); *Peoria City Directories* (Peoria, Ill.: J. W. Frank and Sons), 1888–89, 1891–92; *Peoria City Directory* (Peoria, Ill.: Transcript Publishing), 1890–1891; *Bloomington-Normal City Directories* (Bloomington, Ill.: Pantagraph Publishing and Stationary Co.), 1893–99; CRCMC; CRC, last will and testament, written Nov. 1, 1883, and filed Sept. 18, 1900, in McLean County Clerk's Probate and Will Records, available at the Illinois Regional Archives Depository, Illinois State University, Normal, Ill. Although Colby apparently stayed briefly with Branch in St. Louis while Rose attended Radcliffe, she joined her in Ann Arbor, when Rose returned in 1884 to pursue her master's and doctorate degrees. When Rose left for Peoria in 1888 to teach, Colby purchased a home, and the two women also lived there together. She also joined Rose in the move to Normal, Illinois, after Rose became a professor at the Illinois State Normal University. At the time Colby's estate was settled, she still owned property in Peoria. Her ability to purchase this house perhaps implies some sort of divorce settlement.

25. CRCMC; Minnie Colby to CRC, April 18, 1893, in CRCMC (quote); CRC to Vine Colby, Sept. 6, 1889, in CRCMC (quote).

26. Eva Davis to CRC, Nov. 25, 1892, in CRCMC (quote).

27. CRCMM.

28. Mrs. Frank B. Whitman, "A Thumbnail Sketch of the Purposes of the Normal History club with Apologies to Abraham Lincoln," Feb. 8, 1974 (quote) and "The Normal History

Club: The First One Hundred Years," c. 1994, available from the Normal History Club Collection, held by Illinois State University Archives, Illinois State University, Normal, Illinois.

29. Woloch, *Women and the American Experience,* 292–95; CRCMM; Tuesday Club pamphlet and notebook for 1884–85, CC; Normal History Club Pamphlets, 1895–1900, Normal History Club Collection, held by Illinois State University Archives, Illinois State University, Normal, Illinois.

30. JRC, "A Study," c. 1880–1890s.

31. Ibid.

32. Ibid.

33. CRC Death Record, McLean County Clerk Death Records, available at the Illinois Regional Archives Depository, Illinois State University, Normal, Illinois; CRC's death notice, *Pantagraph,* July, 30, 1900.

Conclusion

1. Betty Friedan, *The Feminine Mystique* (New York: Dell, 1974, 1963).

Bibliography

PRIMARY SOURCES

ARCHIVAL COLLECTIONS

Colby Collection. Illinois State University Archives, Illinois State University, Normal, Illinois.

Normal History Club Collection. Illinois State University Archives, Illinois State University, Normal, Illinois.

University of Michigan Alumni Surveys. Bentley Historical Library, University of Michigan, Ann Arbor, Michigan.

University of Michigan Necrology Files. Bentley Historical Library, University of Michigan, Ann Arbor, Michigan.

University of Michigan Portrait Collection. Bentley Historical Library, University of Michigan, Ann Arbor, Michigan.

BOOKS, CATALOGS, PAMPHLETS, AND MAPS

Ann Arbor, Michigan City Directories, 1872, 1874–75, 1878, 1879. Information obtained courtesy of Bentley Historical Library, University of Michigan, Ann Arbor, Michigan.

Atlas of the State of Ohio: From the Surveys Under the Direction of H. F. Walling. New York: Henry S. Stebbins, 1867–68.

Beecher, Catharine. A Treatise on Domestic Economy. New York: Marsh, Capen, Lyon, and Webb, 1841; Schocken Books, 1977.

Beecher, Catharine, and Harriet Beecher Stowe. The American Woman's Home or, Principles of Domestic Science: Being a Guide to the Formation and Maintenance of Economical, Healthful, Beautiful and Christian Homes. Ed. Nicole Tonkovich. 1869. Reprint, New Brunswick, N.J.: Rutgers University Press, 2002.

Bloomington-Normal City Directories. Bloomington, Ill.: Pantagraph Publishing and Stationary Co., 1893–99.

Catalogue of the Instructors and Students of the Ashtabula County Teachers' Institute. Cleveland, Ohio: Younglove's Steam, 1846.

Catalogues of the Instructors and Students of the Ashtabula County Teachers' Institute. Ashtabula, Ohio: Sentinel Office, 1847, 1849, 1851.

Catalogue of the Instructors and Students of the Ashtabula County Teachers' Institute. Conneaut, Ohio: D. C. Allen, 1848.

Catalogue of the Instructors and Students of the Ashtabula County Teachers' Institute. Ashtabula, Ohio: N. W. Thayer, 1850.

Catalogue of the Officers and Students of Grand River Institute. Cleveland, Ohio: Smead & Cowles', 1850.

Catalogues of the Officers and Students of Grand River Institute. Ashtabula, Ohio: Sentinel Office, 1846, 1848, 1849.

de Tocqueville, Alexis. *Democracy in America.* 1835. New York: Bantam Books, 2000.

Early Church Life in Cherry Valley: Extracts from the Record Book of the Regular Baptist Church, 1830–78. Transcribed from handwritten original. Available at the Newberry Library, Chicago, Illinois.

Flint, Michigan, City Directories, 1881–82. Information obtained courtesy of Bentley Historical Library, University of Michigan, Ann Arbor, Michigan.

Fuller, Margaret. *Woman In the Nineteenth Century.* 1855. Reprint, New York: W. W. Norton, 1971.

The Index. Normal, Illinois: Illinois State Normal University, 1932.

Map of the State of Ohio. New York: J. H. Colton, 1855.

Peoria City Directories. Peoria, Illinois: David Gould, 1887, 1889.

Peoria City Directories. Peoria, Illinois: J. W. Frank and Sons, 1888–89, 1891–92.

Peoria City Directory. Peoria, Illinois: Transcript Publishing, 1890–91.

Trollope, Frances. "Domestic Manners of the Americans." Excerpts available at *Women in America, 1820–1842.* http://xroads.Virginia.edu/~hyper/detoc/fem/home.

CEMETERY AND GRAVESITE RECORDS

Congregational Church of Andover, Andover, Ohio.

Cherry Valley Cemetery, Cherry Valley, Ohio.

Evergreen Memorial Cemetery, Bloomington, Illinois.

CENSUS

United States Census Bureau 2000 Population Summary. http://factfinder.census.gov/home/datanotes/.

United States Historical Web Browser, 1790–1970. http://fisher.lib.Virginia.edu/census/.

United States Federal Population Schedules for Illinois. 1860–1880, 1900–1910.

United States Federal Population Schedules for Michigan. 1880, 1910.

United States Federal Population Schedules for Nebraska. 1880.

United States Federal Population Schedules for Ohio. 1820–1880, 1890–1900.

NEWSPAPERS

Anti-Slavery Bugle (Salem, Ohio).

Ashtabula Sentinel (Jefferson, Ohio).

The Ladies Repository (Cincinnati, Ohio).

The Mayflower (Peru, Ind.).

The Pantagraph (Bloomington, Ill.).

The Woman's Journal (Boston, Mass.).

PUBLIC RECORDS

Ashtabula County Clerk Marriage Records. Available at the Ohio State Historical Society, Columbus, Ohio.

Illinois Department of Public Health Death Records. Available at the Illinois State Archives, Springfield, Illinois.

Illinois Public Domain Land Tract Records. Available at the Illinois State Archives, Springfield, Illinois.

Livingston County Clerk Marriage and Death Records. Available at the Livingston County Clerk's Office, Howell, Michigan.

McLean County Clerk Death Records. Available at the Illinois Regional Archives Depository, Illinois State University, Normal, Illinois.

McLean County Clerk Probate and Will Records. Available at the Illinois Regional Archives Depository, Illinois State University, Normal, Illinois.

SECONDARY SOURCES

Ashtabula County Genealogical Society. *Ashtabula County History: Then and Now.* Dallas, Tex.: Taylor, 1985.

Attie, Jeannie. *Patriotic Toil: Northern Women and the American Civil War.* Ithaca, N.Y.: Cornell University Press, 1998.

Basch, Norma. *Framing American Divorce: From the Revolutionary Generation to the Victorians.* Berkeley, Calif.: University of California Press, 1999.

Baym, Nina. *American Women Writers and the Work of History, 1790–1860.* New Brunswick, N.J.: Rutgers University Press, 1995.

———. *Novels, Readers, and Reviewers: Responses to Fiction in Antebellum America.* Ithaca, N.Y.: Cornell University Press, 1984.

———. *Woman's Fiction: A Guide to Novels by and About Women in America, 1820–1870.* 1978. 2d ed. Urbana: University of Illinois Press, 1993.

Booth, Stephane Elise. *Buckeye Women: The History of Ohio's Daughters.* Athens, Ohio: Ohio University Press, 2001.

Bordin, Ruth. *Woman and Temperance: The Quest for Power and Liberty, 1873–1900.* Philadelphia, Pa.: Temple University Press, 1981.

Boydston, Jeanne. *Home and Work: Housework, Wages, and the Ideology of Labor in the Early Republic.* New York: Oxford University Press, 1990.

Bressler, Ann Lee. *The Universalist Movement in America, 1770–1880.* New York: Oxford University Press, 2001.

Chesebrough, David. *Charles G. Finney: Revivalistic Rhetoric.* Westport, Conn.: Greenwood Press, 2002.

Clinton, Catherine. *The Other Civil War: American Women in the Nineteenth Century.* New York: Hill and Wang, 1984.

Coontz, Stephanie. *The Social Origins of Private Life: A History of American Families 1600–1900.* London: Verso, 1988.

Cott, Nancy F. *The Bonds of Womanhood: "Woman's Sphere" in New England, 1780–1835.* New Haven, Conn.: Yale University Press, 1977.

———. *Public Vows: A History of Marriage and the Nation.* Cambridge, Mass.: Harvard University Press, 2000.

Cowan, Ruth Schwartz. *More Work for Mother: The Ironies of Household Technology from the Open Hearth to the Microwave.* New York: Basic Books, 1983.

Davidoff, Leonore. "Gender and the Great Divide: Public and Private in British Gender History." *Journal of Women's History* 15, no. 1 (Spring 2003): 11–27.

Degler, Carl. *At Odds: Women and the Family in America from the Revolution to the Present.* New York: Oxford University Press, 1980.

Divided Houses: Gender and the Civil War. Edited by Catherine Clinton and Nina Silber. New York: Oxford University Press, 1992.

Dixon, Chris. *Perfecting the Family: Antislavery Marriages in Nineteenth-Century America.* Amherst: University of Massachusetts Press, 1997.

Douglas, Ann. *The Feminization of American Culture.* New York: Alfred E. Knopf, 1977; Anchor Press/Doubleday, 1988.

DuBois, Ellen Carol. *Feminism and Suffrage: The Emergence of an Independent Women's Movement in America 1848–1869.* Ithaca, N.Y.: Cornell University Press, 1978.

D'Emilio, John, and Estelle B. Freedman. *Intimate Matters: A History of Sexuality in America.* New York: Harper & Row, 1988.

Epstein, Barbara Leslie. *The Politics of Domesticity: Women, Evangelism, and Temperance in Nineteenth-Century America.* Middletown, Conn.: Wesleyan University Press, 1981.

Faragher, John Mack. *Sugar Creek: Life on the Illinois Prairie.* New Haven, Conn.: Yale University Press, 1986.

Faragher, Johnny, and Christine Stansell. "Women and their Families on the Overland Trail, 1842–1867." In *Women's Experience in America: An Historical Anthology,* ed. Esther Katz and Anita Rapone, 293–314. New Brunswick, N.J.: Transaction Books, 1980.

Fink, Deborah. *Open Country, Iowa: Rural Women, Tradition and Change.* Albany: State University of New York Press, 1986.

Freedman, Estelle B. *No Turning Back: The History of Feminism and the Future of Women.* New York: Ballantine Books, 2002.

Friedan, Betty. *The Feminine Mystique.* New York: Dell, 1974, 1963.

Fuller, Robert. *Underground to Freedom: An Account of the Anti-Slavery Activities in Ashtabula County Prior to the Civil War.* Jefferson, Ohio: Gazette Printing, 1977.

Ginsberg, Lori. *Women and the Work of Benevolence: Morality, Politics, and Class in the Nineteenth-Century United States.* New Haven, Conn.: Yale University Press, 1990.

Gonda, Susan. "Not a Matter of Choice: San Diego Women and Divorce, 1850–1880." *Journal of San Diego History* 27, no. 3 (1991): 194–213.

Griswold, Robert L. "Apart but Not Adrift: Wives, Divorce, and Independence in California." *Pacific Historical Review* 49, no. 2 (1980): 265–83.

Hampsten, Elizabeth. *Read This Only to Yourself: The Private Writings of Midwestern Women, 1880–1910.* Bloomington: Indiana University Press, 1982.

Hardyment, Christina. *From Mangle to Microwave: The Mechanization of Household Work.* Oxford, U.K.: Polity, 1988.

Hartog, Hendrik. *Man and Wife in America: A History.* Cambridge, Mass.: Harvard University Press, 2000.

Hersh, Blanche Glassman. *The Slavery of Sex: Feminist-Abolitionists in America.* Urbana: University of Illinois Press, 1978.

Hewitt, Nancy. *Women's Activism and Social Change: Rochester, New York, 1822–1872.* Ithaca, N.Y.: Cornell University Press, 1984.

Historical Encyclopedia of Illinois, Vol. 2. Chicago: Munsell, 1908.

Historical Sketch: Grand River Institute. Austinberg, Ohio: Grand River Institute, 1924.

History of Ohio, Vol. 4. Chicago: American Historical Society, 1925.

Hoffert, Sylvia D. *When Hens Crow.* Bloomington: Indiana University Press, 1995.

Hoganson, Kristin. "Garrisonian Abolitionists and the Rhetoric of Gender, 1850–1860." *American Quarterly* 45, no. 4 (December 1993): 558–95.

Howe, Henry. *Historical Collections of Ohio.* Published by author, 1898.

Isenberg, Nancy. *Sex and Citizenship in Antebellum America.* Chapel Hill: University of North Carolina Press, 1998.

Jeffrey, Julie Roy. *Ordinary Women in the Antislavery Movement.* Chapel Hill: University of North Carolina Press, 1998.

Jensen, Joan M. *Loosening the Bonds: Mid-Atlantic Farm Women, 1750–1850.* New Haven, Conn.: Yale University Press, 1986.

Kelley, Mary. *Private Women, Public Stage: Literary Domesticity in Nineteenth-Century America.* New York: Oxford University Press, 1984; Chapel Hill: University of North Carolina Press, 2002.

————. "Reading Women/Women Reading: The Making of Learned Women in Antebellum America." *Journal of American History* 83 (1996): 401–24.

Kelly, Catherine E. *In the New England Fashion: Reshaping Women's Lives in the Nineteenth Century.* Ithaca, N.Y.: Cornell University Press, 1999.

Kerber, Linda K. "Separate Spheres, Female Worlds, Woman's Place: The Rhetoric of Women's History." *The Journal of American History* 75, no. 1 (June 1988): 9–39.

Landes, Joan B. "Further Thoughts on the Public/Private Distinction." *Journal of Women's History* 15, no. 2 (Summer 2003): 28–40.

Large, Moina W. *History of Ashtabula County,* Vol. 1. Topeka-Indianapolis: Historical Publishing, 1924.

Lensink, Judy Nolte. *"A Secret to Be Burried": The Diary and Life of Emily Hawley Gillespie, 1858–1888.* Iowa City: University of Iowa Press, 1989.

Leonard, Elizabeth D. *Yankee Women: Gender Battles in The Civil War.* New York: W. W. Norton, 1994.

Lerner, Gerda. *The Creation of Feminist Consciousness from the Middle Ages to Eighteen-Seventy.* New York: Oxford University Press, 1993.

————. "The Lady and the Mill Girl: Changes in the Status of Women in the Age of Jackson." In *Women's Experience in America: An Historical Anthology,* edited by Esther Katz and Anita Rapone, 87–100. New Brunswick, N.J.: Transaction Books, 1980.

Lystra, Karen. *Searching the Heart: Women, Men, and Romantic Love in Nineteenth-Century America.* New York: Oxford University Press, 1989.

May, Elaine Tyler. *Great Expectations: Marriage and Divorce in Post-Victorian America.* Chicago: University of Chicago Press, 1980.

McGuigan, Dorothy Gies. *A Dangerous Experiment: 100 Years of Women at the University of Michigan.* Ann Arbor: University of Michigan Press, 1970.

McMurry, Sally. *Families and Farmhouses in Nineteenth-Century America: Vernacular Design and Social Change.* New York: Oxford University Press, 1988.

McMurry, Sally Ann. *Transforming Rural Life: Dairying Families and Agricultural Change, 1820–1885.* Baltimore, Md.: Johns Hopkins University Press, 1995.

Moore, R. Lawrence. "The Spiritualist Medium: A Study of Female Professionalization in Victorian America." In *Women's Experience in America: An Historical Anthology,* ed. Esther Katz and Anita Rapone, 145–68. New Brunswick, N.J.: Transaction Books, 1980.

Morgan, Robin. *Going Too Far: The Personal Chronicle of a Feminist.* Originally published by author, 1968; New York: First Vintage Books, 1978.

Motz, Marilyn Ferris. *True Sisterhood: Michigan Women and Their Kin, 1820–1920.* Albany: State University of New York Press, 1983.

James, Edward T. et al., eds. "Catharine Maria Sedgewick," *Notable American Women, 1607–1950: A Biographical Dictionary.* Cambridge, Mass.: Harvard University Press, 1971.

Painter, Nell Irvin. *Sojourner Truth: A Life, A Symbol.* New York: W. W. Norton, 1996.

Riley, Glenda. *Divorce: An American Tradition.* New York: Oxford University Press, 1991.

———. *The Female Frontier: A Comparative View of Women on the Prairie and the Plains.* Lawrence: University Press of Kansas, 1988.

Riney-Kehrberg, Pamela. "The Limits of Community: Martha Friesen of Hamilton County, Kansas." In *Midwestern Women: Work, Community, and Leadership at the Crossroads,* edited by Lucy Eldersveld Murphy and Wendy Hamand Venet, 76–91. Bloomington: Indiana University Press, 1997.

———. "Separation and Sorrow: A Farm Woman's Life, 1935–1941." *Agricultural History* 67, no. 2 (Spring 1993): 185–96.

Roberts, Mary Louise. "True Womanhood Revisited." *Journal of Women's History* 14, no. 1 (Spring 2002): 150–55.

Robertson, Stacey M. *Parker Pillsbury: Radical Abolitionist, Male Feminist.* Ithaca, N.Y.: Cornell University Press, 2000.

Rosenthal, Bernard. "Introduction." In Margaret Fuller, *Woman in the Nineteenth-Century.* New York: W. W. Norton, 1971.

Russo, Ann, and Cheris Kramarae, eds. *The Radical Women's Press of the 1850s.* New York: Routledge, 1991.

Ryan, Mary P. *Cradle of the Middle Class: The Family in Oneida County, New York, 1790–1865.* Cambridge, Mass.: Cambridge University Press, 1981.

———. "The Public and the Private Good: Across the Great Divide in Women's History." *Journal of Women's History* 15, no. 2 (Summer 2003): 10–27.

———. *Womanhood in America from Colonial Times to the Present,* 3d ed. New York: Franklin Watts, 1983.

Schlissel, Lillian. *Women's Diaries of the Westward Journey.* New York: Schocken Books, 1982.

Sizer, Lyde Cullen. *The Political Work of Northern Women Writers and the Civil War, 1850–1872.* Chapel Hill: University of North Carolina Press, 2000.

Sklar, Kathryn Kish. *Catharine Beecher: A Study in American Domesticity.* New Haven, Conn.: Yale University Press, 1973.

Smith, Daniel Scott. "Family Limitation, Sexual Control, and Domestic Feminism in Victorian America." In *Women's Experience in America: An Historical Anthology,* edited by Esther Katz and Anita Rapone, 235–57. New Brunswick, N.J.: Transaction Books, 1980.

Smith, Kimberly K. *The Dominion of the Voice: Riot, Reason, and Romance in Antebellum Politics.* Lawrence: University of Kansas Press, 1999.

Smith-Rosenberg, Carroll. "The Female World of Love and Ritual: Relationship Between Women in Nineteenth-Century America." In *Women's Experience in America: An Historical Anthology,* ed. Esther Katz and Anita Rapone, 259–91. New Brunswick, N.J.: Transaction Books, 1980.

———. "The Cross and the Pedestal: Women, Anti-Ritualism, and the Emergence of the American Bourgeoisie." In *Disorderly Conduct: Visions of Gender in Victorian America,* 129–64. New York: Alfred A. Knopf, 1985.

———. "The Hysterical Woman: Sex Roles and Role Conflict in Nineteenth-Century America." In *Women's Experience in America: An Historical Anthology,* ed. Esther Katz and Anita Rapone, 315–38. New Brunswick, N.J.: Transaction Books, 1980.

————. "Puberty to Menopause: The Cycle of Femininity in Nineteenth-Century America." In *Disorderly Conduct: Visions of Gender in Victorian America,* 197–216. New York: Alfred A. Knopf, 1985.

Steinhagen, Carol. "The Two Lives of Frances Dana Gage." *Ohio History* 107 (Winter 1998): 22–38.

Sterling, Dorothy. *Ahead of Her Time: Abby Kelley and the Politics of Antislavery.* New York: W. W. Norton, 1991.

Strasser, Susan. *Never Done: A History of American Housework.* New York: Pantheon, 1982.

Talcott, Kathryn H. "Cherry Valley." *Ashtabula County Historical Society Quarterly Bulletin* 6, no. 4 (Dec. 15, 1959).

Tillson, Christiana Holmes. *A Woman's Story of Pioneer Illinois.* Chicago: Lakeside Press, R. R. Donnelley, 1919; Carbondale: Southern Illinois University Press, 1995.

Turbin, Carole. "Refashioning the Concept of Public/Private: Lessons from Dress Studies." *Journal of Women's History* 15, no. 1 (Spring 2003): 43–51.

Ulrich, Laurel Thatcher. *A Midwife's Tale: The Life of Martha Ballard, Based on Her Diary, 1785–1812.* New York: Alfred A. Knopf, 1990.

Venet, Wendy Hamand. *Neither Ballots nor Bullets: Women Abolitionists and the Civil War.* Charlottesville: University Press of Virginia, 1991.

Welter, Barbara. "The Cult of True Womanhood: 1820–1860." In *Women's Experience in America: An Historical Anthology,* edited by Esther Katz and Anita Rapone, 193–213. New Brunswick, N.J.: Transaction Books, 1980.

————. "The Feminization of American Religion." In *Clio's Consciousness Raised: New Perspectives on the History of Women,* edited by Mary Hartman and Lois W. Banner, 137–57. New York: Harper Torchbooks, 1974.

Wickham, Gertrude Van Rensselaer, ed. *Memorial to the Pioneer Women of the Western Reserve.* Evansville, Ind.: Whipporwill Publications, 1896; Ashtabula County Genealogical Society, 1981.

Williams Brothers, eds. *History of Ashtabula County, Ohio with Illustrations and Biographical Sketches of Its Pioneers and Most Prominent Men.* Philadelphia, Pa.: J. B. Lippincott, 1878.

Woloch, Nancy. *Women and the American Experience, 3d ed.* Boston: McGraw-Hill, 2000.

Young, Elizabeth. *Disarming the Nation: Women's Writing and the American Civil War.* Chicago: University of Chicago Press, 1999.

Index